AFTER THE BEGINNING
Creation Revealed in Science and Scripture

ANTHONY L. EDRIDGE

WESTBOW
PRESS
A DIVISION OF THOMAS NELSON

WestBow Press books may be ordered through booksellers or by contacting:

WestBow Press
A Division of Thomas Nelson
1663 Liberty Drive
Bloomington, IN 47403
www.westbowpress.com
1-(866) 928-1240

Because of the dynamic nature of the Internet, any web addresses or links contained in this book may have changed since publication and may no longer be valid. The views expressed in this work are solely those of the author and do not necessarily reflect the views of the publisher, and the publisher hereby disclaims any responsibility for them.

Any people depicted in stock imagery provided by Thinkstock are models, and such images are being used for illustrative purposes only.

Certain stock imagery © Thinkstock.

ISBN: 978-1-4497-5463-1 (e)
ISBN: 978-1-4497-5462-4 (sc)
ISBN: 978-1-4497-5461-7 (hc)

Library of Congress Control Number: 2012909664

Printed in the United States of America

WestBow Press rev. date: 6/25/2012

DEDICATION

This book is dedicated to my sister who raised questions
about creation that need answers. I hope and pray
this book provides some of those answers.

CONTENTS

Acknowledgments		ix
Chapter 1:	Introduction	1
Chapter 2:	Theories Of Origins Overview	5
Chapter 3:	The Beginning of Everything	27
Chapter 4:	Abundance Of Life	45
Chapter 5:	Very Good Indeed	61
Chapter 6:	Life And Death In Eden	79
Chapter 7:	Fallout From The Fall	95
Chapter 8:	Life and Death East of Eden	115
Chapter 9:	The Great Flood	125
Chapter 10:	Legends and Evidence for the Flood	147
Chapter 11:	Revelation in Creation	175
Chapter 12:	Mindless Evolution or Intelligent Creation	195
Appendix A:	Major Biblical Themes	219
Appendix B:	Guidelines for Interpreting Scripture	222
Appendix C:	A Day in Creation	225
Appendix D:	Old Is Good	234
Appendix E:	The Fourth Day	241
Index		247

ACKNOWLEDGMENTS

I am indebted to many authors who have contributed to my understanding about creation issues, both as outlined in the Bible and as discovered by modern science. Over the years these authors caused me to lean alternately between the Young Earth and the Old Earth positions on many occasions. And I am grateful to my pastors, who gave many good sermons contributed to my knowledge about God's purpose in creation.

The one person, however, who had most impact on my understanding of the majesty of the Bible and its story of God's involvement with mankind, was Fount Shults, Dean of the Bible College that I attended in Texas. His devoted walk with God and his thorough understanding of Hebrew and Greek inspired me to look for the deeper meanings in Biblical texts.

I am deeply grateful to my friend, Linnea Nelson, who helped with her expertise in both writing skills and in creation topics. I was greatly encouraged by her assistance.

I value the help of my family and friends who provided many useful suggestions. Above all, I appreciate the patience of my wife, Tricia, who has been so gracious as a book widow for so many years.

The front cover picture of the earth, looking down on the Middle East, is courtesy of NASA and is available at Visible Earth's website: http://visibleearth.nasa.gov/.

1
INTRODUCTION

Truth consists of having the same idea
about something that God has.
—Joseph Joubert

Despite vigorous attempts by defenders of different creation models to demonstrate that they have the one true interpretation of Genesis, the Bible does support different creation scenarios. Bible scholars over the centuries have agreed that the brevity and style of the Genesis text is sometimes ambiguous. In other words, the text supports different interpretations of the creation narrative. In the past, science has provided clarification for Biblical interpretation, and it can be expected to do so again. An intermediate period can exist, however, where different theories compete for acceptance, and to some extent, we are in such a period.

Ambiguities arise in Genesis because it is very brief, and also because science has brought to light many discoveries that the Biblical text does not address. Many Christians do not see ambiguity in certain passages; instead they see only one possible interpretation, usually based on translations in English. My objective is to show that the Bible supports valid interpretations for an Old Earth model as well as the Young Earth model. This means that scriptures cannot be used to negate either position conclusively.

When it comes to the science of origins, I differentiate between theories that have been proved with scientific data and theories that are interpretations of circumstantial scientific data. Circumstantial evidence has turned out to be incorrect countless times in court rooms and occasionally in science journals as well. In some ways, the jury is still out in the case against evolution, but as I try to show, the case for creation has gained considerable credibility. I believe that the science of origins and the creation account in Genesis reflect the historical events that actually occurred; my premise is that God both created the universe and inspired the Bible. Readers will want to determine for themselves the extent to which the Bible and science agree.

I have attempted to provide an interpretation that is consistent with the Genesis account, with the proven science we know today, and with the major themes of the Bible (outlined in Appendix A). In addition, I show how the creation story in Genesis is reflected throughout the Bible, in much of our history, and within our own humanity.

The topic of this book concerns our origins, starting from the beginning of the universe until the catastrophic Flood of Noah, all of which are described in the first ten chapters of Genesis. Much of the Biblical narrative is too brief to give any clues as to how it all happened with any detailed scientific understanding. This should not be surprising because the study of science had to wait thousands of years after Genesis was first written.

Both creation and evolution are supported by scientific evidence, all of which is circumstantial. In the last hundred years, science has accumulated a considerable amount of data that strongly supports creation; or at least the concept of intelligent design. Although some fossil evidence exists for Darwin's view of the common descent of man, it is all circumstantial, just as any science for creation is also circumstantial. A brief summary of arguments for and against evolution is provided in chapter 12. Rather than debating Darwin's Theory of Evolution, which concerns the common descent of man from primitive life, I consider it more effective to consider the origin of life itself. The necessary starting point of evolution is *abiogenesis*, which is the accidental assembly of living cells from naturally occurring chemicals. Scientists have not been able to resolve the mystery of life with theories or experiments about abiogenesis, whereas creation scientists are discovering the reasons why creation is the way it is and the amazing complexity of even the simplest life forms.

In general, I have considered just two broad points of view for Genesis: Old Earth and Young Earth. Both have scriptural support, so we can examine scientific evidence to determine which perspective may be preferable. Many Christians (and non-Christians) believe that science has already provided all the evidence that is needed to determine the age of the earth. Nevertheless, we can expect science to continue providing evidence that may eventually lead to consensus. Not that I am putting the Bible in second place, but sometimes in matters concerning the cosmos, Christians have to wait on general revelation (discovering what God did in the natural universe) to help understand those same topics in special revelation (the Bible).

When we have found everything there is to find, we will not know all the answers about our origins. And in the grand scheme of things, what we believe about Genesis does not affect our salvation one little bit. Jesus asked, "Who do men say that I, the Son of Man, am"? He did not ask about the age of the earth. Salvation is about knowing God, not about knowing the length of the creation day. The meaning of Genesis, however, is not an insignificant issue, and the apparent lack of harmony with science promotes mistrust of the Old Testament for many who might have otherwise have accepted the authority of Jesus.

After becoming interested in creation topics, I realized that there ought to be agreement between the Bible and the valid discoveries of science. This means that I should be able to find valid interpretations of relevant Biblical texts that match proven scientific data. Where scientific evidence is circumstantial, preferred interpretations are appropriate. Not all Christians, however, have such an optimistic outlook, leading me to write about the history of creation so that others could be confident in the authenticity of the Bible. Sometimes such reconciliation of science and scripture requires a little faith to begin with, until more complete understanding is gained about the issues. It was that way in my life.

The debate between proponents of Young Earth and Old Earth models could be analogous to two family members doing research on their common ancestry but disagreeing on ambiguous records. One of them may suspect they were descended from royalty, the other that their ancestors were common laborers going all the way back to the Dark Ages. Such disagreement should not affect their relationship nor give rise to unpleasant criticism. In matters of our cosmic origins, Christians above all, should not view with disdain anyone who disagrees with them about the age of the earth, evolution, and related topics.

The final point I would like to make concerning attitudes about origins is that we should not confuse any given interpretation of Genesis with the Bible itself. I believe the Bible is inerrant, although modern versions do not always capture the full meaning of some passages in Genesis. This leads us back to the original Hebrew Scriptures, which in places have been interpreted in different ways by Jews and Christians. In a similar way, the English New Testament has been interpreted in so many different ways that we now have hundreds of Christian denominations, in part because some scriptures are ambiguous. Through the centuries, Christian misunderstanding of scripture has had tragic consequences. Even though we have improved our understanding on most of these issues, we should not think that our own interpretations of ambiguous scriptures have the same weight as the Bible itself. Neither the Young Earth nor the Old Earth position is supreme just because it appears to agree with what the Bible states. The Bible is holy, not our interpretations.

All quotations from the Bible are taken from the New King James Version, unless noted otherwise.

2
THEORIES OF ORIGINS OVERVIEW

In the beginning was the Word, and
the Word was with God, and the Word was God.
He was in the beginning with God. All things were
made through Him, and without Him nothing was
made that was made. (John 1:1–3)

The unimaginable beginning of the universe is described in just the first verse of Genesis: "In the beginning God created the heavens and the earth." It uses merely seven Hebrew words, so it is not surprising that we cannot determine when or how God did this phenomenal task. Did creation take place a very long time ago, or was it more recently within the last few thousand years? This is perhaps the most intriguing and certainly one of the more divisive issues within Christianity today.

At the heart of this controversy are major differences in the interpretation of the first few chapters of Genesis. Many Christians believe that God created both the universe and then living organisms just a few thousand years ago, based on our current English versions of the Bible and the possible meanings of certain Hebrew words. Others believe that the Bible does not say when God created the universe and living creatures; instead, they rely on what appears to be overwhelming scientific evidence for an old earth. Both Young Earth and Old Earth proponents are at odds with people who do not believe in a created universe, believing instead that the universe and life are a chain of cosmic accidents that started billions of years ago. Not everyone falls into one of these three positions. Several variations exist in the details of creation based on how Genesis is interpreted.

Regardless of these differences, all who believe that the Bible is the revealed word of God would agree that if we knew what the Bible really meant, and if we knew what actually happened long ago, there should be no discord. God is the author of both His written revelation and of creation.

It is important for Christians and for Christianity in general that the Bible not be found invalid. If there were anything seriously in error, it would cause misgivings about the rest of the Bible, especially because Jesus quoted on many occasions from the Hebrew Scriptures, including Genesis. The passages that are most contentious are in the first ten chapters of Genesis, which concern creation and the Flood.

Belief in the accuracy of the Bible is more than simply a matter of faith because so much of it has been verified. The veracity of the Bible has been well documented by Josh McDowell in his book *The New Evidence that Demands a Verdict*. Although scholars in the last two hundred years have claimed that dozens of historical references in the New Testament were in error, all such claims have been refuted by modern archaeological evidence. Similarly, historical references in the Old Testament about events after the Flood have withstood the examination of archaeologists, although there is still some controversy over references concerning the early nation of Israel. Nevertheless, no conclusive evidence has been found that contradicts historical passages in the Bible; in fact, many archaeologists use the Bible as a guide to identify sites and artifacts.

Where the Bible refers to historical events that have not yet been verified by archaeology, an element of faith might be required to believe those particular scriptures. This kind of faith is different from other Christian beliefs. The most important aspect of Christian faith concerns the gospel, which is about the person and ministry of Jesus Christ. Another kind of faith concerns the promises of God that are revealed in the Bible but are yet to be fulfilled. Believers also have personal faith about issues that God has revealed to them but which are not revealed in the Bible. They not only trust God but also believe He has communicated His promise for the outcome, perhaps in a "still small voice". None of the issues in the creation debate directly affect these other elements of Christian faith.

RELIGION

A simple definition of religion is belief in a higher power. By that I mean a power that transcends our material world; otherwise, we would simply control it or at least adapt to it. In some religions, this higher power has personhood, unlike the impersonal "force" of *Star Wars* movies: "May the force be with you." Religions that deny the existence of a higher power should be considered more philosophical in nature than religious. It is difficult, however, to make a clear-cut distinction between all religions and philosophies.

Christian faith is about a God who created the universe and who gave inspiration to the Bible over many hundreds of years. The essence of Christianity is about knowing God through belief in His Son, Jesus.

Without the basic rudiments of logic, it is easy to misunderstand some of the Bible, which is one reason why so many Christian denominations and heresies arose over the last 2,000 years. The Bible illustrates doctrines such as the Incarnation, the Trinity and the combined humanity and deity of Jesus. These concepts can be difficult to grasp, with the result that from time to time certain church leaders developed alternative doctrines. From the beginning of church history, sects sprung up with teachings that early church fathers viewed as heretical, based on how far these teachings strayed from conventional doctrine. Over the centuries, church councils were called together to evaluate potential heresies, as well as to confirm the New Testament Canon. Church leaders, such as Justin Martyr, Tertullian, and Gregory, relied on logic to explain and define the meanings of controversial doctrines in terms of Biblical texts; at the same time they revealed the errors within the heresies. By the time of the reformation, Christian theology and doctrine were firmly established, although that has not prevented sects arising with new twists on old heresies. Theologians are still refining more obscure concepts of Christian theology. Books on Christian philosophy and systematic theology reveal the struggles that church leaders went through as they refined their arguments and developed Christian doctrine to be logically sound and consistent with the Bible.

Some atheist leaders portray religions as evil, responsible for much suffering in the world. These opinions amount to demagoguery: religions do not do anything; people with evil motives have perpetrated evil in the name of their religions, regardless of what these religions may actually teach. Such accusations against Christianity fail to address the murder and mayhem carried out by irreligious people. Moreover, they ignore the great benefits that Christianity has brought to society, including rights for women and children, abolition of slavery, building of hospitals, caring for the poor, and education for the public.

PHILOSOPHY

Philosophy is the study of how we think about things. The basic discipline is logic, the ability to reason, so that we all have a measure of philosophical experience. Philosophy can be used to examine any discipline including theology, science, and the study of origins. In the discipline of science, philosophy has established the scientific method that best minimizes error in practice and theory. It may also be used to suggest areas where science should not proceed, such as cloning humans. Philosophy embraces such ideas as values, morality, common sense, and wisdom. It also extends to epistemology, the study of how we know what we think we know.

When scientific measurements indicate the appearance of design, philosophy can create a bridge to conclusions about the existence of the God who created those designs. In addition to its impact on science, philosophy can be used to evaluate arguments for or against the existence of God, and it can also be used to compare merits of theologies between different religions.

Although philosophy appears to be very powerful, it has limitations. Ancient Greek philosophers developed codes of morality, some elementary science, and some ideas about origins. Their efforts, however, lacked input from scientific experiments, which have since proved many of their ideas to be incorrect. Philosophy about the material world needs scientific tests to anchor it in reality. When philosophy is applied to government, the results can be catastrophic, unless it is balanced with the morality and spirituality of religion that Christianity provides.

SCIENCE

Science is based on the scientific method, which starts with an ordered process for examining phenomena in the natural world. Repeatable measurements lead to hypotheses that can be examined by peer review and tested to ensure that failures do not occur under any foreseeable circumstance. After theories and then laws have been established, refinement may occur as greater accuracy is obtained and more comprehensive tests are developed. Such methods can be applied to the properties of historical artifacts such as fossils and sediments, but the results apply only to the artifacts and usually do not yield direct evidence of historical events surrounding those artifacts. Any conclusions reached about such historical events are based on interpretations of the scientific data. For example, sequences of fossils that show significant development towards new species over long periods of time may be characterized with the hypothesis of evolution, although evolution itself would not have been observed. Sequences of fossilized bones do sometimes suggest natural evolution, but they can also be explained by creation.

Science has brought mankind amazing technology, awe inspiring understanding of the universe, and intriguing glimpses of our origins. Nevertheless, it does have limitations and dangers. Without philosophy and Christian virtue, science could take us into the horrors of a *Brave New World* or *Nineteen Eighty-Four.*

All sides of the creation debate use science to support their positions. Science, however, can be mismanaged in different ways, such as neglecting peer review at the end of the process and ignoring philosophical assumptions at the beginning. Peer review is a vital part of scientific discovery. Without the peer review process, scientists can end up losing touch with reality. When Christians promote scientific theories or models without peer review, nothing useful is gained by merely appealing to the Bible for support. Science must stand on its own merits. On the other hand, when philosophical assumptions are not honestly stated, scientists may also end up out of touch with reality, proclaiming invalid conclusions.

SYNERGY OR ISOLATON

At the end of January in 2009, the Daily Telegraph published the results of a survey on Darwinism taken in England by Com Res, a leading polling consultancy: "In the survey, 51 percent of those questioned agreed with the statement that 'evolution alone is not enough to explain the complex structures of some living things, so the intervention of a designer is needed at key stages.'" This is despite the statistic that only 15 percent of the population attended church at least once a month, according to the 2007 Tearfund survey. Apparently people in the UK, and all over the world presumably, come to conclusions that are not based solely on science or religion.

It appears that a majority of people are not convinced that scientific evidence proves that life started by accident. Christians in particular should not let their faith be shaken by statements such as that made by atheist Frank Zindler, Professor of Philosophy at New York University:

> The most devastating thing though that biology did to Christianity was the discovery of ... evolution. Now that we know that Adam and Eve never were real people the central myth of Christianity is destroyed. If there never was an Adam and Eve there never was an original sin. If there never was an original sin there is no need of salvation. If there is no need of salvation there is no need of a savior. And I submit that puts Jesus, historical or otherwise, into the ranks of the unemployed. (*Atheism or Christianity: Where Does the Evidence Lead?* a debate between Frank Zindler and William Lane Craig on June 27, 1993. Video and audio copies of the debate are available from Zondervan Publishing House.)

Frank Zindler was speaking from an isolated position that was essentially philosophical. He might have had a valid conclusion if science had demonstrated test tube life. It has failed to do so; and its chances of succeeding appear to be diminishing. Without doubt, the casual acceptance of evolution has had a serious impact on Christianity, primarily because abiogenesis was assumed to have occurred. But now that the amazing complexity and organization of living cells is coming to light, the underlying assumption of abiogenesis is becoming weak and untenable.

The philosophy of naturalism, which denies any supernatural involvement in the world of any significance, explains everything that exists with one type of phenomenon, the interactions between particles of matter. All that exists and all that has ever happened in the universe are the result of seemingly random variations of molecular, atomic, sub-atomic, and quantum states. Christianity does not deny the existence of these phenomena but ascribes reality to the intervention and power of God in a way that was appropriate for each step of creation. Different stages of creation include the origin of the universe, the formation of our solar system, transformation of our planet for habitation, the origin of life, the expansion of life, and finally the creation of man. Also, because of its significance in the early history of mankind, the Noachian Flood can be included in discussion of our origins. Evidence for each of these events should be examined with appropriate scientific methods.

Scientists have tried to explain the origin of the universe and the origin of life with the assumption that God, even if He exists, was not involved. But this approach is not necessarily correct because there is no scientific evidence that God was not involved. Lack of scientific evidence is to be expected; science only deals with material phenomena and not with spiritual beings. Because the scientific method cannot resolve the question of God's existence, denying the possibility of God and His role in creation is the result of a philosophical position, which can be labeled in various ways such as materialism, naturalism, and of course atheism.

Scientists use philosophical assumptions when interpreting scientific data to show that mechanistic evolution must have occurred, while other scientists are using philosophy to interpret scientific data to show that biological systems must have been designed. It cannot be overemphasized that philosophical beliefs rather than scientific data are the motivation for both Evolutionary Theory (materialistic origin of the universe) and the Theory of Evolution (materialistic origin of living forms). The latter is now generally considered to embrace the origin of life as well as Darwin's theory about the common descent of species from existing life forms.

In his book *When Science Meets Religion*, Ian Barbour proposed four ways of viewing the relationship between science and religion, which in our circumstance is Christianity. These four points of view are conflict, independence, dialogue, and integration.[1] All of these relationships may exist for the many different subjects that science and religion cover. The question might be asked if a preferred connection exists between science and religion on the topic of origins. Stephen Jay Gould, in his book *Rocks of Ages,* proposed the answer to be independence, which he called "non-overlapping magisteria". Without doubt, the means of acquiring knowledge are different. Nevertheless, they do share common topics so that science is not totally divorced from religion.

Without God, either the universe must have created itself at some point or it has always existed. The former option is opposed by both science and Christianity. On the other hand, a perpetual universe would have wound down to be cold and lifeless, or would exist in a steady state in which matter is continuously appearing on a small scale. The steady state solution was proposed as an alternative to the Big Bang Theory, but recent scientific observations do not support it. Currently, most scientists believe that most of what we know about our universe can be explained by the Big Bang Theory. An initial point of intense energy appeared some 13.7 billion years ago, from which the whole universe expanded. The origin of this singularity, or seed of energy, which started the universe, has not been explained with any confidence on simply materialistic grounds. The reasonable implication is that the beginning was supernatural, and quite a few scientists have come to this conclusion.

GUIDELINES FOR INTERPRETING THE BIBLE

In order to understand the limited information that the Bible presents about creation, we need to be familiar with the basic tools that should be used for interpreting the Bible. Guidelines for this purpose are provided in Appendix B, which includes basic rules that address the following: context, figurative language, cultural background, and clarification from other passages.

Although we may have the best possible interpretation for a given passage, it may remain ambiguous. An example of ambiguity occurs in the first three verses of Genesis, where it does not state how much time passed between the very beginning of the universe and when light first appeared on earth. The Bible does not give that information. When it comes to events of long ago, we must sometimes rely on scientific or scholarly research to add details to the Biblical account.

CREATION OR EVOLUTION

Both of these concepts attempt to explain our origins, although no scientific evidence was available for what may have happened throughout the course of events until modern times. We have only archaeological and geological remains of ancient creatures, objects, and events on this earth, whereas astronomy can tell us what appears to have happened in the heavens. Archaeological and geological measurements do not yield a direct narrative of what may have occurred, so that any scientific data must be interpreted; in other words the evidence is circumstantial. Some of the interpretations and theories that are based on the scientific data are compelling, but they are frequently revised as new discoveries are made.

Perhaps the strongest evidence for evolution is the fossil record, in which some sequences of fossils appear to have evolved over long periods of time. Nevertheless, all fossil evidence can be explained in terms of creation. In addition, there is considerable fossil evidence that contradicts evolution, some of which is described in chapter 12.

COMPETING CREATION ACCOUNTS

Christianity has many variations of the Genesis creation account. For the sake of convenience I will call them theories, although technically they are really explanations and interpretations of the Genesis creation narrative. At one end of the spectrum is the belief that the universe was created over a period of six 24-hour Days, typically about 6,000 years ago, commonly known as the Young Earth theory. Most estimates for its age vary between 6,000 and 7,500 years; a few go as far as about 20,000 years. At the other end of the spectrum is the belief that God used mechanistic evolution over billions of years to achieve the same end, one variant of theistic Old Earth theories. In between, progressive creation theories explain how God supernaturally created all life forms without resorting to mechanistic evolution of species: but He did so over a very long period of time, within the current scientific age for the earth of about 4.5 billion years. Old Earth views rely on a figurative interpretation for the word Day; thousands to billions of years in length. Appendix C provides arguments for and against the 24-hour and the figurative Day interpretations. Believers of all these views affirm that the Bible supports their positions. To a large extent this is true because the Bible is ambiguous in certain passages.

In addition to the several variants of Young Earth and Old Earth theories that strive to adhere to a literal interpretation of the scriptures, allowing figurative meanings where appropriate, the Framework Theory takes an allegorical approach. The six Days of creation are not considered to be chronological, but they were written in a literary pattern to indicate what God had created. Some arguments for and against Old Earth, Young Earth and Framework Theories are discussed in *The Genesis Debate*, edited by David Hagiopan. Another book with a discussion format, *Three Views on Creation and Evolution*, edited by J. P. Moreland and John Mark Reynolds, looks at Young Earth, Old Earth, and Theistic Evolution. Theistic evolution, as proposed by Howard Van Till, is in effect, essentially the same as natural evolution, but such that the properties of matter and biological organisms were designed by God to have the capability to evolve into ever more complex living structures of their own accord. Therefore there appears to be no scientific way to distinguish between theistic and natural evolution. Further discussion of the many variations on these basic theories is outside the scope of this book.

The creation debate among Christians should involve the original Hebrew text, which may have alternative meanings that are significantly different from our current English Bibles.

THE HEBREW LANGUAGE

I have relied on the expertise of Hebrew scholars to define the various issues that occur in the Hebrew text of Genesis, such as alternative word meanings and the ambiguity of tenses. I think we expect too much from our English versions of the Old Testament because we do not think in the same terms as Hebrews of long ago. Such differences include emotional instead of rational arguments, words derived from actions rather than concepts, relationship being more important than doctrine, poetry rather than prose, and self contained blocks of reality rather than logical steps that connect ideas together.[2]

One of the many differences between English prose and the Hebrew text used in Genesis is the relatively few words available in Hebrew compared to modern English. There are fewer than 10,000 words in a Hebrew dictionary and over 150,000 words in large English dictionaries, ignoring most modern technical words.[3] Nonetheless languages with fewer words overall sometimes have more words to convey the meaning of certain English words, such as the many Sami words for snow. Consequently, we might expect some difficulty in defining the exact meaning of words and phrases, and indeed volumes have been written on some of the more obscure passages, such as the phrase "without form and void" found in Genesis 1:2.

A related difficulty concerns idioms that may have been lost. The expression "so the evening and the morning were the second day" is strange to us, and it may reflect an ancient Hebrew way of referring to a 24-hour day, or again it may imply something other than a 24-hour day. Further details on this topic are given in Appendix C.

Originally, Hebrew writing did not include vowels, which were added after the time of Christ. As a result, some written words could have different spoken alternatives. This meant that the earlier readers of Genesis had to determine what these written words meant, relying in part on oral tradition and also on context.

Another difference that significantly affects interpretation of Genesis is that Hebrew verbs do not convey information about past, present and future in the same way as English verbs. Hebrew verbs indicate the state of an action rather than its relative time. An action was either complete or incomplete, corresponding to past (perfect) and future (imperfect) tenses. Unique textual customs helped define the time frame of each verb, whether past, present, or future.

Genesis 1 was written with one format for the verbs, excluding information that would indicate our pluperfect tense (described in Appendix E). Use of only the simple past tense carried over into subsequent translations that eventually led to our modern English versions. The first translation from Hebrew was the Septuagint, a Greek version of the Hebrew text, thought to have been written before 200 BC. Even though Greek had a pluperfect tense, translators used the Greek aorist tense that indicated a simple past. Much later in the fifth century, Jerome completed the first Latin Bible, known as the Vulgate, basically from Hebrew texts. Although Latin also had a pluperfect, Jerome did not make use of this tense where none was written previously in his sources. Nevertheless, he was aware of the tense issue and the order of creation events, employing conjunctions that implied a sequential narrative. For example he started the second verse with "However the earth was" instead of the more ambiguous "And the earth was".

Similarly, when King James VI ordered a new English version, the translators did not feel the freedom to incorporate the pluperfect tense or even to vary the translation of the single Hebrew conjunction translated "and", which is used in about ninety instances within just the first Chapter of Genesis. Other translations use where appropriate, however, but, or then instead of "and", as explained in the preface of the New King James Version of the Bible. This highlights the major choice confronting translators, whether to try for consistent word for word equivalence or to employ phrases that catch the meaning without strict word equivalence. The former approach is even more difficult when it is impossible to convey a special meaning of the original text because it is the result of Hebrew word order. The significance of the pluperfect tense will be explained in the next chapter.

Hebrew was the language of the nation that God chose to perpetuate the story of Genesis. As a result, the culture, thought processes, and linguistic customs that existed long ago are still buried in the Hebrew text. Some of this culture has recently come to light but has not been incorporated in major versions of the Bible. Rather than trying to bend English versions of Genesis to fit scientific theories, the full expression of ancient Hebrew understanding should be established first.[4] Only then should Genesis be compared to modern scientific knowledge; but not as an equal in scientific terms.

THE GENRE OF GENESIS 1

Many books have been written about the first chapter of Genesis. Some authors attempt to use its literary genre to help establish interpretations. Usually, only poetry and narrative prose are considered, because these are the two common literary forms we use today. The first chapter of Genesis, however, is really a combination, in which the poetic style is distinctly Hebrew. Our Western style of poetry, with rhyme (repeated syllables at the end of phrases) and meter (repeated syllable count), is very different from Hebrew poetry, which uses parallelisms and Semitic inclusions. In the latter, phrases are repeated at opposite ends of a passage, with other pairs of phrases nested inside the outer phrases.[5] For example each letter in the following patterns represents a word or a phrase:

ABC cba   AB C ba   AB -b-a

The lower case letters represent repeated phrases, and the negative sign indicates an opposite meaning. When the echoing phrases are reversed, such as AB ab they form a chiasm (from the Greek chi, X, that looks like a cross). These structures can be found in several books of the Bible. In addition, both Hebrew and English make use of alliteration, which is the repetition of letters, usually at the beginning of adjacent words. Genesis also places similar sounding words in a thematic word play. Consequently, the full impact of the Hebrew in Genesis is difficult to replicate in English, with the result that we miss a great deal of the original textual artistry, emphasis, and even some of its meaning.[7] Because of the unique narrative format and poetic style, words and phrases in Genesis 1 and 2 should not necessarily be interpreted on the basis of normal word usage in the rest of the Old Testament.

Hebrew poetry was easier to remember than plain prose, a significant benefit for most of the Hebrew nation that did not have access to written texts. Scripture was memorized by hearing it rather than by reading it.

Hebrew texts and other Middle East literature commonly used multiples of seven to express the concepts of completion and perfection.[6] By choosing seven creation Days, six of work and one of rest, God expressed completion as well as the length of a working week. The structure of Genesis 1 is enhanced by the number seven; several key words and phrases occur in multiples of seven. These include: God, heavens, created, earth, light, day, water, it was good. As a result, some repetition occurs, and conversely it may also lead to ambiguity about details that God did not include in Genesis.

The brevity of the creation account can be compared to a painting made with broad-brush strokes that lack detail. Some of the finer topics that are missing from Genesis include the creation and existence of microbes, moss, fungus, soil, plankton, and seaweed. No mention is made of plants that propagate by spores, so ambiguity exists as to whether they were included in the creation of seed bearing plants and trees, or if they were created at some other time. Genesis is not an encyclopedia of all that God created. Instead, God selected specific kinds of animals to reveal His purpose in creation. This will be considered in more detail in the following chapters.

DAY BY DAY

The first chapter in Genesis exhibits an easily discernible form of repetition; the beginning and ending phrases of each creation day. Each day starts with "Then God said" and ends with "So the evening and the morning were the [X] day", where X stands for second, third, and so on through sixth. The leading words, *then* or *so*, can be translated *and*, as context demands because they are translated from the same Hebrew conjunction. From the phrase at the end, we understand that each section corresponds to a creation day, which because of its significance will be written Day, rather than day, throughout this book. This repetitive structure reinforces the chronological character of the narrative. It is reasonable to conclude from the sequential numbering of the six Days that the events recorded in the creation account are also sequential. The creation events are listed in an order that starts with the basic requirements for a habitable earth, the creation of animals, and last of all, the creation of mankind. This order makes sense; light and then land were needed before plants could exist, which in turn were needed before animals could survive.

We should also notice that the first two verses are not included in the literary structure of the first and subsequent Days, which adds significant meaning to these verses. The initial creation event of verse 1 took place before the start of the first Day, which is indicated by "Then God said". The initial creation in verse 1 is often referred to as creation *ex nihilo*, a Latin phrase meaning out of nothing. In other words, no matter existed before the beginning of creation.

FIGURATIVELY SPEAKING

Although conservative Christians agree that the creation account gives us a literal story of God's activities, we should not discount the presence of poetic and figurative language. The combination of poetic and narrative structures implies that some of the text may be figurative. This is particularly important with respect to the length of the creation Day. The straightforward meaning of day is that of a 24-hour day, but figuratively the creation Day could have been any finite length of time. In particular the expression, "So the evening and the morning were the second day" does not necessarily mean a 24-hour day had taken place. The more meaningful words, day and night, are not used. In addition, the Bible does not support the interpretation that a 24-hour Day is defined by the phrase "the evening and the morning"; Appendix C provides a full explanation. One view of the figurative approach is that evening means closing, and morning means opening.[10] A simpler approach, however, is to consider the sequence as it is written. After God's working Day, there was evening, (then night, which was not mentioned, during which no work was done), and then morning. After that, the next Day of work started.

Ancient Hebrew literature is somewhat like our spoken language in that hyperbole or exaggeration is common. For example we might hear ourselves saying: you always say that; you never put things away; everybody knows that; everybody does it. The Bible, especially the Old Testament is full of hyperbole used in all manner of situations (and here too as you can see). It was the Hebrew way of communicating, and much of it is readily discernable as exaggeration and should be understood by context.

Two problems exist with so much hyperbole. First, interpretation of some passages with an absolute sense might be unreliable because we cannot be sure how much exaggeration was intended. Secondly, if the hyperbole is not detected, believers may come away with the wrong impression. A rule of thumb to bear in mind is to treat absolute quantitative expressions with caution. This does not apply to specific numbers that indicate such concepts as people's ages and populations. In subsequent chapters, consideration of hyperbole will offer a more realistic understanding of certain scriptures than would be gained by ignoring the possibility of this common literary technique.

CULTURAL BACKGROUND

Genesis was not written in the cultural background of Adam but in the time of Moses. It was written in stark contrast to the pagan cosmogonies that were prevalent in Moses' time.[8] Almost every statement in Genesis opposes pagan beliefs such as deification of sun, moon, and stars. God was telling the Hebrews how creation really happened but without making the creation account into a scientific treatise. With this limitation and its unique literary genre, some ambiguity must be expected from a scientific perspective. Ambiguity and lack of clarity are also found occasionally in other passages of the Bible without diminishing the intended message.[9]

A HARD DAY'S WORK

The length of each creation Day is at the heart of what is an important, but not necessarily vital, difference among Christians; we believe a creation Day was either a 24-hour Day or a figurative Day of thousands to billions of years. The 24-hour Day, with an associated age for the earth of several thousand years, is categorized as a Young Earth position, and a Day that is figuratively thousands to billions of years is an Old Earth position. Christians on both sides of the debate are using science to justify their beliefs, but some of the arguments are not scientific at all. At some point the better scientific evidence should prevail and possibly settle the issue for most Christians.

Anyone studying Genesis for the first time might be unsure which makes more sense, a 24-hour Day or a figurative Day. The issues, which can be complex, are discussed in Appendix C. More insight can be gained by looking at the function and purpose of a day, as revealed in the Bible. We find that daytime is frequently related to work. God worked during the daytime of each creation Day, and man works during the daytime of his working week, at least when Genesis was written. This concept is at the heart of the relevant Bible verses, providing background for making a decision on the length of the creation Day.

THE NARRATORS PERSPECTIVE

Except for the first verse, where the location is simply *in the beginning*, all descriptions in the first Chapter of Genesis refer to the earth's surface. During the first four Days, the environment of the earth's surface was transformed into a suitable habitation for animals and mankind. In the second Chapter, the location of the narrative is further restricted to the garden of Eden. The creation account ignores such topics as galaxies and microbes that were irrelevant topics for man at that time. Everything described in Genesis was visible to the naked eye. Nevertheless, all that was not visible was also created by God.

Genesis provides six snapshots, one for each Day, of the major events that took place on the earth. This sequence of creation is examined in the next chapter. Many minor and perhaps even major events that must have occurred are not recorded. These include creation of fungi, bacteria, and marine plants. In the first four Days, God modified the existing earth's surface and atmosphere without creating any new matter. In the last two Days, again, no new matter was added, but God created life through very special biochemical arrangements of atoms and molecules. All creatures were made from dust, which contained all the elements necessary for life. In Days five and six, God again created something new, not physical matter; instead He created the souls of each of the creatures that had been assembled from dust.

INTERPRETATION GUIDED BY PURPOSE

An important principle for interpreting Bible passages is to allow the Bible to provide relevant background information. Although it might be tempting to use only relevant creation scriptures, we should also consider God's ultimate intention. His overall purpose adds insight to the creation story. In brief, creation and all of mankind's history lead up to a future heaven, in which God and His chosen people dwell intimately together in perfect unity:

> Now I saw a new heaven and a new earth, for the first heaven and the first earth had passed away. Also there was no more sea. Then I, John, saw the holy city, New Jerusalem, coming down out of heaven from God, prepared as a bride adorned for her husband. And I heard a loud voice from heaven saying, "Behold, the tabernacle of God is with men, and will dwell with them, and they shall be His people. God Himself will be with them and be their God." (Rev 21:1–3)

> I do not pray for these alone, but also for those who will believe in Me through their word; that they all may be one, as You, Father, are in Me, and I in You; that they also may be one in Us, that the world may believe that You sent Me. (John 17:20,21)

God did not create everything and then let it go, as Deists generally believe. He walked with Adam and Eve in the cool of the day, and even after the fall of man, He enjoyed the presence of His people

(Gen 3:8, Prov 8:31). Furthermore, Abraham and Jesus' disciples are called friends, not exactly a remote relationship (Is 41:8, John 15:14). Even after repeatedly arousing God's anger in the wilderness, God said that He dwelled in the midst of His people, conversing continually with Moses and Joshua. (Num 35:34) The Bible illustrates that God is involved with the lives of His people, and that He is creating a spiritual family in which close relationships are paramount.

In God's heaven, no place exists for evil and sin. Consequently, until the Last Day, believers are being transformed to exhibit the fruit of the Holy Spirit, rather than the deeds of our sinful natures (Gal 5:19–21). When mortal flesh ceases, any residual sinful nature will be cast off, so that heaven will not be contaminated. The concept of God having a close relationship with each one of His people is woven throughout the Bible. This provides insight into creation, as we will consider in the next chapter.

WHEELS WITHIN WHEELS

The history of differences between the church and scientists offers caution for both sides. The well known confrontation between Galileo Galilei and the Roman Catholic Church was based on the church defending a literal view of figurative passages. These coincided with ancient theories of geocentrism, proposed prior to Christianity by Aristotle, Plato, and Ptolemy. We can understand how the church theologians determined their geocentric beliefs from the scriptures, although they were not totally opposed to the figurative perspective of these same scriptures. Many of them, including the Pope, valued dialog about the two concepts. Galileo may have won over the church hierarchy if it were not for the arrogance that he displayed in his book, *Dialogue Concerning the Two Chief World Systems*. In his book, Galileo created a parody of Pope Urban VIII, greatly offending the Pope. The result of Galileo's conceit was that the geocentric controversy festered for another 200 years. In addition to lacking diplomacy, Galileo was not always correct scientifically. Nevertheless, his legacy was a considerable advance in the methods, findings and inventions of science.

The scientific observations and heliocentric models, developed by Copernicus, Galileo, and Kepler, prompted church theologians to defend their position by designing and building mechanical models to replicate geocentric circular orbits. These models were extremely complex, requiring epicycles, or wheels within wheels within wheels, to even approximate the motions of the planets. In a similar way today, Young Earth scientists have proposed complex mechanisms to explain scientific observations that otherwise negate the possibility of a very young earth. To account for huge intergalactic distances, such hypotheses have included stellar light created just to give the appearance of age, and a drastic reduction in the speed of light since creation began. To give credit to the Young Earth movement, some of their scientists have accepted that many of these ideas are not credible.[11] More recent attempts to explain a young earth include large changes in the decay rates of radioactive elements and relativistic time frames during the creation week. These ideas in turn require further explanations to account for unintended consequences that resemble the wheels within wheels of geocentricism. Some of their arguments may have merit, but the principle of Occam's razor should cause us to be quite skeptical.

CREDIBILITY

The creation account presented in the Bible is by far the most credible of any of the many creation stories that involve one or more gods. Biblical creation unfolds in a simple but technical manner without recourse to fanciful events. In addition, the creation narrative is supported by scientific evidence for origins of the universe. The Biblical God has purpose, impeccable character, was not involved in immoral activities with mortals, and reasoned with mankind as sin began to take its toll. The God of the Bible was and is self sufficient, not being born or emanating from some other god.

The first chapters in Genesis are quite different from the bizarre stories of other creation genres. The Bible does not have mythological stories involving multiple gods and demigods, which have all our human frailties as their hallmark. Bill Arnold expressed it well: "God has no genealogy, no ancestors, no rivals."[12]

The creation narrative is one of orderly steps in a process that is in broad agreement with modern science. It was not intended to be a complete description of all that God did, and in that sense, the six Days of creation are snapshots within the overall process. The remaining steps within each Day may be discovered by science, but full understanding of creation must wait until we meet our maker.

In the time of Moses when Genesis was written, it is quite likely that no one knew the details of the Biblical creation story. In addition to the various gods and fanciful creation myths that were part and parcel of the many religions of that time, the universe was thought to have always existed, and heavenly bodies were the result of erratic behavior of mythological gods. The concepts that Genesis revealed were not commonly understood. These include: one God creating the whole universe, the earth originally being uninhabitable, gradual transformation of the earth to make it habitable, and life being introduced gradually with increasing complexity. Most, if not all of civilization, had it wrong. The correct version of creation, which appeared with the writing of Genesis when science was too young to provide any help, is in itself good evidence for the divine origin of the creation account.

REFERENCES

1. Barbour, Ian. *When Science Meets Religion*. New York: HarperCollins, 2000: 2–4.
2. Wilson, Marvin. *Understanding Hebrew Thought: Jewish Roots of the Christian Faith*. Grand Rapids: Eerdmans, 1989: 135–153.
3. Whitefield, Rodney. *Reading Genesis One*. San Jose: R. Whitefield, 2004: 4.
4. Young, Davis, and Ralph Stearley. *The Bible, Rocks and Time*. Downers Grove: InterVarsity Press, 2008: 152–153.
5. Godfrey, W. Robert. *God's Pattern for Creation*. Phillipsburg: P&R Publishing, 2003: 49–50.
6. Alter, Robert. *Genesis*. New York: W. W. Norton & Co., 1996: ix–xxxix.
7. See Reference 4, 194–200.
8. Ibid., 154.
9. Ibid., 179–180.

10. Errico, Rocco. *The Mysteries of Creation, the Genesis Story.* Smyrna: Noorah Foundation, 2001: 100.

11. Humphreys, D. Russell. *Starlight and Time.* Green Forest: Master Books, 2003: 43–50.

12. Arnold, Bill. *Encountering the Book of Genesis.* Grand Rapids: Baker Publishing Group, 1998: 50.

3

THE BEGINNING OF EVERYTHING

In the beginning God created the heavens and the earth.
The earth was without form, and void; and darkness was on
the face of the deep. And the Spirit of God was hovering
over the face of the waters. (Gen 1:1–2)

The first verse in the Bible states with elegant simplicity that God created our earth and the heavens that lie so far beyond. The phrase "the heavens and the earth" is equivalent to the whole universe: the earth and the rest of creation. These heavens declare the glory of God, with immeasurable numbers of stars and galaxies spread over unreachable distances. The second verse transfers our focus to the earth, where its surface was found to lack any recognizable features, except that it was covered with water. No length of time is given after which the earth arrived at this condition. It could have been hours, years, or even billions of years. The Bible provides only controversial clues for the age of the universe. In contrast, scientists have developed theories that determine the age of the universe, based on a considerable body of evidence, some of which is given in Appendix D.

In the Old Testament, the Hebrew for the phrase "in the beginning" never refers to an instantaneous event but always to a preliminary period of time. However long this beginning may have lasted, the moment when matter and energy came to exist, was also the beginning of time. It was when everything appeared from nowhere; God was not merely rearranging matter that already existed. This was the beginning of all material existence.[1]

CREATION FROM SOMETHING OR FROM NOTHING

In Genesis 1, the Hebrew word for created is *bara*, which is used in the Bible only when God created something from material that had no prior existence, otherwise known as *ex nihilo* creation.[2] Conservative Christian theologians defend the *ex nihilo* concept against the opposing idea that God started with all the physical matter of the universe already in place and merely fashioned it anew. The Bible does not support an eternally existing universe, nor indeed do generally accepted scientific theories (the Steady State Theory is now largely discredited). The Hebrew word *bara* is used elsewhere in the creation story, either in reference to the first verse or later when living creatures were created with souls. The bodies of these creatures were made from existing material, but the totally new part of creation was their souls.

The next appearance of the Hebrew word *bara* occurs in verse 21, where God created great sea creatures. The Hebrew for these creatures is *nephesh chay,* which means creatures that have souls. This includes whales, dolphins, and other marine mammals, as explained in chapter 4. When God created souls, He created something new that was not physical DNA and organic material that He assembled from dust. On the sixth Day, God created land animals, but the word *bara* is not used, perhaps to keep the number of occurrences to seven; as explained in the last chapter. The same concept of a brand new creation, however, is strongly implied because of the similarity with the creation of marine animals and mankind.

In verse 27, the word *bara* occurs three more times, emphasizing the unique culmination of creation, mankind. This was God's crown jewel, confirmed in the New Testament with James 1:18: "that we might be a kind of first fruits of His creation." In Genesis 2, 5, and 6, the word *bara* is used again but in reference to the previously mentioned verses in Genesis 1.

When God was not creating *ex nihilo*, the word used for God's work in Genesis is *made,* which in Hebrew is *asah.* This has the meaning of making or fashioning something from existing materials. In some verses, however, neither *asah* nor *bara* is used in the Hebrew; instead the word *let* occurs in English. This is translated from the Hebrew jussive form, which expresses a command to the earth: "Let there be"; "Let the waters under the heavens be gathered into one place"; "Let the earth bring forth grass"; "Let the waters bring forth"; "Let the earth bring forth". Again, no new material is involved. The word *let* gives the impression that the earth could have changed or brought forth living creatures of its own accord, but in reality, God made these events occur though His commands.

The reader may have heard the expression "God spoke and the universe leapt into existence." This may indeed have happened, but Genesis neither states that God spoke when He created the universe in the beginning, nor that it occurred instantaneously. It is true that God spoke during each of the following six Days, but then God was rearranging matter that had already been created. In effect, The Bible defines two major stages of creation, described in Genesis 1:1–3 and Genesis 1:3–2:3. Almost all early church theologians were in agreement on this issue.[3] After the universe was initially created during the first stage, an intermediate state was reached in which the earth was "without form, and void". Then during the second stage, which took place during the six creation Days, the earth was transformed for life and then filled with life.

It may be a small point, but in the first verse, the heavens are mentioned before the earth, and perhaps if there is any significance to this it is because the earth was a product of the heavens; at least from a scientific and Old Earth perspective. After the brief creation statement in verse 1, the emphasis immediately changes in verse 2, as God transfers attention from the universe as a whole to conditions on the earth.

THE PRIMORDIAL PLANET

At the transition stage described in verse 2, the whole earth was covered with water, above which, an opaque atmosphere blocked sunlight. The implication here is that the solid earth beneath the waves was relatively flat without any really high mountains. If we could have looked out from an Apollo spacecraft circling the earth at that time, we would have seen the earth, moon, planets, sun, and stars; but not quite as we see them today. We could not have seen the water that covered the earth's surface because no light was able to reach it, somewhat like Venus today, which is covered with clouds of sulfur dioxide and sulfuric acid in an atmosphere of carbon dioxide.

After the universe had been created, the earth was initially found to be uninhabitable. We might ask why God included this intermediate stage in Genesis. Perhaps it was to show that His creation did not appear suddenly. Arguably, God could have created a habitable planet in the very beginning. Instead, it was God's wisdom to form a habitable planet in stages, the first of which had a lifeless and barren surface.[4] This condition is sometimes translated as chaotic, which might be a fitting description for the Old Earth model, in which many asteroids and meteorites struck earth during the Late Heavy Bombardment phase about four billion years ago.

At this point in the earth's existence the Holy Spirit was hovering over the deep. The Holy Spirit remained actively involved throughout the six Days of creation. The presence of the Holy Spirit is found throughout Biblical history, and until the end times, the Bible provides no indication that the Holy Spirit leaves the earth (2 Thess 2:7). Although it may be possible for God to have allowed natural processes to transform the earth during Days 1 through 4, there is good reason to believe that God actively intervened. A habitable planet, such as earth, is so unusual in our very hostile universe that it is reasonable to believe that God orchestrated the transforming events on earth's surface. The location of the earth in a life-friendly solar system appears to have been specially chosen to support a great variety of species, especially mankind.[5]

Old Earth: Scientists believe that the earth was formed from an accumulation of orbiting solar material that included vast quantities of water. At some point, water completely covered earth's initial rocky core. During this early phase of earth's history, the Holy Spirit was seeding the earth with bacteria, the first form of life. Bacteria are thought to have generated oxygen for the atmosphere and converted toxic minerals into more stable ores that would eventually prove useful to mankind.[6]

Young Earth: All of creation would have taken place over six 24-hour Days, based on the narrative in Genesis 1 and also the reason that God gave in the fourth commandment: "For in six days the Lord made the heavens and the earth, the sea, and all that is in them, and rested the seventh day. Therefore the Lord blessed the Sabbath day and hallowed it." (Ex 20:11) In this verse the word *made* is translated from the Hebrew word *asah*, not the word *bara* used in Genesis 1:1. Therefore, this verse in Exodus concerns the six Days in which God changed the earth and filled it with creatures, and does not include the *ex nihilo* creation of Genesis 1:1. This highlights a weakness in the Young Earth position that does not do justice to the well-defined textual structure in each of the six Days, in which God spoke, transforming and filling the earth. Exodus 20:11 provides only a very brief summary of these six Days and should not be used to define the length of the six creation Days.

DID THE EARTH ALWAYS HAVE A SUN?

Before continuing with the creation narrative, we need to investigate a significant debate concerning the point in time when God created the sun, moon, and stars. Although we have already determined that they were created before the first Day, verses 14–19 appear to mean that they were created on the fourth Day. This apparent contradiction can be resolved by considering Hebrew grammar.

Is the first verse a summary about creation of the heavens and the earth, followed by amplification in subsequent verses? Or is the first verse an independent statement about the initial event of creation and the following verses describe subsequent events? Most conservative Hebrew scholars consider the latter alternative to be true.[7] Detailed arguments for this perspective are provided in Appendix E. If the former view were true, then it could mean that creation of the sun, moon, and stars occurred on the fourth Day as verses 14–16 appear to convey in English:

Then God said, "Let there be lights in the firmament of the heavens to divide the day from the night; and let them be for signs and seasons, and for days and years; and let them be for lights in the firmament of the heavens to give light on the earth"; and it was so. Then God made two great lights: the greater light to rule the day, and the lesser light to rule the night. He made the stars also. (Gen 1:14–16)

These verses appear to make the first verse a summary of creation, with the result that many Christians believe that the sun, moon, and stars were all created on the fourth Day. This apparent contradiction can be resolved when we consider that the Hebrew language did not have a pluperfect tense.[8] The author of Genesis could not write in verse 16, *God [had] made*, but wrote what we currently read in English, *God made*. In practice long ago, the readers or listeners of Hebrew would have remembered the context of the first verse, which in Hebrew was understood as an initial and completed action. They would have then understood the pluperfect sense for the fourth Day. This is critical to understanding the sequence of events in Genesis. In addition, we should use an alternative translation for verse 14, where God said, *Let there be lights*. This phrase can also be translated, *let lights appear*, as described in Hebrew lexicons. These two features of Hebrew allow verses 14–19 to mean the heavenly bodies became visible on the fourth Day. Grammatical details and support for this argument are provided in Appendix E.

Old Earth: The interpretation given above is in accord with conventional scientific ideas about the order of creation as shown in chapter 11. Existence of the earth before the Sun was created is not in accord with science, and it does not follow from the preferred interpretation of Genesis 1:1–3.

Young Earth: The Young Earth model states that the sun, moon and other heavenly bodies were created on the fourth Day, although it is not a necessary requirement for an earth that is only a few thousand years old. In an attempt to reconcile the apparent contradiction of when the heavens were created, Young Earth proponents have suggested that the word for heavens means empty space or possibly a spiritual heaven, rather than the sun, moon, and stars. This argument fails because Genesis 2:1 summarizes the creation week: "Thus the heavens and the earth, and all the host of them, were finished". This passage refers to the heavenly bodies described in Genesis 1:14–19, in addition to the changes made to the earth and the creatures placed on it. *Heavens and earth* is the same phrase, however, that is used in Genesis 1:1. Therefore, Genesis 2:1 provides a descriptive meaning to Genesis 1:1, indicating that the heavens in Genesis 1:1 contained the sun, moon, and stars.

DAY BY DAY SUMMARY

During each creation Day, God used matter that He had previously created in the very beginning (verse 1). During the first Day, light from the sun reached the earth's surface as a result of changes to earth's atmosphere; the atmosphere was, however, opaque. On the second Day, God separated surface water into two layers, so that the atmosphere was clear beneath the clouds above. On the third Day, God raised existing rock formations from beneath the oceans and made land appear. Later that Day, plants and trees were created, presumably from the dust that had accumulated. This assumption is reasonable because animals and humans were created from dust. On the fourth Day, God changed the atmosphere again so that the heavenly bodies could be clearly seen and identified. Sea creatures were created on the fifth Day, again presumably from dust. Finally, on the sixth Day, God created animals and humans from the dust of the earth.

God chose six Days to describe his work when He could have arranged creation over a different number of Days. The reason for six Days is given in the Ten Commandments, which state that man is to work only six days before resting on the seventh, as God had done. This was God's purpose in selecting six Days for His work, which required that two creation events take place on both the third and fifth Days. Without the commandment that defined the length of a working week, God could have explained creation in terms of seven or eight Days, or even many more if He included in Genesis the many things that were not mentioned.

FIRST LIGHT

> Then God said, "Let there be light"; and there was light.
> And God saw the light, that it was good; and God divided
> the light from the darkness. God called the light Day, and
> the darkness He called Night. So the evening and the
> morning were the first day. (Gen 1: 3–5)

In the first Day, the earth's atmosphere was modified so that light
shone through to the earth's surface. This is all that Genesis informs us
God did that Day. Nevertheless, it continues to be sufficient to provide
the energy needed for almost all life forms. Previously, sunlight had
been blocked by an opaque atmosphere that was probably composed
of very thick clouds of water vapor evaporating from the surface of the
deep. We can get an idea of the effect of such clouds by considering
thick thunderclouds that we see today. They are almost totally opaque
and the little light that we do see comes from around their sides.
Changes that occurred in this early atmosphere, over an unspecified
time, allowed the sun's light to penetrate and to illuminate the surface
of the deep. God called the presence of light on the earth's surface *Day*,
and darkness He called *Night*.

When God changed the atmosphere to allow light to reach the
earth, the sun, moon and stars were not visible as discrete entities.
The atmosphere was translucent, which allowed plenty of light to
reach the earth, just as it does today when total cloud cover prevents
us from seeing the sun. This understanding of events is consistent with
the heavenly bodies becoming visible on the fourth Day, as described
in Genesis 1:14 and discussed later in this chapter. On that Day, the
atmosphere was changed a second time, becoming totally transparent
and allowing the heavenly bodies to be seen and identified.

Old Earth: The Bible gives no indication that the nature of this first
light was any different from light seen throughout recorded history.
Scientific measurements show that light has constant velocity, both
through space and time. No matter how fast the source or observer of
light may be travelling, scientists find that the speed of light never varies
for a given medium. This discovery gave Einstein the information he

needed to formulate his Special Theory of Relativity, in which gravity is not involved. What we can understand from this theory is that we are unable to tell how fast we are moving in an absolute sense. No reference point exists that can be used for zero velocity within the universe. All we can do is to compare our own velocity with that of any other object; hence the concept of relativity.

Knowing the velocity of light, we can determine how long it takes for light to reach the earth from any given star, assuming we know the distance between the star and the earth. The distance light travels in a year, known as a light-year, is about six trillion miles. For stars that are relatively close to earth, distances can be determined by precise optical measurements, which indicate that some stars are as much as tens of thousands of light years away. Most of the billions of stars that can be seen only with telescopes are much further away. Other scientific methods are used to determine distances to more distant stars. Stars and galaxies can be seen throughout the universe, some at distances of many billions of light years.

Young Earth: Young Earth scientists agree about the size of the universe. If a star, however, were just one million light years away, and if the universe were only 6,000 years old, we could not see that star for another 994,000 years. In order to overcome this contradiction with observed reality, Young Earth proponents have suggested various solutions, including an initially high velocity that quickly fell to its modern value. Nevertheless, attempts by Young Earth believers to show that the velocity of light has decreased since measurements were first taken do not stand up to scientific scrutiny and have been abandoned.[9] The velocity of light is fundamental to many physical processes. If it were significantly different, a habitable universe could not exist. The velocity of light does not change, except for gravitational dilation as required by the General Theory of Relativity.

A *white hole* cosmology was proposed in attempts to solve the problem of distant stars being too far away to be seen within a few thousand years of earth's creation.[12] This theory proposed that as the universe expanded on the second Day, the waters were separated between one mass on the earth and another at the edge of the universe. It fails to keep the chronological sequence of Genesis, because the earth, instead of just water, would not have existed until after the second Day. Also, because Genesis describes what can be seen from the earth, rather than invisible matter in the far distant universe, the outer firmament of water should not be placed at the edge of the universe.

A new theory for the beginning of the universe was then proposed by Dr. John Hartnett in his book *Starlight, Time and the New Physics.* In this theory, based on Carmeli's Theory of Cosmological General Relativity (CGR), the earth was created at the center of the universe where it experienced time at a much reduced rate, while the far-flung universe experienced time much as we do today. As a result of this time dilation, earth's years are far fewer, just a few thousand compared to the billions in outer space. Because it is essentially a big bang theory, it generates similar cosmological processes and structures that we see today, including solar systems. Most scientists believe that solar systems did not appear for billions of years after the big bang, and our solar system in particular started after about eight billion years. Dr. Hartnett tweaks CGR for the earth to be created mainly from water and proposes that the sun was created on the fourth Day. Also, in order for Adam to see starlight two days later, his theory requires that God created and then stopped massive expansion of the universe on the fourth Day.

Because the velocity of light is constant, we can determine whether clocks on earth or those in the rest of the universe yielded the correct time in the beginning stages of this model. As light traveled across the universe, where negligible time dilation occurred, we know that time would have been normal, as we experience it today, and about 13.7 billion years would have elapsed. Meanwhile, nothing much would have happened in the vicinity of earth, just a few days would have passed by in a time warp. Normal galactic and planetary processes would have been suspended, and our solar system could not have developed. So God would have had to disregard this theory and separately create our solar system as we know it today. Essentially Dr. Hartnett has concocted a Young Earth in a very old universe, with many wheels within wheels to account for observed reality. Without Dr. Hartnett's tweaks, CGR may provide solutions to some conventional big bang problems, and in essence, it does not contradict an Old Earth perspective.

Although the Young Earth belief that the sun did not exist until the fourth Day may be an acceptable interpretation of Genesis, it does raise serious problems with other parts of the creation narrative. In order to account for the light that was created on the first Day, Young Earth believers have devised alternative sources of light. The Bible makes no statement about alternative light sources, so they can only imagine what kind of temporary light source God was supposed to have created. Was it physical or spiritual? Was it located near earth or in the sun's position? When did God stop or destroy this alternative light source, which was only to provide light until the fourth Day? Another difficulty with this approach is that *day* and *night* were both defined by the light created on the first Day, so that it is reasonable to assume that it has been the same light source that causes day and night ever since. The Bible does not support a source of light other than the sun.

ATMOSPHERICS

> Then God said, "Let there be a firmament in the midst of the waters, and let it divide the waters from the waters." Thus God made the firmament, and divided the waters which were under the firmament from the waters which were above the firmament; and it was so. And God called the firmament Heaven. So the evening and the morning were the second day. (Gen 1:6–8)

The Hebrew word for *firmament* has a variety of translations, including vault, canopy, and a three dimensional expanse; the sky, or our existing atmosphere beneath the clouds conveys the meaning. The *firmament* was created to form a clear atmospheric layer above the ocean but beneath the clouds above. Previously the surface of water that covered the earth had been evaporating and forming thick clouds and fog that completely covered the earth down to its surface. The *firmament* is simply a term for what we can see, in other words the sky. The Genesis narrative describes objects that are visible to the naked eye. The waters that surrounded the atmosphere formed a translucent barrier, just like clouds do today. Light from the sun penetrated through the clouds, but the sun itself could not be seen.

The Hebrew word for heaven is *shamayim*, which is derived from the concept of lofty. It has more than one application and can mean the sky immediately above us, space where stars and planets exist, and also the spiritual concept where God exists.[11] In the context of making an atmosphere during the second Day, it means the sky above the earth's surface. Until the fourth Day, the sky was completely covered by clouds.

Old Earth: The Biblical description of the earth's early atmosphere is not in conflict with scientific discoveries. Recent work on ancient fossils of bacteria, thought to be about 3.4 billion years old, led to this description of the earth: "hot, and violent, with volcanic activity dominating the early Earth. The sky was cloudy and grey ... Any land masses were small, or about the size of Caribbean islands".[12] This fits in well with the Biblical second Day.

Young Earth: Some Young Earth believers have suggested that the outer layer of water was a continuous band of liquid water, rather than clouds of water vapor. This proposed *water canopy*, some thousands of feet in height, has been used to account for the Flood, when it would have turned into rain that flooded the earth to depths that covered the mountains. Scripture provides little support for this idea, and it has insurmountable scientific problems. As many people have said, it does not hold water.

LAND AND SEA

> Then God said, "Let the waters under the heavens be gathered together into one place, and let the dry land appear"; and it was so. And God called the dry land Earth, and the gathering together of the waters He called Seas. And God saw that it was good. (Gen 1: 9–10)

On the third Day God brought land from out of the depths of the sea. This may have given rise to the single continent called Pangaea, which is believed to have existed before our continents became separate land masses. The substance of the land had been created previously, and during the third Day, the earth's crust rose and became visible above the oceans.

Old Earth: Some scientists believe that about 500 million years ago the earth was covered by water, and the first single continent arose about that time. This is in agreement with the Biblical description of the fourth Day. It took eons for the earth's continental crust to be formed and then to be pushed up by tectonic forces. As the barren rock weathered with the elements, soil was eventually created, aided by the action of bacteria and other organisms designed for this purpose. The new fertile land was then ready for plants that God created later that same Day.

Young Earth: A single continent, several thousand miles across, would have risen out of the ocean in a matter of hours. As the new land surface emerged from the ocean, any loose sediment would have washed away with the draining waters. Water that had been lifted up in the middle of a continent would have taken days or weeks to flow back into the ocean. Massive tsunamis would have battered the new coastline. In order for the vegetation to survive that God created later this Day, God would have had to physically push the waters off the continents and to quell the violent waves. Only then could vegetation have been planted. But not until God had also created soil in which plants and trees could grow. Soil is full of organic materials, worms, bacteria, fungi, and other organisms, the existence of which are not mentioned in Genesis.

As important as the aquatic turmoil above the earth's surface may have been, the processes below ground in the earth's crust and mantle would have been far more significant. Science has no explanation for Pangaea rising out of the ocean in only a few hours. Earth's rocks are far too viscous to allow such rapid movement. This means God would have had to manually shape the earth like a lump of clay. The 24-hour Day model requires a lot of special treatment to allow plants and trees to grow in what was originally virgin rock awash with turbulent and salty oceans.

VEGETATION

> Then God said, "Let the earth bring forth grass, the herb that yields seed, and the fruit tree that yields fruit according to its kind, whose seed is in itself, on the earth"; and it was so. And the earth brought forth grass, the herb that yields seed according to its kind, and the tree that yields fruit, whose seed is in itself according to its kind. And God saw that it was good. So the evening and the morning were the third day. (Gen 1:11–13)

God appears to have been somewhat removed when He created plants and trees. He gave instructions, and the earth brought forth vegetation, almost as if He had allowed the earth to generate plants of its own accord. In later verses, this situation changes as God becomes more involved in the creation of animal life, and then even more so with creation of man. The vegetation mentioned in Genesis was of three types that propagate by seed: grasses, plants, and trees.[13] The Hebrew words for *grass, herb,* and *tree* can have a wide variety of meanings, allowing an alternative interpretation in which two types of vegetation existed: plants with seeds and trees with fruit that contained seeds. The Hebrew words could imply all forms of vegetation or only specific types, such as the grasses, shrubs and trees that grow today. The latter would exclude certain prehistoric plants and ferns, which means this ambiguity leaves these verses open to either Young Earth or Old Earth interpretations.

Old Earth: The wording in Genesis implies that all vegetation created on the fourth Day was growing and recognizably so. It does not appear that God made plants grow or multiply more rapidly than usual. Rather, once life forms were created, they had the power to grow and multiply with natural abilities preordained by God, with the implication that it would take many years for each species to multiply and fill the earth.

Once land had appeared, thousands or even millions of years elapsed before soil with microorganisms became established. After God had created different varieties of plants, similar periods of time passed by as they spread across the world. Virgin rock does not support plant growth well, as scientists with the European Space Agency discovered when they attempted to grow seedlings in pure crushed rock. The addition, however, of certain bacteria made all the difference, presumably because the bacteria were releasing vital nutrients from the rock.

The fossil record shows that extinct giant ferns are found near the bottom of the geological column of plants. If God had made large ferns and seed bearing trees on the fourth Day, we would expect to find fossils of all kinds of trees in the same geological layers. The seed bearing trees, however, are all found above the earliest ferns. Adam could not have seen giant ferns, so that God would have had little reason to include them in Genesis. A more detailed discussion of the fossil order is given in chapter 11.

Young Earth: When God made creatures, He made a limited number and then commanded them to "be fruitful and multiply". Probably, God used the same method with plants and trees, in which event, a 24-hour day could not suffice, or there would not have been sufficient vegetation for the herbivores that He was about to create.

HEAVENLY BODIES

> Then God said, "Let there be lights in the firmament of the heavens to divide the day from the night; and let them be for signs and seasons, and for days and years; and let them be for lights in the firmament of the heavens to give light on the earth"; and it was so. Then God made two great lights: the greater light to rule the day, and the lesser light to rule the night. He made the stars also. God set them in the firmament of the heavens to give light on the earth, and to rule over the day and to rule over the night, and to divide the light from the darkness. And God saw that it was good. So the evening and the morning were the fourth day. (Gen 1:14–19)

As noted earlier, the sun, moon, and stars already existed before the first Day. In a similar situation to the appearance of land that had been previously created, so here the heavenly bodies appeared, having been created long before. On the fourth Day, in Genesis 1:14–15, God made them visible and stated the purposes for their existence. From the perspective of the earth's surface they appeared as lights in the sky. In Moses' time, nobody knew that stars were millions and billions of light years away. Before the fourth Day, the sun was not directly visible, and it served to provide only diffuse light through the clouds, sufficient for growth of vegetation that had been created on the third Day. Night would have been pitch-black. With the introduction of creatures during the fifth Day, some light was necessary for nocturnal creatures. The full purpose for the sun, moon, and stars was realized only when men began to populate the earth and were able to use them for "signs and seasons".

God had intended the stars to be useful signs that would reveal His message of hope to the world. The message He created, however, has been corrupted by thousands of years of astrology.[14] When God created the nation of Israel, He forbade them from pursuing astrology and other occult practices because they circumvented God's provision for Israel and directed them away from their allegiance to God. Nevertheless, many Israelites relied on astrologers, who used positions of stars and planets to seduce people into thinking that stars in the sky contained meaning for their everyday lives. In contrast, God's intention for the stars was for men to see the key events that God had planned for mankind, not what might befall men on a daily basis.

The constellations show God's plan for Jesus, from His virgin birth to the coming of the Lion of Judah. The zodiac was established thousands of years before the birth of Christ, indicating a supernatural origin. Ancient records show that all major ancient civilizations had twelve constellations, most of them arranged in the same order. Although their meanings have been distorted through the ages, the most ancient records give meanings consistent with the gospel. Early carvings show Virgo at the starting point and Leo at the end.[15] A full explanation of the original Zodiac, its meanings, and the astrological distortions that followed can be found in *The Real Meaning of the Zodiac* by the late Dr. James Kennedy.

Prior to the birth of Jesus, Magi used the conjunctions of planets and stars to find the birth place of the King of the Jews in order to worship Him. These Magi were not necessarily astrologers: many of them understood astronomy and its relationship to future events that were predicted by the signs of the zodiac. The amazing stellar and planetary conjunctions that occurred during the birth and crucifixion of Jesus have been recreated with computer models of the solar system. These can be seen on a DVD, The Star of Bethlehem, available at the web site of Rick Larson.[16]

Genesis 1:16–17 must be translated with the pluperfect tense to agree with the creation event of verse 1. We should read: "And God [had] made two great lights", and "God [had] set them in the firmament". The sun, moon, planets, and stars looked just like lights shining from within the immediate sky above and still do. Now however, we know they are so very far away beyond our sky and atmosphere.

Old Earth: The interpretation of Genesis given above provides a sequence of creation events that is in agreement with the conventional scientific description of when these events occurred.

Young Earth: The Young Earth interpretation of Genesis is that the sun, moon, and stars were all created on the fourth Day. This belief in itself does not have much bearing on the age of earth. This poor interpretation, however, does keep Young Earth scientists striving to explain how much conventional science on this topic is not valid.

REFERENCES

1. Bavinck, Herman. *In the Beginning*. Grand Rapids: Baker Books, 2000: 34–39.
2. Phillips, John. *Exploring Genesis*. Grand Rapids: Kregel Publications, 1980: 38.
3. Copan, Paul, and William Craig. *Creation out of Nothing*. Grand Rapids: Baker Academic, 2004: 118–144.
4. Godfrey, W. Robert. *God's Pattern for Creation*. Philipsburg: P&R Publishing Company, 2003: 24–26.

5. Ross, Hugh. *More Than A Theory.* Grand Rapids: Baker Books, 2009: 121–171.

6. Ibid., 152–153.

7. Errico, Rocco. *The Mysteries of Creation, the Genesis Story.* Smyrna: Noorah Foundation, 2001: 72–74.

8. Gray, Gorman. *The Age of the Universe.* Washougal: Morning Star Publications, 2005: 183.

9. Humphreys, D. Russell. *Starlight and Time,* 2003. Green Forest: Master Books, 2003: 43–51.

10. Wilson, William. *Old Testament Word Studies.* Grand Rapids: Kregel Publications, 1978: 213.

11. Brasier, Martin. *Oldest Fossils on Earth Discovered.* Science Daily Website. 22 Aug 2011. <http://www.sciencedaily.com/ releases/2011/08/110821205241.htm>

12. See Reference 9, 34–35.

13. See Reference 2, 42.

14. Kennedy, D. James. *The Real Meaning of the Zodiac.* Fort Lauderdale: Coral Ridge Ministries, 1989: 7.

15. Ibid., 8.

16. Larson, Rick. *The Star of Bethlehem.* DVD, <http://www.bethlehemstar.net/>

4

ABUNDANCE OF LIFE

Earth is crammed with heaven
And every bush aflame with God
But only those who see take off their shoes.
—Elizabeth Barrett Browning

The first animals created by God that are recorded in Genesis were aquatic. At about the same time, birds were created to fill the air, and then the next Day, animals were created to dwell on land.

> Then God said, "Let the waters abound with an abundance of living creatures, and let birds fly across the face of the firmament of the heavens." So God created great sea creatures and every living thing that moves, with which the waters abounded, according to their kind, and every winged bird according to its kind. And God saw that it was good. And God blessed them saying, "Be fruitful and multiply, and fill the waters in the seas, and let birds multiply on the earth." So the evening and the morning were the fifth day. (Gen 1:20–23)

> Then God said, "Let the earth bring forth the living creature according to its kind: cattle and creeping thing and beast of the earth, each according to its kind"; and it was so. And God made the beast of the earth according to its kind, and

everything that creeps on the earth according to its kind,
And God saw that it was good. (Gen 1:24–25)

God had personally created animals suitable for all three habitats, land, sea, and air. Two categories of sea creatures are mentioned, *great sea creatures* and *every living thing* (presumably *every living thing* does not include *great sea creatures*). Birds were simply a single category. On land, three categories of creatures are mentioned: *cattle*, *creeping thing*, and *beast of the earth*. These descriptions do not match our modern scientific classifications, but they were practical and relevant for people at the time Moses wrote Genesis, about 1,400 BC.

The Bible describes creatures with which mankind was familiar. The creation narrative mentions only extant species; if God had included extinct species, such as dinosaurs, it would have had little if any meaning. Other species that were not mentioned include microscopic species, many of which could not be seen by mankind for thousands of years. Missing classifications that are essential parts of our ecology include: bacteria, fungi, crustaceans, amphibians, and possibly fish and reptiles, depending on the meaning of certain Hebrew words that will be discussed in the next section.

THE ESSENTIAL SOUL

English translations do not capture the specific meanings of the Hebrew words used to describe the creatures that God created. In particular, the final creation event was of man who is described in English as a *living being*: "And the Lord God formed man of the dust of the ground, and breathed into his nostrils the breath of life; and man became a living being." The Hebrew words for *living being* are *nephesh chay*, which refer to a creature (*chay*) with a soul (*nephesh*). This is indicated in the New King James Version with a translation note to that effect. Souls have non-material existence, which includes the capacity for feeling emotions. Emotional expression in animals may be limited in comparison to humans, depending on the species. In the Bible, *chay* is often translated animal or beast, whereas *nephesh* is always used for non-material existence. A fundamental difference, however, exists between man and beast; it is the spirit that God breathed into man; we are much more than creatures with souls.

In the Old Testament, *nephesh* occurs 753 times. The King James Version translates this word as soul 475 times, a life 117 times, a person 29 times, and mind or heart 30 times. The overwhelming meaning is a soul that occupies a body but is not the body itself. When a person dies, the soul departs, leaving the body behind.

In Genesis there are ten instances of *nephesh chay*. Three occur in verses that describe the creation of animals, and one in the verse that describes the provision of vegetation for their food. Genesis 2:7 describes how God breathed life into man, and he became *nephesh chay*. When Adam named the animals, this term was used again. The final four instances occur after the Flood, when God made His covenant not to flood the world again. Genesis is consistent about the creatures (*nephesh chay*) that God described in creation, about those that Adam named, and about those that Noah took on the Ark. They were all creatures with souls.

The Hebrew words *nephesh chay,* which are used for the creatures that God introduced in the sea and on land, are shown below for the appropriate verses:

> Then God said, "Let the waters abound with an abundance of living creatures [*nephesh chay*], and let birds fly above the earth across the face of the firmament of the heavens." So God created great sea creatures and every living thing [*nephesh chay*] that moves, with which the waters abounded, according to their kind, and every winged bird according to its kind. And God saw that it was good. (Gen 1:20–21)

> Then God said, "Let the earth bring forth the living creature [*nephesh chay*] according to its kind: cattle and creeping thing and beast of the earth, each according to its kind"; and it was so. (Gen 1:24)

In order to simplify discussion of verses with *nephesh chay,* this phrase will normally be translated in this book as Mammals and Birds, creatures that exhibit soul like behavior, even if it is very limited in some species.

God created species that are not mentioned in the six creation Days, such as reptiles, fish, and amphibians. These do not exhibit emotions, and they are not included among species that have souls. They lack the limbic structure of the brain that is responsible for emotions.

THREE IN ONE

Adam was created a *living being* when God breathed life into him. (Gen 2:7) At this point, Adam became unique among all of creation, he was given spiritual life. God did not breathe this life into animals. The spirit of man is inextricably entwined with his soul, so much so, that separation would only be possible through the word of God. (Heb 4:12) When people die, both soul and spirit leave the body. Often we refer to just the soul or just the spirit in such circumstances, depending on the context. Each person is three natures in one; body, soul, and spirit. Some people, however, think of the soul and spirit as a single entity, which is not a big issue for most of us.

THE MAGNIFICENT SEVEN

Genesis 1:20–25 describes creation of six different kinds of animals, all belonging to the classification of Mammals and Birds. On the sixth Day, one more creature in this classification was added; man, bringing the total to seven and symbolizing the perfection of creation. These were the Magnificent Seven that to some extent demonstrated the character of God. The apostle Paul remarked: "His invisible attributes are clearly seen, being understood by the things that are made". (Gen 1:20)

Genesis informed Moses and the nation of Israel that God alone created these animals, which they had seen and heard about; they were not the result of any pagan pantheon of gods. Although God had also created all extinct species, these were not included in the creation narrative because at that time, they were not observable in nature. Moses and the Israelites could not have understood a list of extinct animals. All of the animals described in Genesis are extant kinds of

Mammals and Birds (at the time Genesis was written), which still populate the earth.

Six of these kinds of creatures were mammals. The other kind was birds, which are also warm-blooded and have similar limited emotional capabilities as mammals. All these creatures had souls.[1] Although fish are mentioned in verse 28 as creatures over which man was to have dominion, they were omitted from the previous verses that dealt with creation. This is one example of other kinds of animals that God had created but was not mentioned in the creation narrative. Serpents were another kind.

This interpretation, that the emphasis of Genesis is about Mammals and Birds, becomes compelling when we look at other passages in Genesis. For example, in Genesis 2, God asked Adam to find a creature comparable to him. The animals that God brought to Adam were Mammals and Birds, specifically cattle, beasts of the field, and birds; all of which he named. After the Flood, God made a covenant never to flood the whole earth again. He made it with Noah and also with the Mammals and Birds; specifically birds, cattle, and beasts of the earth. God did not make His covenant with insects, amphibians, and reptiles; nor does it seem appropriate to have done so. The common theme in these passages about animals is that of relationship. God wanted mankind to understand that His ultimate intention was, and is, to have a close relationship with His people.

FRIENDS

God wanted Adam to understand the dynamics of having a friendship with other creatures. Most of us who have pets understand this kind of friendship, sharing emotions and observing their ability to think, although to very different degrees.

Well documented examples exist of pets showing amazing intellect and devotion. Even wild animals have been shown to share these characteristics: for example, dolphins are known to protect humans from sharks. An anecdotal example was reported in a Denver newspaper about a parrot that was instrumental in saving a baby that was choking, while the babysitter was in another room. The family parrot was in the same room as the baby, and raucously called out "Mama, baby" repeatedly, until the babysitter came to the rescue. In this instance the parrot had to recognize the graveness of the baby's situation and then to care enough to do something about it. Finally, the parrot had to know how to get help and how to vocalize the solution. I do not think this kind of behavior, or any kind of reciprocal relationship, is possible with cold-blooded reptiles.

We can make educated guesses about the types of animals created on the fifth and sixth Days. Both on land and in the seas, the overall description is Mammals and Birds. Only two categories are given for the oceans: *great sea creatures*, and *every living thing*. *Great sea creatures* must refer to whales, so that *every living thing* includes smaller mammals such as dolphins, which are also warm-blooded air-breathing creatures. Dolphins and other cetaceans live in pods, which are constantly on the move, agreeing with the description of Genesis 1:20. Fish were not mentioned in this phase of God's creation because they do not possess souls but were included in Genesis 1:28, which lists creatures over which Adam was to have dominion. The Hebrew for fish, *dag*, could include species such as crustaceans.

On land, cattle were the kind of animals that man could domesticate, even keep as pets. Beasts of the earth were mammals that were wild, although some of these creatures such as large cats have also been tamed. *Creeping thing* in general can mean any small creature, but in this context of mammals, it does not include reptiles, amphibians, and insects; they do not have souls. This category of *creeping things* includes small mammals such as mice and other rodents.[2] They are warm-blooded but do not usually demonstrate much in the way of an emotional relationship with humans.

Old Earth: In an Old Earth understanding, bacteria of various kinds were created soon after the earth had a sufficiently hospitable environment. Over many millions of years, they created oxygen and converted various ores into stable minerals that we recognize and use today.

By restricting aquatic animals created on the fifth Day to mammals, the order of creation fits the fossil record, lending considerable credence to this interpretation. Other sea creatures, such as fish and crustaceans, were created during the fourth Day but before creation of flowering plants. This is consistent with the fossil record that shows fish and most other marine species occurring before flowering plants. More is said about the fossil record and the creation sequence in chapter 11.

Young Earth: The earth's great ore reserves, which scientists believe were laid down by bacterial activity, could not have been deposited within a period of a day or two. Young Earth scientists have no explanation for deposition of metallic ores through bacteria, or any other mechanism for that matter.

The Young Earth model does not agree with the fossil record because all species of land animals do not show up in one geological instant in the fossil record. If they had all been created in a single 24-hour day, fossils of all species should appear in the same early strata. Moreover, there should be no shortage of such fossils because Young Earth scientists claim a vast biomass existed prior to the Flood in order to account for our extensive oil reserves.

Young Earth believers sometimes go to great pains in estimating the speed at which Adam named all the animals that ever existed, all during the daytime of one 24-hour day. This idea requires more than supernatural intervention. God had already used much of the sixth Day to make all land animals, create Adam, and make the garden of Eden. After naming the animals, the remainder of the Day was spent with the creation of Eve. Recognizing the limited number of hours in a day, Young Earth believers claim that Adam named all the animals at superhuman speed. This approach misses the point entirely. God wanted Adam to establish a relationship with these animals, in particular with birds and beasts of the field such as herbivores. In order to do this and determine how each one might help and relate to Adam, he must have spent a few days at least with each animal. He might have found that dogs are for companionship, horses for riding, cats to keep the yard clear of vermin, and so on.

THE CULMINATION OF CREATION

> Then God said, "Let Us make man in Our image, according to Our likeness; let them have dominion over the fish of the sea, over the birds of the air, and over the cattle, over all the earth and over every creeping thing that creeps on the earth." So God created man in His own image; in the image of God He created him; male and female He created them. (Gen 1:26–27)

It was as if God had been somewhat aloof during the previous five Days of creation, saying, "Let there be". For the final event of creation, however, God became personal, saying, "Let Us make man in Our image". This added intimacy; humans were made in God's own image and likeness. Because "God is Spirit", our physical appearance itself is not the image and likeness of God. Probably, no significant distinction exists between the meanings of the two words *image* and *likeness*, both expressing the same concept, which we may find difficult to express. Nevertheless, one aspect of God that we can understand is that He chose to manifest his image through a male and a female, not in a single person. People are able to mirror the oneness of God in relationships, between husband and wife, parents and children, between friends, and also between strangers. Because we are all different from one another, we are able to demonstrate God's likeness in a variety of ways.

Another aspect of the image of God is the strong sense of unity that is found in many passages of The New Testament, stating that the Son of God is one with the Father. This same unity is expressed between God and Jesus' disciples in John 17. God's desire for a close relationship with His people is the one reason for our existence. He did not create us in this universe in order to forget and ignore us.

There can be no higher expression of mankind than when people exhibit the qualities that God created in them. We can be specific about attributes that we share in our limited way with God. Throughout the Bible, He is found to be a God of love, joy, peace, patience, goodness, faithfulness, gentleness, and self-control. In addition to these virtues, God exhibits anger and jealousy, but these are consistent with His inherent truth and righteousness. None of us achieve the full potential that God gave us, but to aim for anything less is to deny the purpose for which God created us.

As much as we may focus on improving our physical appearance, it is not the image of God because God is Spirit. Consequently anyone who is disfigured or an amputee can also exhibit imago Dei. To be more specific, the image of God is in part how we think, feel emotions, create and communicate, plan, have purpose, and take responsibility and authority. This image is so precious that anyone who took another person's life, effectively destroying an image of God, was to be put to death (Gen 9:6).

DEFINING THE FIRST HUMAN

Adam was the first human being, the first man created by God; as human beings, we have the scientific name *homo sapiens sapiens*. All other similar creatures that were created before him, such as hominids, were not human. Even if they appeared almost identical, they were not human. From a creation perspective, they should not be called early human beings or ancestors of human beings because they did not have the likeness of God. There is no doubt that hominids had some intelligence, emotional capability, and could make tools. Consequently, it may be difficult to distinguish between fossils of humans and those of hominids that existed before Adam.

Looking back in time at a sequence of fossils, a scientist might not know how to recognize when the first human appeared. People have a wide range of capabilities and physical attributes, yet they are all human. Beyond man's much greater intellectual and communicative capacities, the essential difference with animals was the spirit that God breathed into man. Without a spiritual nature, man is only a much more sophisticated animal, as many atheists believe.

Mammals and Birds share with mankind, to a limited extent, some emotions, intelligence, and the ability to communicate such things. They lack or have marginal ability for other attributes, such as a language with a vocabulary that can be increased at will, awareness of God, conscience, humor, and musical appreciation. Nevertheless, when in a close contact with humans, they seem to acquire some of these attributes to a small degree.

Archaeologists may be able to use one defining difference to distinguish between humans and hominids, the physical evidence for a belief in God. Two archaeological manifestations are temples and burial artifacts for the afterlife. The latter should not be confused with burial methods for sanitary reasons, or artifacts that hominids may have left for emotional reasons. The site of the earliest known temple is at Göbekli Tepe in Southern Turkey, discovered in 1994 by Klaus Schmidt. Without mentioning mankind's pre-existing knowledge of God, Charles C. Mann described these amazing ruins in his article, *The birth of Religion,* in the June 2011 edition of National Geographic. The beginning of the temple complex has been dated to about 11,600 years ago. Well carved T-shaped stones of up to sixteen tons were quarried and moved to the temple site from up to a quarter of a mile away. These large stones were covered with sophisticated carved animal and geometric decorations. The skills for such building and the date of 11,600 years ago fit well with date for the Flood of 13,900 years ago, discussed further in chapter 10.

Some people might be offended by the thought that humans are the culmination of creation. Nevertheless, we are clearly the highest expression of God in the animal kingdom. This is in accord with God's purpose of creating people with whom He will have an eternal loving relationship. The alternative, that God used evolution through random events, could not be the process God would have used to create mankind; He wanted Adam and Eve to be in His own image and likeness, not some random result of mutations.

God gave dominion of the earth and its creatures to mankind, with the implication that God's purpose in creating them was at least in part to benefit mankind. Man was given dominion over creatures that occupied the realms of land, sea, and air. His authority included stewardship of these resources; nevertheless, they remained the property of God. The Bible does not give support to man being given dominion over or owning other men; instead it supports voluntary submission to leaders, such as children to parents, and citizens to government officials. Human relationships between leaders and followers should also be a reflection of the nature and unity of the godhead.

DOMINION OR DEVASTATION

> So God blessed them, and God said to them, "Be fruitful and multiply; fill the earth and subdue it; have dominion over the fish of the sea, over the birds of the air, and over every living thing that moves on earth." (Gen 1:28)

For Christians, this verse could resolve our approach to conserving the earth's flora, fauna, and mineral resources. God stated that His creation was good, five times during the first five Days of creation, and He went on to call everything *very good* at the end of the sixth Day. Consequently we have reason to avoid destroying the goodness of His creation. Although God told man to subdue the earth and to have dominion over its creatures, God was, and still is, the owner. He had simply transferred stewardship to mankind. A second reason to treat creation with respect is that if we devastate the earth or cause extinctions of species, we have to put up with the consequences. We have the God given right to make use of all that is on the earth but within the caveat that we minimize destruction of its natural beauty. As the human population begins to fill the earth, however, we find an increasingly greater challenge in conserving this beauty and preserving its scarce resources. Although God has given man the wisdom and means to act in concert to look after the goodness of His creation, greed and ignorance sometimes lead to long term destruction of earth's beauty and resources.

The command to fill the earth was intended to spread the image and likeness of God into every corner. God is pleased when mankind exhibits His likeness in all manner of circumstances. He is also pleased when men unlock the secrets of His creation through science, revealing His laws spread throughout all scientific disciplines.

The Hebrew word for *living thing* in Genesis 1:28 is *chay*, the generic word for creature, which would include reptiles and insects. Consequently, no creature is off limits for man's use. Nevertheless, that does not give us the right to abuse animals or to cause unnecessary suffering. God demands that we take good care of our domesticated animals, which we may fail to do with intensive factory rearing of livestock.

DIVINE DIET

God knew what the best diet was for Adam and Eve. In Genesis 1:29, He told them what they should eat: "And God said, 'See, I have given you every herb that yields seed which is on the face of all the earth, and every tree whose fruit yields seed; to you it shall be for food.'"

In this passage, the food for humans appears to be seeds, fruits, and nuts, rather than the trees and plants on which they grow. We do not generally eat the plants or trees themselves, although exceptions would include vegetables. The terms used here appear to be neither totally exclusive nor totally inclusive. This is the first passage in which we should consider the possibility of hyperbole. Is this verse an example of typical Hebrew exaggeration? Not every herb provides food that is nutritious, palatable, or even edible; although it is likely they were in the garden of Eden. Without being aware of hyperbole we might assume that the fruit of any plant over the whole earth was good to eat. An example where the meaning of the word *all* is less than absolute is the phrase "on the face of all the earth". Vegetation does not grow in deserts, on mountains, or in polar regions.

The use of absolute adjectives, such as *all*, *every*, and *each*, must be evaluated by context. In many passages the absolute sense does not apply. Examples of this are throughout the Bible. In judgment against the nation of Israel, Isaiah wrote, "All you beasts of the field, come to devour, all you beasts of the forest." (Is 56:9) Not all creatures in field or forest are carnivorous, so that the word *all* must be qualified by the verb *devour;* that is, the passage concerns only the beasts that devour, not the herbivores. Similarly, in Psalm 104:20: "You make darkness, and it is night, in which all the beasts of the forest creep about." Not all forest creatures are nocturnal, so the meaning clearly concerns only beasts that creep about at night.

When God promised to destroy creatures that dwelled on land with the Flood, He could not have included those He saved on the ark: "For after seven more days I will cause to rain on the earth forty days and forty nights, and I will destroy from the face of the earth all living things that I have made." (Gen 7:4) The Hebrew word for *every* is sometimes translated *whole*, as in Genesis 8:9: "for the waters were on the face of the whole earth." In this account of Noah releasing a dove to find dry land, the dove found no resting place. Forty days previously, however, the waters had already subsided, so that mountain tops were visible (Gen 8:5). The word *whole* can not mean every acre of the earth's surface, because the Flood had been receding from the mountaintops for forty days. The Bible has many other examples where the sense of the words *all* and *every* is limited by context.

In addition to Biblical examples that show the words *all*, *every*, and *whole* do not always have an absolute sense because of context, logical arguments exist that might limit the sense of their use. The seeds and fruits eaten by Adam and Eve and their descendants were restricted because some were unpalatable or even poisonous. It might be argued that God did not create poisonous plants until after the fall, when He cursed the earth; but no scriptures support this idea. The story of creation indicates that God created all life forms, including thorns and thistles and then rested from His creative work. He did not start another round of creation.

Although God gave herbs and fruit for man to live on, we do not know whether all men kept a vegetarian diet until after the Flood, when God gave meat for mankind to eat (Gen 9:3). Before the Flood, there was much wickedness, including murder, so that it is quite possible that animals were killed for food. (Gen 4:23, 6:5) In reality, God did not command Adam to have a totally vegetarian diet. He did not give instructions to refrain from eating meat, and He did not specify a penalty if man did eat meat. The only command in Genesis that God gave about diet was when He told Noah not to eat meat with the blood of the animal. (Gen 9:4) Other commands about food were given later to Moses with the Ten Commandments. Nevertheless, it is reasonable to assume that prior to the Flood, a vegetarian diet was preferable for health reasons. We can speculate that the plants in the garden of Eden were even more nutritious than those in the rest of the world, and probably none of them were poisonous.

The same reasoning concerning hyperbole applies to animals: "'Also, to every beast of the earth, to every bird of the air, and to everything that creeps on the earth, in which there is life, I have given every green herb for food'; and it was so." (Gen 1:29) Animals were given herbs to eat, without any mention of fruit, seeds and nuts. Did every creature eat one or more herbs? Some animals and birds eat only fruit, nuts, or seeds, so we have to interpret this verse with at least some degree of qualification. The meaning here is not about every kind of beast and creature but only about the animals that actually eat herbs and the by products of those herbs, such as seeds. The word *every,* which applies to *beast, bird and everything that creeps,* is qualified by the green herbs that serve as food. In a similar way, *every green herb* must be limited to the particular herbs that each species ate; some species such as Koala Bears and Panda Bears feed only on a single species of vegetation.

If God originally made only herbivores, then we might ask how some were changed into carnivores. We cannot take the fall of man as a direct cause, because only God has the power to undertake such massive reworking of creation. The idea that God changed herbivores into carnivores is not supported by scripture; God had ceased from His work of creation, so that the only mechanism to bring about such a change would have been evolution. That is not possible, however, over the very short time of the Young Earth model.

FIVE STAR RATING

God commented on His own completed creation, all He had made was *very good.* We will examine what this might mean in the next chapter. Whatever it means, we can give praise to God for the wonders of His creation. Each day amazing new discoveries are made concerning vast galaxies, new species from the deeps or from jungles, the incredibly complicated interactions of microscopic cells, complex symbiotic relationships, the food chain, and the many cycles of resources such as water and oxygen. And then we are awed by the inspiring beauty of earth's scenery and so much of its flora and fauna. If Hollywood were to produce a movie about creation, it would surely get a rating of five stars and both thumbs up.

THE DAY OF REST

> And on the seventh day God ended His work which He had done, and He rested on the seventh day from all His work which He had done. Then God blessed the seventh day

and sanctified it, because in it He rested from all His work which God had created and made. (Gen 2:2–3)

The first few verses of Genesis 2 really belong to the narrative of Genesis 1, so we will continue with them here. Usually, the word *rest* is used to mean a state of inactivity, which would allow recovery from weariness. Another meaning is to cease from activity, without any sense of being weary, which is the situation when God rested from His work. The phrase, *And God said,* which initiated each of the previous six Days, is not used. Nor is the ending phrase, which, if present, would indicate that the seventh Day was over, and perhaps another was to follow. It follows that the seventh Day is ongoing, a concept that was employed by the author of Hebrews, who noted that even today we may enter into God's rest. (Heb 4:1–10) The author of Hebrews was referring to Psalm 95:10–11: "For forty years I was grieved with that generation, and said, 'It is a people who go astray in their hearts, and they do not know My ways.' So I swore in My wrath, 'They shall not enter My rest.'"

Mankind can enter into God's rest by ceasing from certain types of work. Such work is done to placate God in order to enter heaven, effectively earning salvation. The writer of Hebrews was telling us to cease from this kind of work, and instead, to believe in the work of Christ on the cross. This implies that God's rest on the seventh Day is still continuing. When God blessed the seventh Day, it was not just one 24-hour day but every day since then. In other words, this seventh Day is a figurative day, giving context to the length of the previous six Days.

The use of a figurative day in Genesis supports the Old Earth position, although it does not prove that the six creation Days were more than 24 hours each. Genesis 2:4 provides another example of a figurative day, which is more than 24 hours: "in the day that the Lord God made the earth and the heavens." This phrase supports the Old Earth position, but again, it is not conclusive. Further discussion on the length of the creation Day is provided in Appendix C, which reviews scriptural positions for literal and figurative meanings of the creation Day.

The seventh Day is mentioned in the fourth of the Ten Commandments: "For in six days the Lord made the heavens and the earth, the sea, and all that is in them, and rested the seventh day.

Therefore the Lord blessed the seventh day and hallowed it." (Ex 20:11) In Hebrew, the word *made* is not *bara,* which is used exclusively for *ex nihilo* creation, such as occurred in Genesis 1:1. The Hebrew word is *asah,* which as noted previously, is used during the six Days when God was fashioning the earth and making creatures from the materials that He had already created. This summary in Exodus does not include the first two verses of Genesis 1; instead it concerns the six Days that God worked on the earth's surface. More importantly, because this verse in Exodus is a summary of most of Genesis 1, it should not be used to define the meaning of words that are more fully described in Genesis itself.

The fourth commandment in Exodus provided a reason for Israel to rest on the seventh day, which is the Sabbath. God worked for six of His Days and then rested, using this pattern as an example for mankind to follow. God was not defining the length of His creation Day.

The seventh Day ends the chronological account of the creation story. Genesis 2:4 starts a second account of creation, which is often described as contradictory to Genesis 1. But that is not really the situation as we will discover in chapter 6.

REFERENCES

1. Ross, Hugh. *The Genesis Question.* Colorado Springs: NavPress, 1998: 49–50.
2. Ross, Hugh. *A Matter of Days.* Colorado Springs: NavPress, 2004: 234.

5

VERY GOOD INDEED

Here finished he, and all that he had made
Viewed, and behold! all was entirely good.
So even and morn accomplished the sixth Day;
                    —Paradise Lost, John Milton

The Creation story in Genesis ends with God's assessment that all He had done was *very good*. The way in which we interpret this phrase makes all the difference in the world. The Hebrew word means good in the sense of pleasing or fitness for purpose. Hebrew words that mean perfect in terms of morality or completeness were not used. Nevertheless, Young Earth believers interpret *very good* to mean perfect, in the sense that heaven is perfect, without death, decay, or even pain.[1] We will look at the complex consequences of this approach. The other approach is to assume that death, decay, and pain, have always been a part of this world. In chapter 7, we will consider if the cause of all death, decay, and pain can be attributed to Adam's sin or God's curse on the ground.

The Young Earth view that creation was perfect cannot extend to Adam's character; he did not have the maturity to obey God. Consequently, *very good* cannot mean perfect in the fullest sense, but it could mean a variety of non-perfect conditions.[2] Nevertheless, it must mean that God's creation was good for His intended purpose.

Whenever we describe something as very good, we give our approval without any significant reservations. Such approval, however, is limited to the intended function or purpose. For example, a landscape painting may convey images that evoke our appreciation of real landscapes, but it will never generate gentle breezes and warming sunlight. It is very good for its intended purpose, in this circumstance artistic. On closer examination, the brush strokes may be found coarse and without suitable texture and the pigments may not duplicate colors accurately. In other words, it is not perfect. Everywhere we look, we find that we live in a world of imperfection, approximations, random events, and design trade offs.

God's creation was very good when completed. Nevertheless, for a brief period, something was not good: "And the Lord God said, 'It is not good that man should be alone: I will make him a helper comparable to him.'" (Gen 2:18) At this point, mankind was a work in progress. Everything was good but not quite good enough in that one respect for God's purpose. After Eve had been created, the work in progress was to continue, especially after Adam sinned and demonstrated that he was not yet mature enough to obey God's protective command.

NATURAL OR SPIRITUAL BODIES

God could have created a perfect world, as distinct from a *very good* world, in either of two ways. The first is a universe that was totally spiritual in nature, just as heaven will be when the new earth and new heavens are created. In this universe of the future, the Bible states in various places that there will be no sin, no death, no decay, and no pain. The second kind of deathless universe that God could have created is a material universe similar in substance to the one we live in today. Although creatures would have been made of flesh and blood, they would not have decayed or shown any sign of aging, and their only food would have been vegetation.

In order for creatures to have avoided death, there would have been some significant differences in the properties of matter as we know them, as well as massive intervention by God to ensure that there was no accidental death. And then, after Adam and Eve sinned, God would have had to completely overhaul the world to cause death, decay, and pain to exist.

Answering the question, what was Adam made of? resolves certain issues within the creation story. The Biblical description for physical or material substance is *natural*. In our natural world, people's bodies are made of flesh and blood, and such bodies grow old. All creatures have limited life spans, which for humans since the Flood, is about 120 years. In addition, with the exception of Jesus, all of mankind commits sin, often with tragic consequences that may include death. In contrast, people who pass on to heaven have spiritual bodies that do not grow old and die, where there is neither corruption nor decay, and sin has no place. A point to emphasize is that people in heaven do have bodies, just as Jesus had when He was resurrected. These are spiritual bodies, so that the saints in heaven will not just be disembodied spirits, whether or not they play the harps of popular caricatures. Angels also fit the description of having spiritual bodies. Heaven is, and will be, populated by spiritual beings.

The Bible has many descriptions about the end times, which will usher in a new earth and new heavens, where there is no death, decay, or pain. Our question is what did God create originally, a spiritual paradise in which spirits dwelled, or a natural earth inhabited by people of flesh and blood? The apostle Paul gave the answer clearly:

> So also is the resurrection of the dead. The body is sown in corruption, it is raised in incorruption. It is sown in dishonor, it is raised in glory. It is sown in weakness, it is raised in power. It is sown a natural body, it is raised a spiritual body. There is a natural body, and there is a spiritual body. And so it is written, "The first man Adam became a living being." The last Adam became a life-giving spirit. *However, the spiritual is not first, but the natural, and afterward the spiritual.* [Italics added] (1 Corinthians 15:42–46)

The last Adam is a reference to Jesus, who was the second and last man to arrive on this earth without a sinful nature. In the italicized sentence, Paul categorically states that God creates natural beings before transforming them into a fully spiritual existence. The natural state has corruption (or decay), weakness and dishonor, and includes death: "And as it is appointed for men to die once, but after this the judgment, so Christ was offered once to bear the sins of many." (Heb 9:27–28) Scripture does not support an originally perfect paradise but fully supports the concept that God's creation was natural, with associated death, decay and pain. The passage quoted above, from 1 Corinthians 15, continues by contrasting the dust of mankind's substance on earth with the image Christ in heaven. Then to put the nail in the coffin of the natural man, so to speak, Paul wrote in verse 50, "Now this I say, brethren, that flesh and blood cannot inherit the kingdom of God; nor does corruption inherit incorruption."

DUST TO DUST

God reminded Adam that he had been made of dust when He pronounced the curse on the ground, saying, "for dust you are and to dust you shall return". God did not change Adam's chemical composition but simply affirmed that Adam was still made of dust. Paul confirmed this in verse 47: "The first man was of the earth, made of dust; the second Man is the Lord from heaven." Here, Paul is referring to Genesis 2:7, which states, "And the Lord God formed man of the dust of the ground." Clearly, Adam did not have a spiritual body when he was first created but had a body made of natural materials. Dust is the result of decay; inorganic from rocks and organic from dead flora and fauna.

Adam and all of mankind have been inextricably entwined with the earth and its dust. Adam's vocation was gardening; his function was to till the soil in the garden of Eden and to grow crops in that soil. Later he had the same vocation outside the garden. He planted trees that grew and seeded. After many generations, those trees were cut down for lumber. Then a carpenter fashioned furniture and perhaps even crosses from the descendants of those trees, before being hung on one Himself.

Not one passage in the Bible states or implies that Adam and Eve had spiritual bodies. Nowhere do the prophets mourn the loss of perfect spiritual bodies that never aged. Not even David wrote Psalms about an eternal future of mankind that had been previously lost in the garden of Eden. Such a concept is totally alien to the Bible. Nor is there any reference to a renewal of creation; instead a new creation is promised.

(2 Pet 3:13, Rev 21:1) I have heard it said that God had originally planned for Adam and Eve to have perfect children, like themselves. Such a paradise may have brought glory to God, but the problem was that Adam was not mature enough to keep paradise from being lost. Even if he had not eaten the forbidden fruit, sooner or later his children would have done because they would have been like their parents, who did sin after all. As with Adam and all of his descendants, we are born unable to meet God's standard for attitudes and behavior.

The long and the short of it is, that in order to exist in heaven with a heavenly body, every man and woman, including Adam and Eve, must first enter this world with bodies of flesh and blood. Then, at the end of our mortal lives, those entering heaven acquire a new heavenly body that in some way will be related to its earthly body. There is no short cut to arriving in heaven. If it were possible to be created with free will and without the propensity to sin, the sacrifice of the Lamb of God would not have been required. Moreover, if God had planned for Adam and Eve to live forever in their natural bodies, without sin, they could not have entered the kingdom of God, because flesh and blood cannot inherit the kingdom of God.

God could have made mankind with natural bodies in two ways. Either they were created in a universe that did not support death, decay and pain, or they were created in this aging and decaying universe that we know today. In the latter situation their lives were limited by the well-known processes of decay, disease, accident, wear and tear, and other phenomena. Some of these phenomena were apparently different before the Flood; some life spans were almost 1,000 years. Aging is a form of decay in which biological processes cease to function properly. Other forms of degradation occur as toxins and radioactive materials are ingested. Many of the nutrients we ingest are toxic at some level. God provided processes for our bodies to maintain a balance so that an excess of potentially harmful nutrients becomes neutralized by other molecules, or if cellular damage occurs, proteins perform repairs.

Other aspects of aging are consequences of the Second Law of Thermodynamics, which affects the whole universe. This law expresses empirical and theoretical findings that sources of energy eventually dissipate, and ordered molecular structures tend to breakdown. Energy, which evolution is supposed to use in the formation of complex and functional structures, eventually causes the same structures to deteriorate. The sun will eventually cool, but we should not worry about this outcome; it would take many millions of years, and in the mean time God has other plans for His creation.

If God had created a natural universe without death, decay, and pain, conditions would have been very different from those of today. We will examine the details of what these differences might be in the next section.

WAS ADAM CREATED TO LIVE FOREVER?

In a spiritual sense, we all have an eternal existence; it is the eventual location of that existence that remains to be determined. Our souls will continue eternally, either in heaven or in hell. After death of the mortal body, we enter a spiritual eternity: if it were to be in hell, there is another form of death, which is the absence of God or any relationship with Him. Life in its fullest sense will be possible only in heaven, because of the ongoing relationship of love with God, a relationship that believers glimpse while still on earth. In one sense Adam was eternal; his soul still exists and always will. His physical body, however, was not eternal.

It was the thought of a fallen human race gaining eternal bodies that prompted God to banish Adam and Eve from the garden of Eden:

> Then the Lord God said, "Behold the man has become like one of Us, to know good and evil. And now, lest he put his hand and take also of the tree of life, and eat, and live forever" — therefore the Lord God sent him out of the Garden of Eden to till the ground from which he was taken. (Gen 3:22–23)

From these verses, it is evident that Adam's body of flesh and blood was going to die sooner or later; unless he ate the fruit from the tree of life. He was not like angels that are eternal spirits, which do not die. No scripture indicates that Adam and Eve were created with bodies of flesh and blood that could live indefinitely. Another scripture that sheds light on this issue is: "And as it is appointed for men to die once, but after this the judgment." This verse does not state that men are cursed with death, but instead we are appointed to die, and no exception is given. Death of our bodies is not judgment, merely the outcome of living in a decaying and non-spiritual world. Judgment will come, but that occurs after death of the body.

Although we might agree that Adam was not created with a spiritual body that could exist forever, the question remains as to whether his body of flesh and blood could have existed indefinitely. If it were true, God would have had to protect him from all accidents, and his teeth would never have worn out. Nevertheless, Adam lived almost one thousand years in a world where death and decay were prevalent. Did God intend that Adam would live longer, or even indefinitely, if he had not sinned? It is really a moot question, because Adam sinned. God knew that he did not have the maturity or love for Him to resist temptation. If Adam were to have gained maturity, he would have needed trials to strengthen his character. Trials often result in pain and suffering, which is not consistent with the Young Earth view of the garden of Eden.

When God spoke to Adam about the two unique trees in the garden, Adam was a spiritual being with a natural body, and his spiritual nature would have lived indefinitely in communion with God, until he disobeyed. Having eaten from the tree of knowledge of good and evil, Adam and Eve lost their spiritual lives. The tree of life could not undo spiritual death, because that required the death and resurrection of Jesus. Therefore, the tree of life must have been effective for extending the natural life of flesh and blood, and its nourishment would have enabled the natural body to avoid the consequences of decay, and the outcome of eventual death.[3] This is the consensus of Christians; it leads, however, to the conclusion that neither Adam nor the animals were created to live forever in the natural world. If the natural bodies of mankind needed this fruit in order to remain alive, then presumably other creatures would have needed the same kind of fruit to avoid death. They could not all traverse the earth to find the one tree in the garden of Eden, and there could not have been other trees of life in the world, or Adam would have been able to eat from them. The reasonable implication is that God's earthly creatures were not made to live for ever, and death was the natural outcome of having natural bodies, both for mankind and for all other creatures.

Although Adam and Eve died spiritually on the day they sinned, it could be argued that death of their bodies was a delayed result of that sin. This argument, however, is not consistent with God's warning that Adam would die on the day that he ate the fruit. Spiritual death, and its loss of relationship with God, satisfied God's warning that they would die when they ate the forbidden fruit. Physical death is more likely to have been a result of sin in general, where greed, anger, and other stresses took their toll, just as they do today. Environmental conditions such as radiation and poor choices of food may also have contributed.

Perhaps the most persuasive argument against the idea that Adam was created to live forever is philosophical in nature. It implies that God had plan A for Adam if he behaved and plan B in the event that he sinned. Such contingency planning is uncharacteristic of an omnipotent God and decidedly unscriptural. Whenever death may have entered the world, the good news is that one day there will be no more death: "Then Death and Hades were cast into the lake of fire. This is the second death."

DEATH AT SEA

The Bible does not state the kind of food that was suitable for marine creatures. This could mean they were exempt from the statement of Genesis 1:30, which applied to land animals and birds: "Also to every beast of the earth, to every bird of the air, and to everything that creeps on the earth, in which there is life, I have given every green herb for food; and it was so." The omission of a diet for sea creatures is not necessarily a black and white issue; they could have been included conceptually with the instructions for land animals without being mentioned. But then we need to consider if this makes sense.

Baleen whales and related species are unable to eat seaweed because their closely spaced baleen filters do not allow them to ingest long strands of weed. They feed by straining massive quantities of plankton and krill from the sea. Some species of plankton devour other species, which in turn consume vegetation and minerals in order to maintain the lower end of the food chain. The existence of large whales makes it impossible to have a food chain of purely minerals and vegetation. Similar arguments apply to sharks and large fish that feed on smaller fish. Another example of marine ecology is the food chain of penguins. In addition to there being no vegetation in their environment, they have to eat fish with high fat content to stay alive in the harsh winters.

It appears that carnivores were created to live in the oceans, so it is not unreasonable to contend that they were also created to live on land. The Bible has no compelling scriptures against this position, although philosophical and perhaps theological arguments may differ.

DEATH ON LAND

In this section we will examine the Young Earth position that before the fall, animals lived without growing old or suffering death for any reason. We will consider what organisms had to die, which could not include plant life because it was food for all animals. Microorganisms must be included with plants, because they are prevalent everywhere and are eaten with fruit and vegetation. Some of these microorganisms were responsible for ensuring that the nutrients within fallen fruit and dying vegetation were returned to the environment by some of the many natural cycles that God had implemented.

When considering animal life, an obvious demarcation can be made between insects and higher life forms. Many insect species have life cycles of less than a year and die in so many accidental ways that God would have had to intervene continuously to keep them alive. Another demarcation is between parts of the body and the whole body. Our skin cells continually slough off, mostly caused by abrasion that cannot be avoided in a natural world. Also we should be aware that hair and nails are made of cells that have already died. Therefore, some aspects of death must have existed in the original Young Earth animal kingdom. To prevent animals from dying, however, God would have had to eliminate death caused by accidents, old age, disease, seasonal conditions, overpopulation, and becoming dinner.

Accidents occur from many conditions, for example: volcanic and seismic activity, lightning, drought, floods, tar pits, falls, high winds, being stepped on, and freezing weather. God would have had to intervene in all of these situations to prevent the death of millions and perhaps billions of birds, mammals, reptiles, and amphibians.[4] The overall picture is barely imaginable but perhaps possible. Nevertheless, we should not expect God to micro-manage His creation to such an extent, and the Bible gives no indication that God was involved with such intervention, perhaps billions of times each day.

In a deathless world, the debilitation of old age would not have occurred for any creature. All animals would have lived indefinitely. For humans, most of the body regenerates continuously as cells die, and this could conceivably occur without end, as long as teeth were to continue growing as they wore down. Nevertheless, the existence of indefinite life in the animal kingdom raises the problem of overpopulation.

The number of rats and mice would rapidly become unbearable. Many species multiply exponentially when there is no predation, followed by starvation as a result of insufficient food sources. Genesis states that God told man and sea creatures to multiply, so we can assume that land creatures had to do the same. In a few years, overpopulation would have been inevitable without present day mortality rates. Explanations for why there would have been no death as a result of overpopulation must be purely philosophical, because the bible provides no help. A short term solution might be that God altered reproductive rates to avoid overpopulation, but this is pure conjecture, which is not in agreement with God's command to multiply.

Disease may not have been as commonplace in the pristine new world as it is today. Currently we are becoming more susceptible to disease as our DNA mutates and degenerates.[5] Extrapolating backwards, we can reason that early man may have been relatively free from disease. Looking forward, it seems that in the long run we could be doomed to extinction unless medical discoveries outpace harmful mutations; or God intervenes.

Seasonal conditions imposed a severe challenge to animal populations that spread across the earth. God had ordained stars to indicate seasons; so we know that seasons existed by the fourth Day. When winter came, many smaller creatures could not have survived because of diminishing food and increasing cold. Nonetheless, they could have stored food, as marmots do today. Larger animals could have migrated to warmer zones to find sufficient vegetation. God could have orchestrated weather, hibernation, and other methods to avoid all death caused by seasonal variations. But this is an imaginary scenario because the Bible is silent about the death of animals prior to the fall of man.

RED IN TOOTH AND CLAW

Perhaps the cause of death that is most offensive to people is predation. Scriptural support for the absence of carnivores in the original creation is based on Genesis 1:30: "'Also to every beast of the earth, to every bird of the air, and to everything that creeps on the earth, in which there is life, I have given every green herb for food'; and it was so." Despite the implication that all animals created on the fifth Day were herbivores, Biblical considerations may indicate otherwise. Support for this alternative view is found in the instructions given by God to Noah after the Flood. Although God changed man's diet to include meat, He did not change the diet of animals, which implies that they continued to eat what they had been eating since they had been created. God was not ignoring animals because He included them in His covenant of the rainbow, in which He promised man and beast that there would never again be a worldwide flood. The implication here is that since the beginning of creation some animals have always been carnivores. In addition, no dietary restrictions were placed on marine creatures, and as discussed above, oceans must have supported carnivores.

So the question remains, when God said that He gave herbs and fruit to *every beast*, *every bird*, and *everything that creeps*, did He mean absolutely all of these creatures? The use of *every* and *all* was discussed in chapter 1, where it was shown that scripture frequently uses these two words in a less than absolute sense, just as we do today. In the creation narrative, God did not segregate the animal kingdom into herbivores and carnivores, so that *every green* herb may represent the primary food source of the food chain.

Proverbs 8:22-31 provides a description of earth's creation through the skill and understanding of God (Jesus), personified as wisdom.

Creation of the universe required not just power but great wisdom, more than mankind will ever fully understand in this mortal world: "Then I was beside Him [God] as a master craftsman; and I was daily His delight, rejoicing always before Him, rejoicing in His inhabited world, and my delight was with the sons of men." This passage refers to a time after the fall, when many descendants of Adam and Eve had filled the world, and at a time when we all agree that carnivores inhabited the earth. At that time, Jesus was rejoicing in creation, which included carnivores, making it difficult to justify a philosophical position that neither death nor carnivorous activity existed prior to the fall.

God takes credit for the natural world as we know it, including predation of one species on another. In Job 39, God describes wonders of creation, including various kinds of animal behavior such as eagles feeding prey to their young. All of creation reveals the attributes of God, as Paul stated in Romans 1:20. This is true today as it was during the creation week. God has not apologized for His creation, which is *red in tooth and claw*. We may not like the thought of so much killing and death in the natural world; nevertheless, our world is a glorious place, full of beauty and amazing creatures.

RESTORATION

Young Earth believers claim that certain passages in the Bible speak about restoration or renewal of the earth, to a state that existed before the fall of man, in which there was no death.[6] We will examine these verses to see if there is any truth to these claims.

The prophetic passage in Isaiah 11:6–7 has been used for this purpose. In these verses, however, it is the future, not the past, which is portrayed by the wolf dwelling with the lamb, the leopard with the goat, the lion with the calf, the bear with the cow, and straw being the food of the lion. Such eschatological language is typically figurative, even confusing at times. Whether or not these verses are merely symbolic, the new earth will not include carnivores that eat other animals. Nevertheless, if a similar situation existed prior to the fall, it is strange that there is no reference in any scripture back to that time, no mention that God would restore His creation back to its original state. That particular concept is entirely missing in the Bible, which has no reference to the absence of death and decay in the original creation. If God had created it without death, He would have had to radically alter and revise creation after the sin of Adam. Scriptures that are used to support this idea are examined below.

In Romans 8:19–25, Paul wrote about creation becoming free from the bondage of corruption, which would include death and decay. A previous time, when creation was free from corruption, is not mentioned. Because creation was subjected to corruption at some point, the passage is ambiguous about the time it occurred, either during creation or as a result of the fall.

Acts 3:21 refers to the "restoration of all things", which could be applied to the Young Earth argument. This verse, however, goes on to say, "which God has spoken by the mouth of all His holy prophets". By examining the words of the prophets in the Old Testament, we can determine what was to be restored. What we find is that the prophets spoke about the land of Israel and of restoring relationships between God and man and between men. The prophets do not mention restoration of a pre-fall existence, where death did not exist.

Colossians 1:15–20 concerns reconciliation, which cannot refer to any pre-fall condition but must be about events after the fall. Finally in Revelation 21–22, there is no mention of pre-fall conditions, just a statement that "there will be no more curse".

DECAY

Death is often the result of some kind of decay, perhaps the natural function of an organ has deteriorated, or teeth have rotted to the point that sufficient food cannot be eaten. Nevertheless, decay is much more prevalent after death. Decay is inherent in our universe, from the spontaneous splitting of radioactive isotopes to the death throes of a supernova. Another perspective of decay is entropy, which is a measure of a system's disorder. In general, systems without external influence tend towards a maximum entropy value, that is, they run down to an equilibrium condition of maximum disorder. The laws of entropy can be applied to the thermodynamics of matter, as expressed by The Second Law of Thermodynamics, and to information theory, as expressed by Shannon's work on communication systems. Both concepts have application in arguments against naturalistic evolution.

The natural world includes radioactive elements that cause background radiation and small amounts of nuclear decay and damage within all living matter. The result is some cellular damage occurs in living tissue. In an attempt to contend that the earth is young, some creation scientists have proposed that radioactive decay rates were greatly increased during the creation week.[7] In reality the consequence of this idea would have been lethal levels of internal and background radiation.

PAIN

Adam and Eve inhabited a natural world that included death, decay, and pain. Because our mortal bodies are made of flesh and blood, pain should not be viewed as a curse. Without pain, we would easily suffer injury to our relatively fragile bodies. Pain acts as a warning to keep our limbs from becoming damaged. In our future heavenly home there will be no need for pain because our spiritual bodies will be indestructible. A certain amount of pain serves another purpose in God's economy; in the development of discipline, which we have already discussed.

One of God's instructions to Adam and Eve was to have children. The garden of Eden may have been a painless paradise in which childbirth was without pain, but this does not appear to be how God created things. In the curse on Eve, God greatly multiplied her sorrow and conception, implying that childbirth would not have been painless in the garden.

THE BIG PICTURE

Perhaps the big question is why would God create a universe that has so much evil and suffering on earth? The answer is that God has a purpose for mankind that is worth evil and suffering. The end that God has in mind is the new earth and the new heavens, to be ushered in at the end of this age. He will fill every need and desire, and evil and suffering will be no more. Our lot may not seem fair in this life, but only God can see the beginning from the end and determine our best interests. The alternative belief, that there is no God, is even worse. For in such a universe we still have death and suffering but no promise of future perfection and of endless delight for those who persevere to the end. For this and many other arguments, we must not give up on God.

An issue that we have to face is whether or not God is responsible for death, decay, and pain: either these evils were part of creation originally, or they were inflicted on the universe when Adam first sinned. One way out of this dilemma, for anyone who cannot accept that God is ultimately responsible for death and suffering, is to blame Adam. Adam's sin is said by many Young Earth Christians to be the reason for all death, decay, and pain. Before we examine what the Bible says about this idea in chapter 7, we can already see one weakness of such an argument. Because God created Adam, God is really responsible anyway, just as we are responsible for our children as they grow up. Nevertheless, God is not accountable to us for His actions, and He does not need our permission or approval to proceed with His plans.

It does not make sense to blame all death and suffering on Adam's sin because God takes responsibility for many of these evils, possibly all of them. One must be careful in making such a statement. God did not personally carry out evil in the course of mankind's history, and we need to allow that for sinners, evil may actually be divine justice, or for their advantage in the long run. The Old Testament is full of stories about nations defeating other nations in battle, and about natural disasters that destroyed thousands. God takes credit for all of the victories. At the same time, people took the initiative themselves to kill and destroy, and catastrophes occurred that appear to be as much part of the natural order as tides.

Ultimately, God is responsible for all that happens, whether or not He appears to intervene, because He created everything. When wars coincided with God's plans for judgment on people, then God can rightfully claim the credit, even though people may have planned and executed death and destruction themselves. Conversely, the Bible shows that God averts calamity on those people for whom He has mercy. An example is provided by the story of Lot and the destruction of Sodom and Gomorrah. God did not allow one righteous person to die, even vacillating Lot. In the process of saving Lot and his family, the wickedness of the other citizens was revealed. The natural event that destroyed these cities was preceded by God discussing His plans with Abraham, followed by the rescue of Lot and his family. The story indicates that if only ten righteous people could be found, God would have spared those cities. This event indicates that God has standards for judgment that we do not fully understand because we do not see the overall picture.

When the apostle Paul wrote that the cross is foolishness and an offense to unbelievers, he was commenting on the natural philosophy of people who do not accept God's method for salvation. The offense is taken in two parts, first that anyone should need to be saved, and secondly that it was necessary for Jesus to suffer such barbarity. The latter offense is based on a natural philosophy that suffering is evil. We find it necessary, however, to discipline our children, not necessarily with corporal punishment, but with some kind of suffering to restrain them from antisocial and even dangerous behavior. Without some discipline and suffering, children may grow up to be rebels and run the risk of further suffering at the hands of the judicial system, or from anyone seeking vengeance. If we find it necessary to impose discipline and punishment within our society, then it would make sense for God to do the same.

Scripture does not give explicit support to the idea that death and suffering existed only after the fall of man. Philosophically, this idea is not acceptable either, because God would have had to interfere continually in nature to maintain creation without death. An excellent book on the subject is *Peril in Paradise* by Mark Whorton. He compares two ways of looking at creation based on philosophical approaches, the Perfect Paradise Paradigm, and the Perfect Purpose Paradigm.

Although it is appealing to think that God did not create a world with the suffering that we see today, the Bible shows that God uses suffering for the good of those who endure it. The apostle Paul understood this when he wrote in Romans 8:18, "For I consider that the sufferings of this present time are not worthy to be compared with the glory which shall be revealed in us." Paul was stoned and beaten many times and endured all kinds of hardships; nevertheless, he believed that the promises of God were worth all the suffering. Because we are not in a position to second guess God, we can trust His righteousness as revealed in the Bible, invent our own standard for what is right and wrong for God, or sadly reject the notion of God altogether.

REFERENCES

1. Morris, Henry. *The Beginning of the World*. Green Forest: Master Books, 1977: 59–70.

2. Whitefield, Rodney. *Reading Genesis One*. San Jose: R. Whitefield, 2003: 128.

3. Henry, Jonathan. *Did Death Occur Before the Fall?* Creation Research Society Quarterly, 43.3 (2006): 163.

4. Ham, Kenneth. *Adam and Ants*. The Institute for Creation Research, 1 Sep 1991: <http://www.icr.org/resources-for-scientists>

5. Crow, James. *The High Spontaneous Mutation Rate: Is it a health risk?* Proceedings of the Natural Academy of Sciences, 94.16 (1997): 8380–8386.

6. Mortenson, Terry and Thane Ury, ed. *Coming to Grips with Genesis*. Green Forest: Master Books, 2009: 383–385

7. DeYoung, Don. *Thousands … Not Billions*. Green Forest: Master Press, 2005: 141–154.

6

LIFE AND DEATH IN EDEN

... Can it be a sin to know?
Can it be death? And do they only stand
By ignorance? Is that their happy state,
The proof of their obedience and faith?
—Paradise Lost, John Milton

The contents of Genesis 2 are often referred to as the second account of creation, having a more detailed rather than chronological perspective. This second account of creation, however, appears to contradict the sequence of events listed in Genesis 1, which is clearly chronological. For example, plants do not seem to be present before Adam was created, implying a different order to that given for Days three and six in Genesis 1. When context is taken into account, however, there are no conflicts. The six Days of creation are concerned with the events that took place over the surface of the whole earth. The focus of Genesis 2, however, changes to just Adam and Eve in the garden of Eden on the sixth Day. Other potential conflicts between the two accounts are resolved when the pluperfect tense is assigned to actions that God had taken previously, as explained in Appendix E. Instead of saying God made something, it is sometimes appropriate to say God had made something. In English we have the advantage of a pluperfect tense to remove ambiguity, but in Hebrew, which did not have this tense, context and grammar must be considered in order to avoid ambiguities.

The second part of the creation story starts in Genesis 2:4. Two points of view exist as to which part of verse 4 introduces the second account, either at the beginning or half way through it. The beginning of verse 4 is preferable because it is consistent with other occurrences in Genesis of the opening phrase: "This is the history of". This phrase in Hebrew means *these are the generations of*, which in this and the other instances precedes the following relevant text. Another reason for believing that the story of Genesis 2 starts at the beginning of verse 4 is that Genesis 2:1–3 forms an *inclusio* with Genesis 1:1. The three topics of creation, God, heavens and earth, are written in reverse order in Genesis 2:1–3, thus forming the inclusio, a common poetic Hebrew structure, which appears like nested brackets around the story of Genesis 1.

The word *day* is used here in a sense that means more than 24 hours; "in the day that the Lord God made the earth and the heavens." A somewhat ambiguous reference to time is the word *history*, which means generations in Hebrew and implies a much longer time than six days. These verses lend support to the Old Earth position, in which the creation Day is much longer than 24 hours, but they are not conclusive.

The events in Genesis 2, which occurred on the sixth Day, start with an echo of Genesis 1:2. Emptiness existed in both situations: "without form and void" after the initial creation, and in the garden, an absence of plants (of an agricultural variety), rain, and man. The middle section of Genesis 2 describes the geography and mineral content of the garden, and the last section concerns God's direct involvement with Adam and Eve.

THE FIRST FARM

This is the history of the heavens and the earth when they were created, in the day that the Lord God made the earth and the heavens, before any plant of the field was in the earth and before any herb of the field had grown. For the Lord God had not caused it to rain on the earth, and there was no man to till the ground; but a mist went up from the earth and watered the whole face of the ground. And the Lord God formed man of the dust of the ground, and breathed into his nostrils the breath of life; and man became a living being." (Gen 2:4–7)

The plants and herbs that grew in the garden were *of the field*, different from the wild species of grass, herbs, and trees that God had created on the third Day. The Hebrew word used here for *plant* implies that special varieties for cultivation were planted in the garden.[1] God had not made it rain on the earth, referring to the land in the vicinity of the garden of Eden, not to the whole earth. The Hebrew word for earth can also mean land, such as the land of Nod. The Hebrew word for *mist* can be translated in various ways, including dew, fog, or streams of water coming up from the ground, such as a spring for example. It was in this environment that God placed Adam. The next verse describes the trees that God had planted for Adam:

The Lord God planted a garden eastward in Eden, and there He put the man whom He had formed. And out of the ground the Lord God made every tree grow that is pleasant to the sight and good for food. The tree of life was also in the midst of the garden, and the tree of the knowledge of good and evil." (Gen 2:8–9)

In English translations, the story is quite ambiguous at this point. Did God make the trees grow before He put Adam in the garden, or was it the other way round? To remove the ambiguity, we should make use of the pluperfect tense, and say, "the Lord God [had] made every tree grow". This passage is then in agreement with the chronology of Genesis 1. The New International Version has this wording with the pluperfect tense.

Another question is, how long did it take for the trees to grow? When trees grow they require nutrients, water, and sunshine. They also require considerable time to absorb nutrients because there are physical restrictions on how quickly plants take up nutrients. To grow a tree in one day is impossible by natural means. The Hebrew word for *grow* means to spring up in the sense that plants normally do, which means these trees did not suddenly appear; the implication being that trees in the garden took many years to grow.[2] Some of the vegetation in the garden may have been unique, perhaps with more abundant yields and nutritional value than wild species. We will never know what they were because the trees and plants were washed away in the Flood.

In Genesis 2:15, we find that Adam was assigned the role of gardener. Adam prepared the soil, planted crops (the plants and herbs of the field), and kept other vegetation at bay. Vegetation in warm climates quickly overpowers a landscape when left unchecked, as gardeners can readily testify.

Even with the extra details provided in Genesis 2, questions remain about the events of the sixth Day, such as when did it first rain? In the context of Adam's brief tenure, rain may have been seasonal, as it is in many parts of the world. Eden must have had a warm climate because, at first, Adam and Eve did not need clothing. Genesis 3:8 mentions evening times were cooler, implying that there was little cloud cover. This would have allowed warm bodies of water to create fog, which as it drifted over the cooler land, would condense into dew. Dew may have sustained some vegetation, but the thirstier plants and trees would have had to grow next to rivers and lakes. Because Genesis 2 is about the garden of Eden, the lack of rain is relevant only to the garden and not to the world at large. The sense of these verses is not exactly about an earth that was just a few days old.

HOW GREEN DOES YOUR GARDEN GROW?

The garden of Eden appears to have been a paradise, in that God designed it for companionship with Adam and Eve. This was a place close to God's heart, a place of peace and fellowship that He enjoyed in the cool of the evening. Some plants and creatures that existed outside the garden did not belong inside because of their disruptive characteristics.[3] Born in England, I can associate with the concept of garden; my wife and I have always delighted in our gardens. Many people feel the same way.

The garden was a paradise in other ways. Meals were easy to

prepare because tasty fruit of every kind was readily available, providing complete nourishment. The relatively hard work of farming, hunting, and preparing meat was not required. Moreover, some trees had been planted just because they were beautiful, and perhaps the garden had many flowers as well. The wording of Genesis 2:10 indicates a river flowed into the garden, supplying it with water, and then divided into four smaller rivers, giving some idea of the garden's size, at least several acres, probably much more. Although the garden may have been created without unmanageable weeds or destructive insects, Adam was not expected to be idle.

God placed Adam and Eve in the garden to cultivate and maintain it; Adam was supposed to keep paths cleared and prevent the garden from becoming an untidy jungle. He was not only to work but also to be creative because he was made in God's image. Nor was he left alone. As he and God walked in the garden during the cool of the evening, they may have discussed the various merits of different varieties of plants and trees and where they should grow. Somehow, Adam acquired the knowledge to make tools and implements with which to tend the garden; this knowledge was readily available through his friendship with God. Perhaps this was the way that humans gained most of their early technology, such as metallurgy, mentioned in Genesis 4:22. With only four men rescued in the ark, much of the antediluvian technology was lost in the Flood, so that thousands of years of trial and error were needed afterwards to regain skills such as metallurgy.

Gold and gems were available in the neighborhood of Eden, although Adam and Eve may not have used them. The presence of these materials indicates long term geological and mineralogical processes had taken place prior to Adam's existence. Young Earth believers, however, must assume God had placed gold and gems in the ground so that they had the appearance of having been through such processes. Such arguments for God creating the universe with the appearance of age are not generally acceptable, even to Young Earth believers.

Minerals and metals that were available to Adam had either beauty or usefulness, sometimes both. It was the same way with the trees in the garden; they were either useful for food or beautiful to behold. These two values of our natural resources should provide guidelines for managing them.

The garden was probably on relatively high ground to allow the four outgoing rivers to flow downhill. We have only one direct clue as to the location of the garden of Eden; we are given the names of two of the rivers flowing out of it. These were the Euphrates and the Tigris (Hidekel in Genesis). I have read about two reasonable suggestions for its location. One is in eastern Anatolia where the Euphrates and Tigris still have their headwaters.[4] The other two rivers, Pishon and Gihon, can be identified with ancient rift valleys that head south. The Pishon would have flowed through what is now the rift that includes the Jordan River and the Dead Sea. The Gihon is associated with a rift that is now under the eastern end of the Mediterranean Sea and continues through the Red Sea to the land of Cush (associated with Ethiopia).

The other location is just north of where the Shatt-al-Arab flows into the Persian Gulf. This short river is formed by the confluence of the Tigris and Euphrates, about sixty miles northeast from the Persian Gulf. An alternative translation of the somewhat ambiguous Hebrew text supports this arrangement of rivers.[5]

THE ONE AND ONLY COMMAND

> And the Lord God commanded the man, saying, "Of every tree of the garden you may freely eat; but of the tree of the knowledge of good and evil you shall not eat, for in the day that you eat of it you shall surely die." (Gen 2:16–17)

It was only one commandment, and one that did not even require any effort or diligence. Adam and Eve had complete freedom in everything they did, except for eating from that one tree. They did not have to continually follow laws and rituals, not even one. Perhaps life was too easy for Adam and Eve, and a little discipline would have given them the resolve to refrain from breaking that one commandment. Discipline, however, is what was missing, as will be discussed in chapter

7. There is also something we cannot fully understand, because we have never known complete innocence. How could Adam listen to the serpent and watch as Eve ate the fruit? knowing the dire warning that God had given him. Why did he not intervene? This disquieting topic is explored in *The Silence of Adam* by Dr. Larry Crabb.

Adam and Eve died spiritually that day. It was not physical death; after all, they continued to live on the earth for almost 1,000 years. Spiritual death is a broken relationship with God and an inability to be completely moral or righteous (righteous as God requires, not as man sees fit). Nevertheless, mankind is able to make good decisions from a personal and human perspective. Such decisions would not be prompted by God, and may not please God.

THE FIRST LADY

In Middle Eastern and some other cultures, it is common for wives to be treated merely as property. But that is not how God planned the institution of marriage, nor did Jesus teach that way. God intended all along to provide Adam with a wife, not only so that they could have children, but also to reflect the nature of God in unity and in equality. This can be seen in Genesis 1:27, where male and female were made in the image of God as a couple, not just as individuals. Before creating Eve, God gave Adam the opportunity to understand the kind of relationship he should have with the wife he was about to receive. God brought all kinds of animals to Adam to see how they could support him. Strength, size, and friendliness were characteristics that were readily available. But for all their different attributes, none were comparable to Adam in emotional or intellectual ability.

> And the Lord God said, "It is not good that man should be alone; I will make him a helper comparable to him." Out of the ground the Lord God formed every beast of the field and every bird of the air, and brought them to Adam to see what he would call them. And whatever Adam called each living creature, that was its name. So Adam gave names to all cattle, to the birds of the air, and to every beast of the

field. But for Adam there was not found a helper comparable to him. (Gen 2: 18–20)

We should note here that the pluperfect tense is needed in the second sentence to reconcile this sequence of events with that recorded in Genesis 1, as explained in Appendix E. The sentence now becomes: "Out of the ground the Lord God [had] formed every beast". Each *living creature* named by Adam was one of the Mammals and Birds, creatures with souls that Adam could relate to in some way. In particular, Adam named cattle, beasts of the field, and birds.

A comparable helper was not just for companionship and functional purposes. The word *comparable* means corresponding to, and in Hebrew the word implies a position of before, rather than under, against, or in opposition. Adam was to look for someone, who in addition to standing beside him to help him, could stand in front of him as an equal in stature, not necessarily physically or in function, but in essence. A wife is known for being a "weaker vessel", but the contents of our human bodies are equally precious, whatever the strength of the vessel. We might draw the analogy of comparing a piece of fine bone china to an earthenware pot. They may have the same contents, even though the vessels themselves are so different. The New Testament always includes women as heirs of the kingdom of God, treating men and women as equals in all aspects of worth.

The Bible and common sense tell us that men and women have different roles as well as different attributes. Everyone knows that on average, women have beauty, whereas men have physical strength. Men prefer conquering, adventure, and using their physical prowess. Women prefer relationships, talking, and decorating. Men usually predominate in leadership, but not always. Most would agree that Queen Elizabeth I and Margaret Thatcher were effective leaders. Similarly, in the patriarchal society of Israel, Queens ruled from time to time, and Deborah, one of Israel's judges, was a heroic leader. In any group of people it is customary to appoint or select a leader, who will act as spokesman, set direction, and hold others accountable. God has given the lion's share of leadership to men, a role that in the family is not easy to fulfill. (Eph 5:25–33)

Adam considered the creatures that had some characteristics similar to his own. They were all Mammals and Birds with souls, so he was able to build friendships with them. The Hebrews had a concept that naming a person was a result of having a superior relational position. This gives some meaning to the task Adam had of naming the animals that God brought to him. Adam was not just giving names to animals; he was establishing relationships with them and determining how much of a comparable helper each one could be. This task provided Adam with understanding of how he might relate to autonomous creatures, without recourse to instinct. Perhaps Adam saw the similarity in the relationship he had with God. Although no creature was found to be comparable to Adam, we know from our own relationships with animals that Adam had a rewarding experience in making friends with many of them. Naming and befriending these animals took many days and could not have taken place within a single day.

Today, people have friendships with cats, dogs, horses, elephants, parrots, and many other animals. Above all, we understand the adage that a dog is a man's best friend. I believe such friendships are possible only with warm-blooded creatures, and that it is not possible for cold-blooded reptiles to exhibit emotions. In addition to land mammals, warm-blooded creatures include birds and sea mammals; the latter excluded from Adam's experience, presumably for practical reasons. Smaller mammals such as mice, designated by *creeping thing* in Genesis, do not appear to have the same level of emotional capability and reciprocal relationship as the larger mammals. Adam did not name any *creeping thing*, probably for this reason. It may seem strange that God would let Adam look for a comparable helper among the animal kingdom, but God was letting Adam find out how to relate to friends that were autonomous. When Eve appeared before his eyes, he knew that the deeper longings of his heart had been met.

These animals did not include any that might be dangerous. The beasts that God brought to Adam were not *beasts of the earth*, instead they were *beasts of the field*, which browse and graze. Such animals might include herbivores, apes, and non-human hominids; the latter would depend on when such hominids became extinct. Not all of these animals were resident in the garden. One or two elephants can wreak havoc in any cultivated area. Eventually Adam realized that no animal met the desire of this heart, and then God created Eve, just as He had planned to do all along.

God had created Adam's body from dust, which contained all the necessary elements for life. Because dust is the result of many years of erosion and organic decay, the Young Earth creation model requires this dust to have been specially created within one or two Days. Although God could have created Eve *ex nihilo,* it is likely that Eve was also made from dust because in addition to Adam, all animals and birds had been created from dust. (Gen 2:19) Eve, however, was not only made from dust, she also had a more personal substance, Adam's own flesh and blood, taken from his side (normally translated rib). It was more meaningful for Adam to obtain a wife based on his own human nature, instead of one that had been merely taken from another pile of dust. Of the different creatures in Genesis, only Eve is stated to have been created from the male, although others may have been. Adam must have been intrigued by their differences. Her DNA matched Adam's DNA, with modifications for female gender and suitable emotional and intellectual tendencies. These include the love of shopping in malls, talking and listening to six others at once, and so on. It was appropriate for God to have created Eve from Adam and not the other way round, because men have both X- and Y-chromosomes, whereas women have only a pair of X-chromosomes.

DNA – THE KEY TO LIFE

Whatever God took out of Adam, whether just a single cell, a drop of blood, or even a larger part such as a rib, God altered his DNA, changing the Y-chromosome to an X-chromosome. God tweaked Eve's genome to reflect her female and feminine nature and added more dust to complete her body, as discussed above. It is possible that God used this method of creation throughout the six Days of creation. At appropriate times, God would have taken a part of an existing species, modified it, and made the remainder of the new creature's body from dust. This approach to creation is consistent with fossil evidence that shows long periods of stasis followed by relatively sudden appearances of new species; creation is revealed in the fossil record by the *incremental introduction* of new species. God would have chosen a certain species of very advanced hominid that had DNA suitable for modification into the blueprint of man. The alternative view of this pattern in the fossil evidence is known as *punctuated equilibrium,* caused by random mutations, according to the Theory of Evolution. It is not supported by the Bible because random mutations could never lead to men and women who had been made in the image of God.

Scientists have not been able to determine the hominid species that directly preceded the human race and perhaps never will. I am not saying that we are descended from apes, but that God modified the DNA pattern of an existing hominid. A hominid by itself could never evolve into a human, but God suitably modified its DNA in order to create a man. This is not evolution by random mutation; instead it is a process of intentional creativity, which built upon previous designs. After all, we share the same elements, the same carbon chemistry, the same four DNA bases, the same twenty amino acids found in proteins, and more or less the same proteins. There is no logical or theological reason for God to take a pile of dust and design a completely new DNA blueprint each time that He introduced a new creature. The fossil record reveals that living creatures display a continuity of design in their DNA from the first created life forms until the last, mankind.

Evidence for this approach to creation is found in a complex genetic defect found in both man and chimpanzee but not found in other mammals. We share the same inability to create vitamin C from normal food sources. We also share defective genes for hemoglobin. These two genetic defects are too complex to have arisen twice by chance mutations but almost certainly show a common DNA source.[6] This means that the hominids used by God as a starting point for mankind also shared these genetic defects, along with earlier species.

LOSS OF INNOCENCE

The first recorded instance of any evil in the garden of Eden was the planned subversion by the serpent of Eve's allegiance to God and to Adam. Animals, especially serpents, are not known for their ability to talk unless a supernatural power gives them words to say. The serpent's questions and statements are attributed to Satan, who had opposed God from the beginning. (John 8:44) Satan is not just a fallen angel who rebelled from God. He became an instrument of God's will, perhaps without knowing that his evil plans would eventually be thwarted. Angels and humans have intelligence and free will, and both are able to resist and rebel against God. The result of not having a proper relationship with God is that we tend to find or develop our own gods. In Satan's situation, it was himself.

Satan fulfilled the role of instigator for the temptation of Adam and Eve. The Bible describes how he also tempted Job, Jesus, Judas and Peter amongst others. He was successful in the hearts of Eve and Judas, but he did not thwart God's overall plan. Another function of Satan was actual implementation of evil, as seen in the story of Job, the attacks against the apostle Peter, and the crucifixion of Jesus. Nevertheless, in the lives of all these people, Satan's power and the extent of his evil were limited by the will and command of God.

Adam was present when Satan was seducing Eve: "She also gave to her husband with her, and he ate." (Gen 3:6) Adam had the opportunity at that time to seek God about the tragedy of Eve's succumbing to Satan's temptation. Instead, he took matters into his own hands and set his course with that of Eve and Satan. Perhaps God could have restored the situation if Adam had not eaten the fruit. We can only guess whether he was tempted in the same way as Eve, or whether he did not want to be separated from Eve. Perhaps both elements were present in his decision to disobey. Whatever his reasons, his heart was more selfish than his love, trust, and obedience towards God, with the following consequence:

> Then the eyes of both of them were opened, and they knew that they were naked; and they sewed fig leaves together and made themselves coverings. And they heard the sound of the Lord God walking in the garden in the cool of the day, and Adam and his wife hid themselves from the presence of the Lord God among the trees of the garden. (Gen 3:7–8)

The earth did not shake, the sky did not fall, nor did the world change in any way, except in the hearts and minds of Adam and Eve; they felt for the first time self-consciousness and the effects of their consciences, both the result of losing spiritual life. They became self-conscious in a way that we understand. They may have had that capacity before sin, but with God's loving presence, they had no cause to feel ashamed in any way. After their sin of betrayal, they realized that they had lost God as their closest friend. Ever since, nakedness has always been a source of embarrassment for mankind, although nudists are able to persuade themselves that there is nothing wrong with exposing naked bodies in public. They miss the point; it is the presence of others that reveals our nakedness, and that the shame of physical nakedness is a reflection of what exists in the soul. The shame felt in Eden was awareness of internal nakedness, a result of no longer having God's spiritual covering, a robe of righteousness that saints will wear in heaven. Consequently, they made coverings of fig leaves for themselves to hide their shame.

Later, God made Adam and Eve some clothes from animal skins, showing them that animals were for their use, although animals were not given to mankind for food until after the Flood. Clothing is one of the distinctions between humans and animals. Where clothes have survived in the fossil record with skeletons, they may indicate human bones rather than the remains of hominids, which had not been made in the image of God. A more reliable indication of human burial is where the dead were buried with hope for the afterlife, with precious artifacts and everyday necessities that were thought to have been needed for a future existence. Animal sacrifices also reveal human activity, although without suitable temple structures it would be difficult to determine if animals had been sacrificed or merely eaten.

The fall was not just loss of innocence. As long as Adam and Eve walked with God, the spiritual life that they had enjoyed gave them wisdom and good character. Agreeing with Satan extinguished the source of these virtues, which good men and women have strived for ever since.

CURSES AND EVICTION

When God arrived in the garden and called for Adam, as though God did not know where he was, an interesting three-way conversation developed. At first, God did not reveal anything that He knew about the events that had transpired, merely asking questions based on what Adam said. Adam responded initially that he knew he was naked, whereupon God asked him if he had eaten the forbidden fruit. Adam replied by blaming Eve, and then Eve blamed the serpent. Adam also blamed God by implication in a somewhat petulant remark about Eve. Here we see evidence of the fallen nature of mankind; Adam and Eve were trying to pass the blame instead of admitting to their failings. It is what children do, as well as adults, because they have not grown up and matured. It takes both time and trials to develop character, and that had not occurred in the garden of Eden.

God punished each of the three persons individually for his or her specific role of disobedience and disloyalty. This follows the Biblical concept that people should be judged for their own sins. God spoke first to the serpent, then Eve, and finally Adam. Each punishment was specific and limited in scope. The curse for Adam was not so much on Adam but for him: "Cursed is the ground for your sake". This curse was an appropriate punishment for Adam's disobedience, in that it was his role as gardener that was affected. Although no punishment was given to any other person or creature as a result of Adam's disobedience, consequences ensued for all his descendants; they would all share his punishment, as well as his sinful nature. The punishment for Eve was an increase in pain during childbirth. This was appropriate because her role was to bear children as God had commanded. The punishments for Adam and Eve were not only appropriate because the roles they had been assigned were made more difficult, but they were ultimately for their benefit. Without trials and tribulations, they could not begin to mature and develop character that would be fitting for a future home in heaven.

The curse on the serpent may have been applied directly to the reptile that spoke for Satan. If it had legs prior to the curse they were lost as it was turned into a snake. More likely the curse was on Satan himself, but it was only manifested when he appeared on earth, where he would be constrained to crawl along its surface. This curse also revealed the first of many promises that God made about His plans to remedy the effects of the fall. The first person in the promise concerns the seed (singular) of Eve, which must mean a male descendant because women do not have seed. This seed is Jesus in Christian theology. The second person in the promise is the seed (plural) of Satan, which must be figurative in meaning, and applies to men and women who would serve Satan. Some of them opposed Jesus, who said that they had Satan for a father. (John 8:54) The promise was that God would put enmity between these two seeds, and that Eve's seed would crush the head of Satan, the heel of Eve's seed becoming bruised in the process.

The immediate result of the curse affecting Adam was that he was no longer able to rely on easily available fruit from the garden. Instead, he had to plant seeds, deal with weeds and pests, harvest, thresh, and grind the grain, and then finally cook each meal. From this time on, life included toil and sweat in order to put food on the table for each meal. Thorns and thistles that would grow with his crops were a result of his being removed from the garden and having to live outside where these weeds were growing already. Whatever God did to curse the ground, it appears that it may not have been just a matter of weeds growing in the soil. In some way the soil appeared to be less prolific, as Lamech bemoaned at the birth of his son Noah: "This one will comfort us concerning our work and the toil of our hands, because of the ground which the Lord has cursed." (Gen 5:29)

Adam and Eve had become like God in at least one respect; they knew both good and evil and also the difference between them, which is more than we can say about much of our postmodern culture. As mentioned earlier, Adam and Eve did not get the chance to eat from the tree of life. If they had done so after the fall, they would have had their sin nature for all eternity, or at least indefinitely. But because they did die in the flesh eventually, they could be resurrected in the spirit. Paul wrote about this: "But someone will say, 'How are the dead raised up? And with what body do they come?' Foolish one, what you sow is not made alive unless it dies." (1 Cor 15:35–36) Also, if Adam and Eve had eaten from the tree of life, would they have remained under the dominion of Satan? Would God have had a different plan of salvation? These and other questions imply that God had plan B, whereas scripture and theology indicate He had only one plan. His plan was for the Lamb of God to be slain, as decreed before the foundation of the world, in order to redeem God's people from Satan's power. (Rev 13:8)

Adam and Eve were evicted from the garden of Eden to prevent them from eating from the tree of life. As an additional measure, cherubim with a flaming sword protected the tree at the east end, which was probably the only accessible entrance. It is likely that the Flood destroyed the garden and the tree of life, removing any need for a guard.

A PLACE IN HISTORY

Because the garden of Eden was inhabited for such a short time, we tend to ignore its existence and purpose in the overall scope of history. God created the garden in order to start the process of creating many sons (and daughters) to be in glory with Him. The tragic events that occurred did not surprise God, because He had already planned His response for the rest of time. God has always been in control, although this means that because He allowed free choice, various forms of evil took place within His plan. The New Testament makes this predestination of events clear. For example, God chose His people to be adopted as sons before the foundation of the world. (Eph 1:4–5)

REFERENCES

1. Hamilton, Victor. *The Book of Genesis Chapters 1–17.* Grand Rapids: Eerdmans, 1990: 154.
2. Wilson, William. *Old Testament Word Studies.* Grand Rapids: Kregel Publications, 1978: 203.
3. Snoke, David. *A Biblical Case for an Old Earth.* Grand Rapids: Baker books, 2006: 56.
4. Klenck, Joel. *The Region of Eden: Analysis and Debate.* Creation Research Society Quarterly, 46.2 (2009): 93–108.
5. Hill, Carol. *The Garden of Eden: A Modern Landscape.* Perspectives on Science and Christian Faith. 52.1 (2000): 31–46.
6. Behe, Michael. *The Edge of Evolution.* New York: Free Press, 2007: 71–72.

7

FALLOUT FROM THE FALL

… then wilt thou not be loth
To leave this Paradise, but shalt possess
A paradise within thee, happier far.
—Paradise Lost, John Milton

In chapter 5, we demonstrated that the Bible does not support the Young Earth position that God created a universe in which death and decay did not exist. Now, we will look at the related Young Earth position, that the tragic event of Adam's sin led to the introduction of all death and decay, and also suffering and pain.[1] If this were so, did death and decay first occur when Adam sinned, or when God cursed Adam? We will examine the scriptural validity for these two alternatives. Whenever death may have entered the world, the good news is that one day there will be no more death: "Then Death and Hades were cast into the lake of fire. This is the second death." (Rev 20:14)

At the end of this chapter we will examine God's responsibility for the existence of death and suffering. The argument that a good God could not allow, condone, or even cause such aspects of evil should not be ignored. In judging these issues, however, we must consider all the circumstances, and where appropriate, give God the benefit of the doubt. Otherwise, those people who could not believe in God because of death and suffering would run the risk of considering themselves God's equal and perhaps of judging Him.

YE SHALL NOT SURELY DIE

Satan is well known for tempting people with deception that is packaged with an element of truth. His comforting statement to Eve, "ye shall not surely die", had some truth to it because Adam and Eve continued to live for almost 1,000 years. Nevertheless, God had said they would die the same day that they ate the forbidden fruit. This is not a contradiction because there are two forms of death, spiritual and physical. They died spiritually, while their bodies continued to live. Also, God did not warn them of physical death, implying each of them would continue to live a natural life until it had run its course.

The loss of their relationship with God was soon revealed when they attempted to hide from Him. Losing that vital relationship with God is synonymous with spiritual death, which is demonstrated throughout the Bible. For example, until salvation people are seen as walking dead: "And you He made alive, who were dead in trespasses and sins." (Eph 2:1) Spiritual death can be likened to a flower being plucked. It quickly shrivels and dies, no longer having its source of life from the plant. Regeneration of a dead flower would take a miracle, and that is indeed what takes place when someone is born again and becomes one with the only source of spiritual life.

Most people are familiar with the scripture in Romans 6:23 that states, "For the wages of sin is death, but the gift of God is eternal life in Christ Jesus our Lord." Because we are so concerned and familiar with the natural death of our bodies, we might think that this verse concerns taking our last breath on this earth. As in the garden of Eden, however, that is not the case. After we sin we continue to live by God's grace, at least most of us do. Conversely, the gift of eternal life is immediate, although in general, any effect on our physical bodies is not always evident.

Physical death is not necessarily a punishment. Because God knows the future of any given individual, He may find it more beneficial for that person to take his or her life early. This thought was expressed by Isaiah: "The righteous perishes, and no man takes it to heart; merciful men are taken away, while no one considers that the righteous is taken away from evil." (Is 57:1)

Finally, no scripture expresses or even implies that death, pain, and suffering were not present in the garden of Eden prior to the fall. The only scriptures that refer to a place where death, pain, and suffering do not exist concern the future kingdom of heaven. As Isaiah wrote, "The wolf also shall dwell with the lamb, the leopard shall lie down with the young goat, the calf and the young lion and the fatling together; and a child shall lead them." (Is 11:6) These and many other verses, some in the Revelation of John, all point to a time in the future and never express any connection with the past.

WAS ADAM THE COSMIC CULPRIT?

This question asks whether the cause of all death, decay, and pain was Adam's act of sin or whether instead, it was the result of God's curse. Theologians generally agree, and common sense tells us, that only God would have had the power to impose death and decay on a world and its inhabitants that He had previously created to be without death and decay. Adam did not have the authority or the wherewithal to implement the changes to the animal kingdom, such as new digestive systems, hunting instincts for predators, defensive instincts for prey, and the myriad complex symbiotic relationships that exist between predators and prey.

CONSEQUENCE OR PUNISHMENT

The three penalties that God pronounced on the serpent, Eve, and Adam were all very specific and intended as punishment. God was very careful to explain why He described each punishment and what the effects were going to be. The only penalty we need to consider in detail is that placed on the ground for Adam's sake. The other two, concerning Eve and the serpent, are not relevant to the discussion about the entry of death, decay, and pain into the world (except the pain of childbirth was increased).

> Cursed is the ground for your sake; in toil you shall eat of it all the days of your life. Both thorns and thistles it shall bring forth for you, and you shall eat the herb of the field. In the sweat of your face you shall eat bread till you return

to the ground, for out of it you were taken; for dust you are, and to dust you shall return. (Gen 3:17–19)

In order to understand God's curse for Adam, it is helpful to distinguish between a consequence and a punishment. All parents have to deal with this distinction when they warn their children to avoid dangerous situations. When children disobey, they are liable to suffer the consequences of their actions, often dictated by the laws of nature. But afterwards, parents have the option of punishing their children, regardless of whether they suffered any harm as a direct consequence of disobedience. In the situation of Adam and Eve, they suffered the consequence of eating the forbidden fruit and died spiritually that day. This spiritual death caused the loss of their vibrant relationship with God, which is why they attempted to hide when God called for them in the garden. When God found them, He meted out punishment, the most significant being the curse on the ground.

Unless one reads between the lines, the meaning of the curse for Adam can be applied only to the earth, not to creatures, nor to the heavens. Adam was not sentenced to immediate physical death, although that was an option available to God. Instead, he was evicted from the garden and forced to work hard on the land for his bread. However, he and Eve were also denied access to the tree of life. This appears to be a consequence stemming from their punishment, which could be construed to mean that their punishment included eventual physical death; they no longer had access to the tree of life.

The Hebrew word for ground is comparable to our word earth, which in the context of these verses means soil or the land to be tilled. It does not include the heavens or the whole universe. A curse on animals is not included, or God would have mentioned them, just as He mentioned them when He made His covenant not to flood the earth again. The curse did not introduce worldwide death, or any death at all; Adam and Eve died spiritually as a result of disobeying God, not because of the curse.

The curse implies that thorns and thistles were not present in the garden, although their previous existence outside the garden is not mentioned. God did not say that he created them at the time of the curse, but He may have done so. In general terms, the extent of the curse was limited to growing crops. It describes how Adam had to cultivate herbs of the field in order to make bread, and that it would take a lot more effort than he was accustomed to. The curse was not applied to animals. Various herbivores did not suddenly start preying on and eating other animals. Carrion eaters had not been starving until the fall and then found their first meals.

Scripture reinforces the idea of only the ground being cursed. When Noah was born to Lamech, Noah's family was experiencing the consequences of the curse, about which they lamented: "This one will comfort us concerning the work and the toil of our hands, because of the ground which the Lord has cursed." (Gen 5:29) After the Flood, God mentioned the curse: "I will never again curse the ground for man's sake." (Gen 8:21) Again, the only object of the curse was the ground. For the remainder of man's tenure on earth, no additional curses will be placed on the ground, and humanity will not be destroyed by flooding. If cursing the ground meant that death and decay entered the universe, then it does not make any sense for God to say after the Flood that He would never again curse the ground for man's sake. (Gen 8:21) If the curse for Adam created death and decay for all creatures, it could not logically be repeated after the Flood.

God had spoken to Adam alone about the forbidden fruit. No other creature was warned about the fruit, in part because animals are not held accountable for their instincts, and in part because God was not working in the lives of animals in order to prepare them for heaven. Accountability is based on knowledge of a law or a commandment; therefore Adam alone had full accountability. At the time when Adam and Eve ate the forbidden fruit, the rest of creation was not affected.

THE NEW TESTAMENT PERSPECTIVE

The New Testament has much to say on the issue of spiritual death entering the world, all of which confirms the interpretation outlined above for Genesis. In his epistle to the Romans, the Apostle Paul deals with the involvement of Adam in the death of mankind. The first half of this book is a great theological treatise that spells out most of our Christian doctrine. It was this book that transformed the life of Martin Luther. In particular he is said to have received revelation as he read Romans 1:17: "For in it the righteousness of God is revealed from faith to faith; as it is written, the just shall live by faith." Many others have found similar inspiration.

In Romans 5, Paul compares the sin of Adam and its consequences with the righteousness of Christ and its consequences:

> Therefore, just as through one man sin entered the world, and death through sin, and thus death spread to all men, because all sinned – for until the law sin was in the world, but sin is not imputed when there is no law. Nevertheless, death reigned from Adam to Moses, even over those who had not sinned according to the likeness of the transgression of Adam, who is a type of Him who was to come. (Rom 5:12–15)

This scripture plainly states that death spread to all men, but other creatures are not mentioned. To be precise, spiritual death was the penalty for sin that applied to man. In this respect, animals were not mentioned by Paul, which is because they do not sin and were not given a spiritual nature. For Adam, the consequence of death was the result of disobeying the one and only command that God had given him. For all of Adam's descendants who did not know God's commandments, conscience was the equivalent of those commandments, except for those who were under the Law of Moses. (Rom 2:12–16) In contrast, animals do not have the capacity to sin; as far as we know they were not given any instructions to obey. When sin entered into the world through Adam's disobedience, spiritual death was the direct consequence visited on man. Animals are not mentioned, and except for the three curses, no other punishment or consequence was visited upon the world as a result of Adam's sin.

Paul was concerned with the mandatory effect of sin, which is spiritual death, not natural death of the body. The day Adam sinned, he died spiritually. When Paul wrote that sin entered the world, he was of course, referring to the sin of man; when death entered the world, it was the spiritual death of man.

It is worth considering the differences between the deaths of Adam and Jesus. First, Adam died spiritually (long before he died physically), whereas Jesus died in the flesh; He did not die spiritually because He was God, and He did not sin. Adam had to die in the flesh in order to inherit the Kingdom of God. Jesus did not die to save man from physical death; He died so that mankind could be born again in the spirit. Nevertheless, it is the death and resurrection of Christ that will result in believers acquiring bodies that will no longer be subject to death and decay. Physical death has been appointed for all people, regardless of a person's state of salvation. The only exceptions are Enoch, Elijah, and those who will be taken up when Jesus returns. Even these will cease to live in the flesh. We all get to die once in the flesh, whether or not we have been chosen by God.

Romans 5:17, contains another mention of death as a result of Adam's sin. Death is said to reign in all mankind, again "by the one man's offense". In this verse, however, the consequence of death is not stated to be exclusive to mankind, but because of the clearly stated limitation to man in the preceding verses 12–14, we must accept that this limitation is implied in verse 17. In addition, this scripture makes the comparison of the gift of righteousness, made available through the death of Jesus, with the death inherited by all mankind from Adam. For this comparison to make sense, this verse can refer only to humans because only humans are eligible for the gift of righteousness. Death, in this context, must be limited to the spiritual death of man, the original and ongoing result of sin.

Death is often a result of aging, where every living thing, from microbes up to elephants, loses its ability to function properly. Other words that convey this fact of life are decay and corruption. This aspect of corruption or decay is the subject of a passage in Romans:

> For the creation was subjected to futility, not willingly, but because of Him who subjected it in hope; because the creation itself also will be delivered from the bondage of corruption into the glorious liberty of the children of God. For we know that the whole creation groans and labors with birth pangs until now. (Rom 8:20–22)

There is no reference here to Adam, instead it was God who was directly responsible for making corruption part of creation. Adam is not even listed as a contributory reason. This state of futility does not depend on Adam. Instead it was caused by God, in hope that we can have. This hope is for creation to be delivered from corruption when the children of God are transformed into the image of Christ and receive their inheritance. Until then, all of creation groans and not just since Adam sinned. The statement that creation is groaning until now implies that it started to do so from the very beginning. Otherwise there would have been a reference to an event when it actually did start. Again, there is no scriptural evidence that God implemented death, decay, and pain after Adam first sinned.

PHILOSOPHICAL ARGUMENTS

It might be argued that God modified the universe from a deathless state to one that exhibited the cycle of life and death as we know it, but that He did not include this information in the Bible. Instead of Biblical evidence, is there any philosophical argument to support the idea that death did not afflict our world until the time of the curse? When Adam sinned, God had the power to curse the whole world with death, but He did not have to do so because His warning to Adam did not include such an outcome. Moreover, God did not have to visit the world with death at this time for any other reason. If God did react to sin in such a way, it would have been purely volitional because His universe was good (not perfect) in every other respect, and it did not need to be changed. God had provided Adam and Eve with the opportunity to live in their mortal bodies for many years in order to perpetuate the human race. There is no reason of any kind for God to have imposed death, decay, and pain on the world at the time of the fall.

As far as Young Earth believers are concerned, a philosophical argument probably overrides all others. They believe that for moral reasons, God could not have created a world in which death and suffering existed for millions of years before the fall of man. The same death and suffering, however, has existed for almost all of Young Earth history; about 6,000 years. God is ultimately responsible for death, either for 6,000 years or for millions of years; it is just a matter of numbers. More died in one situation than the other. In addition, we should be careful not to anthropomorphize animals, which do not feel pain to the same extent as humans, as discussed later in this chapter.

God may have placed limits on their suffering, not only as prey, but also in disease and old age.

It is one thing for Adam to suffer the preordained consequence of death after he ate some fruit against his maker's orders, and another to say that, in addition, God unleashed death and suffering on the rest of creation. Such an idea violates justice in two ways. First, the sentence of universal physical death goes beyond the prescribed penalty that God spoke to Adam, and secondly the victims of universal death and its consequences were not party to the original sin against God. The spiritual death of Adam and Eve fulfilled the purpose and warning that God had spoken, but implementation of universal death and suffering did not fulfill any purpose related to the fall of man.

If Adam were to blame for all death and suffering, how could he carry such a burden? He was just a man, not a mythological god. Surely, God would have warned Adam about consequences of universal death and suffering if he were to be held accountable for them.

ABSENCE OF BIBLICAL EVIDENCE

If God had originally created a perfect world, without death and suffering, it is strange that the Bible makes no explicit mention of it. Nor is there any indication that man was intended to live for ever without pain and suffering in the natural world. Nor is there any statement about any of God's earthly creatures having an eternal life.

Many Young Earth believers claim that when God cursed the ground, the cycle of life and death that we see today began, and this required many species of animal to be turned into carnivores. This idea is not supported by the Bible explicitly, and it has serious philosophical and scientific ramifications that have already been discussed. We do not find any evidence in Genesis that animals died only after Adam sinned. The ground was cursed but not animals.

FREE WILL

The freedom to act independently from God means that we are not like puppets, or robots, or creatures that operate only from instincts. Creating animals that live by instincts may have been fun for a while, but it was a relatively trivial exercise for an omnipotent God. When creatures are given free will with emotions and intelligence, destructive consequences, caused by disobedience and rebellion, are likely to occur. One-third of the angels rebelled, despite living in the heavens beholding the glory, kindness, and love of God. (Rev 12:4) Mankind lives under a different grace, but even so, no man has led a sinless life. Because God's plan was to create a redeemed community of believers, He had to have far reaching plans to achieve this goal.

His method is to show favor to those who believe in Him and accept His loving grace. In this way, God will be able to reveal at the final curtain, a people who love Him and are obedient without coercion. They will have lived on earth with appetites for temptation to offend God and with suffering for which they might blame God. The Bible establishes our purpose for living on earth, which is to eventually die so that we can enter eternity, where He has planned pleasures evermore for those who love Him. God has made an offer we can't refuse, although many refuse who do not believe in Him.

HOW TAME IS OUR GOD?

As we try to come to grips with the nature of God, we might imagine Him as if He thinks like one of us. We would like God to be good and safe. C. S. Lewis, however, had a different perspective. In his book, *The Lion, the Witch and the Wardrobe*, he gave the following words to Aslan the lion, the character that portrayed Jesus: "you can have good, but not safe". We want both, and we like to put God in a box where He is unable to do anything that would offend us. But scripture teaches us about a different God, one who does not need to ask man what is acceptable. The apostle Paul wrote that we know something about God's attributes from His creation: "For since the creation of the world His invisible attributes are clearly seen, being understood by the things that are made, even His eternal power and Godhead, so that they are without excuse." (Rom 1:20) Paul was writing about the ability of all mankind to see the nature of God throughout history. Paul did not limit the revelation of creation to the time that was prior to the fall. Amongst the wonders of the universe, we find creation is "nature, red in tooth and claw", as Alfred, Lord Tennyson wrote. Personally, I am not really comfortable with a God who created such a violent universe, but I am comfortable with His goodness, with His capacity to love each one of us more than we could possibly imagine or deserve. Even Jesus could not escape the violent reality of this present age as he met the demands of justice and mercy: "O My Father, if it is possible, let this cup pass from Me; nevertheless, not as I will, but as You will."

The Bible gives glory to God for the magnificence of His creatures, which were just as we know them today. There are no scriptures that blame man for the existence of predators. God questioned Job about His wisdom in creating the hawk, so it would make no sense for Adam to get credit or blame for the predatory nature of the hawk. (Job 39:26–30).

BEFORE THE FOUNDATION OF THE WORLD

Although we may have a hard time accepting that God created a universe with such evils as death and suffering, we should not think that God placed Himself above and beyond them. Even before the world was created, God had foreseen the temptation and fall of man, followed by the disastrous consequences of man's incorrigible sinful nature and the subsequent need for a sacrifice to rescue mankind. There was no easy fix for man's predicament, and a penalty had to be paid to satisfy the legal requirements of justice. The Father and the Son agreed that the Son would pay that penalty and make that sacrifice, even though the Son would have to endure the most degrading, barbaric and painful death that mankind had ever developed. Long before Adam sinned, the crucifixion of Jesus was predetermined, as attested by the following passage that also warns about the worship given to the beast in the end times: "All who dwell on the earth will worship him, whose names have not been written in the Book of Life of the Lamb slain from the foundation of the world." (Rev 13:8)

EVIL: DEATH, DECAY AND PAIN

Beauty is said to be in the eye of the beholder, and in a sense, evil also depends on one's viewpoint. For example, a convict may see his punishment as evil, but society would see justice. For the sake of brevity, I would classify evil as any perceived injustice or loss of well-being, without going to extremes, such as believing that plants have rights. Third parties may perceive injustice done to others, often without knowing all the details. We all agree that man should not abuse animals. Many animals, however, are eaten by other animals, which some people consider an evil; what did the devoured animal do to deserve becoming supper? When people are swallowed by earthquakes or tsunamis, we might ask the same question; what did they do to deserve such death? Poverty and disease are other evils that plague the world. We have come to accept that death and taxes are inevitable, but sickness and the infirmities of growing old are not seen in the same way. As our bodies age, they lose their ability to function, cellular functions decay, and we struggle to hold off the ultimate evil of death. In the mean time, pain frequently disrupts life, another evil that many battle continuously.

Such evils are the reason that many deny the reality or relevance of God. If we ask the question, how a good God can allow so much pain and suffering? we might be assuming that the ultimate responsibility lies with God. Some observations about God's involvement with evil include:

- God created a universe that was *very good*, but He also created the opportunity for evil to be present and to continue. Men and angels, both creatures of free will, rebelled against God and brought about much of the evil known to man.
- At times God authorized evil to be carried out. It was God who ordained the death of Jesus; it was not an accident. The predetermined outcome is that Jesus is sitting at the right hand of the Father in heaven. God also sanctioned Job's suffering at the hand of Satan.
- When God authorizes an evil for a person, such as suffering, it is either for their ultimate blessing or to ensure that justice prevails.

Observations about evil in the lives of people:

- For those who follow Jesus, all things work for good (Rom 8:28), although we do not always appreciate this truth because we cannot see into the future.

- There are times when perceived evil comes to a person as a result of previous misbehavior, either through direct consequences or through a judicial system.
- People endure evil in hope of better things, and also because evil in the form of trials should be counted as joy for the character it builds.

Observations about evil in nature:

- Evil events, such as dying, occur in the cycle of life and death, in which the death of one organism results in life for others.
- Death and suffering that occur as a result of natural causes, such as floods and earthquakes, appear to have no benefit. The existence of these global catastrophes, however, ensures that the earth continues to provide a generally habitable planet for humans and other creatures, over a very long period of time.

I think that the universe is the way it is so as to provide the best environment, perhaps the only possible environment for God to bring many sons and daughters to glory with Him. If anyone has a better solution, I have not heard it.

We have no right to life and happiness within God's economy: but what we do have is by God's mercy and grace. Also, we have the right to life from our fellow man. A universe without God, however, does not bestow rights. Even if we recognize that God gave us life, liberty, and property, we may find it necessary to defend them from other people and from governments. Nevertheless, God may take such blessings back at any time.

SUFFERING AND MATURITY

The Bible has much to say about suffering, providing some well-known stories such as the trials of Job. The book of Job exemplifies the role God takes in the sufferings of people He has chosen for His kingdom. In brief, Job lost all of his children, most of his servants, all his possessions, and was inflicted with painful sores. It was not that God was punishing Job, after all, God said that Job was righteous and held him up as a paragon of virtue to his friends. Perhaps, God would not have allowed all this grief for Job if Satan had not prompted God to provoke Job so that he would curse God. Satan's purpose has always been to oppose God's glorious plan for mankind. Nevertheless, it was God who authorized the taking of Job's children, the loss of his property, and then finally the loss of his health.

God restrained Satan from taking Job's life, as he sought to make Job curse God. Satan was the instigator and the instrument of death and suffering in the lives of Job and his family. In contrast, God was the authority, the arbitrator, and finally, the one who rewarded Job. Having endured all this suffering, God gave Job twice as much as He had before. Jesus expressed these rules of engagement for Satan when He told Peter that Satan had asked to sift him like wheat. But Jesus had prayed for Peter, that his faith should not fail, and that he would recover and strengthen the brethren. (Luke 22:31–2) In both these instances, Satan had to ask permission to cause suffering.

Another Biblical story of suffering is about Ruth, whose mother, Naomi, lost her husband and two sons after emigrating from Israel to Moab. Naomi's suffering was emotional, and possibly with hardship as well. Nevertheless, God provided for her through Ruth, the one daughter-in-law who stayed with her. When Naomi returned to Israel with Ruth, they settled down in relative poverty. Through a remarkable set of coincidences, Ruth married the most eligible bachelor in town, so that she and her neighbors were able to praise God for all that had happened. In these examples, we see one of the principles of suffering and victory, which is that we only get to experience our own journey through life. We may hear about others who have overcome adversity through the power of God, but that occurs when they are ready to give praise to God for their situations; as did Job, Ruth and Naomi. In the *Chronicles of Narnia*, C. S. Lewis expressed it well when Aslan (representing Jesus) did not allow comparisons of suffering and victory between the different characters.

In these Bible stories, the only people about whom we have any significant information are the central characters, with enough detail perhaps to see that from their perspectives that God could be trusted, despite great suffering. We do not know, however, the personal situations of other persons, such as the children of Job and those of Naomi, all of whom died. If a book were written about each of them, we would be able to appreciate their predicaments and whether or not they had reasons to trust God. The issue is not whether God can be seen to be fair, because "life is never fair", as my father-in-law used to say, frequently. Rather, it is whether, in the last day, God will be praised for His actions.

From my perspective, I believe that God, who created this amazing universe, has put into place a plan of salvation through the work of His own Son, and He is preparing a heaven where there will be no complaints. In the movie, The Godfather, Marlon Brando utters the famous phrase, "... an offer he can't refuse". Unlike the method of coercion contemplated in the movie, God has also made an offer; but it is with love and without coercion. Unfortunately many have a different god in mind, or none at all; but have they worked out all the implications of free will, suffering, and the process of finding a truly perfect heaven? People who do not wish to be associated with the God of the Bible, may one day find their desires granted, only for ever. It will mean spending an eternity without the comfort of people who share the love of God. Philosophically that might prove to be acceptable in this world, but what would they find in the way of virtues without the presence of God?

The pivotal concept for suffering is found in Hebrews 2:10 and 5:8: "For it was fitting for Him, for whom are all things and by whom are all things, in bringing many sons to glory, to make the captain of their salvation perfect through sufferings" and "though He was a Son [Jesus], yet He learned obedience by the things which He suffered". In the last sentence of this passage, the Greek words for *learning* and *suffering* are very similar, giving rise to a play on words. It is hard to imagine that Jesus, sinless and perfect in all His ways, was learning obedience. It might even be hard for us to understand the benefit of suffering in our own lives, but it is a Biblical theme that resonates in our lives.

These verses in the book of Hebrews throw light on Adam's predicament. Although created sinless and in prime physical condition, he had not been perfected and was not yet ready for the kingdom of heaven. In a nutshell, he was not mature and did not love God enough to obey Him, even to refrain from eating just one fruit. Instead of feeling the security of being warned of the only danger in the garden of Eden, perhaps he and Eve felt resentment that God had not given them even more. Consider the scene in the garden as the serpent beguiled Eve. Adam was right there listening: "She also gave to her husband with her, and he ate". (Gen 3:6) The first problem is he said nothing to correct Eve's understanding, and the second problem was his unwillingness to deal with the situation.[2] Sinless until this point, Adam failed to deal with his feelings and his responsibilities.

Another aspect of suffering, that at first sight seems counterproductive, is that the church often grows fastest when it is being persecuted.[3] Conventional wisdom would predict the opposite to be true, and sometimes the church does grow at times of peace and prosperity. But when we think about God's ultimate intention of creating a kingdom of mature believers, who have been proven by adversity, persecution begins to make some sense. Instead of creating a heaven for every immature and faithless person, a recipe for ongoing disaster, God is selecting mortals who have acquired character under all kinds of suffering and have proved their love for Him. This is related to another popular misunderstanding, that we were created to be happy.[4] It is true we want to be happy, but for our own good, God wants us to know and enjoy Him. Our happiness, which depends on our lifestyle and circumstances, is also important to God but not at the expense of our eternal salvation.

Because suffering is part of our natural world and sanctioned by God, we might ask why it should apply to animals. Before trying to answer this question it is best to put some boundaries around the issue. Many creatures do not feel pain as we do. Fish routinely become frozen in ice and swim away. Some frogs hibernate for years underground until rain comes. Livestock are content to stand outside in bitterly cold weather, although if it gets cold enough they would seek shelter. I think their pain threshold is at a different level, although some pets appear to be more susceptible to pain than others. Nevertheless, they need the pain stimulus, as we do, to survive. We cannot be sure how much animals suffer, but I do not think we should anthropomorphize animal suffering. Anyway, most of us do not complain too much about the suffering in this life, at worst it is the price we pay to be alive; the Bible, however, teaches that the benefit of suffering in faith is the good character obtained though it.

God uses the pressures of this world to make us fit for a higher kingdom. He likens Himself to a potter, with us being the clay. Potters make vessels to their own specifications and sometimes tear down what they start in order to make improvements.

FRUIT OF THE GENEALOGY TREE

The expansion of humanity can be likened to the growth of a tree under the care of a master gardener. It started out as a single shoot, and then grew into a fairly large tree. By the time of Noah, however, most of it was rotten, so God pruned away all but a single stem with three smaller twigs on it. As the tree grew again, some of it flourished, but much of it rotted over many generations, so that God had to continually prune it back, often removing whole tribes. Each year, good fruit grew on healthy branches. As the tree continues to grow, good fruit grows on new healthy branches, while decaying branches are still being removed. In a sense, the gardener is unable to control the type of growth, whether healthy or rotten, which in this metaphor is the result of free will. Pruning is necessary to prevent the whole tree becoming rotten, with the undesirable result that no more good fruit would grow.

The Bible illustrates the fall of civilizations as a result of moral decay; a phenomenon demonstrated throughout the course of human history. God allows a certain amount of iniquity in a given nation, and then judges that nation. (Gen 15:16)

JUSTICE

When seemingly good people suffer at the hands of others, or good people who have served the community well lose everything they own in a flood, we think of the injustice, that such circumstances are unfair. We cannot see, however, the beginning from the end. Job, a rich man in every way, might have been feeling very sorry for himself after he lost his health, all his property, his servants, and all his family except for his wife. But after God had restored Job's family and fortunes to him twice over, he did not complain at the treatment he had received: why then should we complain for him? In that sense, we can complain (or show gratitude) only for our own lives and not for that of others. We have no proof that God provides justice for everyone; it is a matter of faith, backed up by verses in the Bible. Part of that faith in God's justice must include the fate of those who do not have faith, those who deny the power of God in their lives. Unfortunately, such people, who do not want to know God and do not want to experience His goodness, will not be able to complain when their wish is granted for eternity; separation from God forever is a reality of hell.

The Flood may be deemed an unjust punishment for almost all of antediluvian mankind. Nevertheless, as explained above with the analogy of a tree, mankind's destruction was necessary because almost everyone had become universally evil and corrupt. For humanity to flourish, a new start was required. God had the right to start over, because He gave life in the first place. Another concern about God's justice is when He directed the Israelites to annihilate whole nations and tribes. In addition to adults, all the children were to be killed in some situations; this is galling because we see children as essentially innocent. Here again, the tree analogy is useful. Wickedness tends to escalate from one generation to the next. Many of the nations encountered by Israel had become so rotten that they were sacrificing their own children to their idols.

Jesus spoke about an eternal hell as well as the eternal kingdom of heaven. His descriptions indicate levels of hell, with the implication that there is justice, even in hell; people who have been most offensive to God's sense of justice will be assigned the worst fate. Hell is illustrated in various ways; as darkness, with eternal fire, or with devouring worms. We might view these descriptions as separate figures of speech because both fire and worms would consume everything after a finite time, and fire extinguishes darkness. We are really at a loss for words here, in part because time will not be experienced within eternity as it is in our temporal existence.

RIGHT TO LIFE

If we suppose that there is no God, then we have no inherent right to life, or any other right for that matter. When governments recognize that God has granted mankind the right to life and liberty, they can protect those rights but only to the extent to which they can be enforced. Otherwise, governments may not recognize either of these two rights, a situation that exists in many countries today.

Unlike other gods, the God of Christianity has made a number of promises, many of which have been fulfilled. One promise, which applies to the present as well as eternity, is that God will never leave those who believe in Him, although no promises have been made in general that guarantee length of life or freedom from suffering. Other promises are for the future, such as the final destinations of all people, either with God or separated from God. If there were no God, suffering would always remain but without purpose; no promises could be hoped for the future, and no reason could exist for believing in fundamental rights.

REFERENCES

1. Morris, Henry. *"The Beginning of the World"* Green Forest: Master Books, 2000: 59–70.
2. Crabb, Larry. *"The Silence of Adam"*. Grand Rapids, Zondervan, 1995: 87–99.
3. Moreland, J. P. and William Craig. *Philosophical Foundations for a Christian World View*. Downers Grove: Intervarsity Press, 2003: 545.
4. Ibid., 544.

8

LIFE AND DEATH
EAST OF EDEN

Neither famine nor disaster ever haunt men who do true justice;
but light-heartedly they tend the fields which are all their care
—Hesiod

THE FIRST FAMILY

When Eve bore her first son, she remarked that she had acquired Cain from the Lord. (Gen 4:1) This was after God had said she would bring forth children with increased pain, and perhaps this caused her to recall what God had said to her. After she had her second son, Abel, the two boys grew up together, one learning husbandry, the other farming; a useful division of labor for the first family. Normally parents have high hopes for a first born son, but these were to be dashed, along with those for their second son. Cain killed Abel in a religious dispute, a motivation all too common throughout the ages. First-born sons are usually expected to succeed; but they did not always do well in Biblical families, especially those that were potentially in the messianic line. Some of these first born sons committed crimes, others God overlooked because He was seeking qualities other than those that mere mortals admire.

We might be able to imagine how Adam and Eve could have sinned by eating some fruit in the pristine garden of Eden. But it is hard to imagine why Cain killed his brother Abel. It just does not make sense. And perhaps that is the answer, man was not always able to act upon common sense, he had become defective. Without the prompting and presence of their loving creator, they were left with unbridled and willful passions.

Although Adam and Eve no longer had the close proximity of their creator, which they had enjoyed in the garden, God's presence was still a very real part of their lives, as indicated by Genesis 4:16: "Then Cain went out from the presence of the Lord and dwelt in the land of Nod on the East of Eden." I doubt that they had worship services every week, but some sort of Sabbath observance was likely. In their communion with God, they came to understand that He wanted men to sacrifice an innocent animal, a glimpse of the ultimate sacrifice yet to come.

Adam's family, children, grandchildren, and so on, were like any family today, each having different personalities. Those that were rebellious or adventurous might have felt the need to escape the family environment and to settle elsewhere. Genesis indicates that at first, the family atmosphere might have been quite religious, with Adam and Eve giving credit to God for the birth of their children. And surely they talked about the times they walked with God in the garden. God Himself was present, and even the murderer Cain was able to converse with God and enjoy His protection. Adam's descendants, who were better behaved and who appreciated any encouragement from their parents to know God, were more likely to stay within the originally settled area outside the garden of Eden; especially because it included God's presence. The others, who rejected God, as people do in every generation, had the freedom to escape. Some travelled east, to the land of Nod, where people were more wicked, living away from God's presence and instruction. The description of Cain's descendant Lamech points to this conclusion:

> Then Lamech said to his wives: "Adah and Zillah, hear my voice; Wives of Lamech, listen to my speech! For I have killed a man for wounding me, Even a young man for hurting me. If Cain shall be avenged sevenfold, Then Lamech seventy-sevenfold." (Gen 4:23–24)

Cain was a murderer, but his great, great-grandson Lamech revealed that he was even more violent; turning further away from the God of his ancestors.

THE FIRST RELIGION

Shortly before the first murder was committed, Cain and Abel brought sacrifices to their God. The act of making sacrificial offerings was in recognition of what they knew about God. Both men brought the end product of their labors; Cain his produce and Abel the firstborn of his flock. At first sight this seems fair, but sacrifices to God are not about us and our labors. Unlike the effort Cain put into the crops that he offered, Abel put little or no effort into his sacrifice because the lamb was raised by its mother. His sacrifice foreshadowed the sacrifice of God's own son that would bring the offer of redemption and salvation to all mankind. The author of Hebrews noted the difference between the two sacrifices: "By faith Abel offered to God a more excellent sacrifice than Cain, through which he obtained witness that he was righteous". (Heb 11:4) If Cain were to make a similar sacrifice, he would have had to buy or barter the best lamb that his brother had available. Instead, his own offering merely reflected the hard work he had put into raising his crops. This effort, however, did not impress God; He wanted to see a heart that understood the need for the eventual atonement of all sins. When God communicated His displeasure, Cain took offense; his efforts had been rejected, and without due respect for God, he was angry.

These two types of sacrifice represent two types of religion that attempt to please God. The first, illustrated by Abel is based on understanding the grace of God, which is unmerited favor that forms the basis for Christianity: "For by grace you have been saved through faith, and that not of yourselves; it is the gift of God, not of works, lest anyone should boast." The second, illustrated by Cain, is based on the merits of one's own works, which is a common theme in most world religions.

God was very much involved in the lives of this prototype family. After letting Cain know that his sacrifice was not acceptable, He counseled Cain, advising him to watch his attitude but to no avail.

Cain then had a little talk with Abel who apparently did not cooperate. Exactly what Cain demanded is not suggested, but it seems obvious that Cain had something against his brother, which would likely be that God was pleased with his brother's sacrifice. This put Cain in a bad light. Was it sufficient cause to kill? Religion is a very important issue for many people, and similar anger, hostility, and murder can be seen today.

God confronted Cain in the same manner that He had confronted Adam in the garden of Eden, asking a non-accusatory question, "Where is Abel your brother"? Cain's response was sarcastic but nonetheless, is a question at the root of all human relationships: "Am I my brother's keeper?" This rhetorical question, asked by the murderer of the second son to be born on earth, was echoed with a similar rhetorical question, thousands of years later, by Pilate, just before he had the first and only begotten Son from heaven executed. He asked Jesus "What is truth"?

There is a great sense of anguish in God's question to Cain, "And He said, 'What have you done? The voice of your brother's blood cries out to Me from the ground.'" The personification of Abel's blood is a reflection that his life was in his blood, as stated in Leviticus 17:11–14. This was behind Hebrew laws concerning death and sacrifice, including the death of Jesus. His life and blood had the power of redemption for sinners. Although Abel's blood had no redemptive power, his death as a righteous victim foreshadowed the coming Christ and Calvary.

God then placed a curse on Cain as punishment for murder that was an amplification of the curse placed on Adam and was equally appropriate:

> So now you are cursed from the earth, which has opened its mouth to receive your brother's blood from your hand. "When you till the ground, it shall no longer yield its strength to you. A fugitive and a vagabond you shall be on the earth. (Gen 4:11–12)

The ground, that had readily produced crops for his unacceptable sacrifice, would no longer do so. Even by working hard on the land, Cain would not be able to farm his land; his crops would fail. In addition, he was exiled, which in part seems to have been for his own safety. Being classified as a *fugitive and a vagabond* implied that some of his family members were after his blood. He would always be wandering, never finding a permanent place of welcome. Consequently, it is not surprising that he complained about his punishment: "And Cain said to the Lord, 'My punishment is greater than I can bear'"! He may have been concerned that some of his family would seek to kill him. Regardless, God provided Cain with a protective mark, about which we can only speculate. Everybody would soon know about these events because that kind of news travels fast, especially throughout the small region inhabited by mankind at that time. Sadly, Cain left his parents and the comforting presence of God to dwell in the land of Nod. As suggested earlier, this land was occupied in part by those who wanted to escape the family home, were driven out because of their unacceptable behavior, or like Cain, were driven out by God.

LEAVING THE PRESENCE OF GOD

We now reach one of the more difficult passages in the Bible: "And Cain knew his wife" (Gen 4:17) Where did Cain's wife come from, and who were all the people that inhabited the city that Cain built? One answer is that God had created another race of people who had always lived outside the garden of Eden. A second is that Adam and Eve had many children in the garden, and a third is that Adam and Eve had lots of children after they left the garden. The first alternative does not agree with the creation story, and the second has no scriptural support. The third alternative implies that siblings married and had children.

Today, that is intolerable, but in Adam's time, there was no prohibition against incest and genetic defects were minimal if any. Without any history of problems with incest, it was entirely natural for a man to take a wife from within his immediate family, as the Egyptian pharaohs are known to have done. Even today, in some parts of the world, marriages between first cousins are acceptable and without any significant genetic problems. If Cain were only forty when he arrived in the land of Nod, he may have had up to thirty or forty siblings, with dozens of sisters and nieces between twenty and forty years old. The Bible does not mention where he chose his wife, either back where his parents lived or in his new home in the land of Nod.

Five generations after Cain, his descendant Lamech became notorious for violence. The bloodthirsty nature of Cain was amplified in Lamech, to the extent that revenge was not just sevenfold but seventy-sevenfold. Lamech boasted about killing a man who merely hurt him. This is in direct contrast to Jesus' answer to Peter about forgiveness: "I do not say to you, up to seven times, but up to seventy times seven." The penchant for violence was growing, leading to a situation that God could no longer tolerate and which culminated in His judgment with the great Flood. The lineage and moral culture derived from Cain was finally washed away but not entirely.

Although so much wickedness existed in the land of Nod and to some extent back where Adam and Eve lived, mankind had acquired impressive technology and artistic skills. Presumably, these were shared between these two centers of civilization and any other colonized areas. These early humans had livestock, developed music with harps and flutes, made tools and artifacts from both bronze and iron, and built permanent dwelling places (cities). As mentioned earlier, mankind may have acquired much of their technology in the garden of Eden, directly from God. Also, each person was able to develop knowledge and skills over a very long lifetime. Perhaps they had other impressive technologies not mentioned in the Bible.

IN THE PRESENCE OF GOD

The remaining verses of Genesis 4 return our attention to the immediate family of Adam and Eve. Because it was 130 years after Adam's creation, the arrival of Seth may have been long after Cain and Abel were born, and in the mean time, Adam would have had many other children. The birth of Seth evoked a response from Eve that was similar to the one she uttered when she had her first son Cain: "For God has appointed another seed for me instead of Abel, whom Cain killed." In both circumstances, Eve recognized that God gave her the ability to have children. When Seth was born, she understood that he was the ancestor of the seed that God had spoken about when He cursed the serpent. Seth was not the child who fulfilled that prophecy, but he was the first in the messianic lineage that would culminate in the birth of Jesus and the final showdown on Calvary. Even though Cain was the first born, Eve realized that he was not part of this messianic lineage, thinking that it would have been Abel, had he lived. (Gen 4:25)

It was not uncommon for patriarchs to know which son was to follow in the messianic lineage. This can be seen in the custom of the father blessing and prophesying over his sons before he died; examples are the blessings by the patriarchs Isaac and Jacob, which are recorded in later Chapters of Genesis. When Seth had a son who was in the messianic line, people were so encouraged that they felt the freedom to "call on the name of the Lord". (Gen 4:26). Here is an indication that life was bleak for a while, and that people had little faith that God would live up to His promise to deal with the fall and its consequences. The promises of God are often tested in our own lives, as they were in the lives of many Biblical heroes, some of whom are mentioned in Hebrews 11.

THE PRE-FLOOD GENEALOGY

Genesis 5 is primarily the genealogy of the antediluvian patriarchs, which includes the age of each patriarch at the time when he had a son who was next in the messianic lineage. This genealogy is important to both Christianity and Judaism because it records the messianic pedigree. Each of the sons in the messianic line may have been the first-born son, but God did not always choose the first born. Of the well-known persons in the messianic line, for which there is sufficient historical detail, we find the following were not first born: Seth, Noah's son Shem, the patriarchs Abraham, Isaac, Jacob, Judah, and Kings David and Solomon. Daughters are not mentioned by name in this first genealogy. Consequently, we can assume that other children were born prior to each of persons listed in the messianic lineage. This argument can also be applied to the situation of Adam and Eve, meaning that they had many children before Seth, possibly even before Cain.

Enoch and Noah are included in this genealogy, both of whom pleased God. All of the ten men in the genealogy lived between 700 and 1,000 years, except for Enoch, who God took directly into heaven. Life spans that approached 1,000 years seem absurd in today's context, but conditions prior to the Flood were different. Reasonable assumptions include fewer diseases, fewer genetic defects, a more nourishing, vegetarian diet, fewer pollutants, and possibly less harmful radiation. At the time of the Flood, God decided to limit the longevity of man to 120 years; this did not take effect immediately, however, but gradually over many generations. Noah died when he was 950 years old, whereas Abraham lived to be 175 years old, and Joseph lived to be only 110.

Of the ten men listed in the pre-Flood genealogy, two are mentioned in the *hall of faith* in Hebrews 11. This passage refers to those God fearing people whom the writer of Hebrews selected as examples of faith. Abel is included, which means he understood the significance of Cain's anger towards him. Although they died long ago, faith in God's promises is something we can share with those heroes. Their faith was focused in looking forward to Calvary, in addition to believing God for the outcome of whatever situation they had to endure. This living by faith is a major theme in the Bible, first expressed directly as a concept in Habakkuk 2:4: "But the just shall live by his faith". We can see such faith in Eve's recognition that God provided her with the messianic seed, and in the desire of men to call on the name of God. Much of what God spoke to these men and women of faith is not written for us to see; but just as Abraham understood the gospel, so too, these early believers understood the rudiments of the gospel. (Gal 3:8)

Genealogies in the Bible are generally given in multiples of ten or fourteen, which may have helped memorization and added safeguards against omissions in copying. The genealogy given in Genesis 5 includes the age when each father had the son that was next in the genealogy. By adding all the years together, a chronology can be obtained for the age of the earth from Adam until the Flood. The same can be done for the generations after the Flood, which are recorded in Genesis 11, bringing us to historical times, for which dates are known. In this way, after considerable research, Bishop Ussher published in 1650 the date when the earth was created, namely, 4004 BC. Remarkably, he went further and determined the day and hour when God did this, although there is no support in the Bible for such detail. These calculations for a date of 4004 BC form the basis for Young Earth creationism. At first sight this reasoning appears to be without fault, but some potential problems exist, identified in the next section.

The textual structure in the pre-Flood genealogy appears to ensure that no names were omitted, each name occurring five times. The genealogy given to Moses, however, may not have included all generations that lived between Adam and Noah. This is because the Hebrew word which is translated *begot* can mean that the father had a descendant, instead of having a son.[1] This genealogy may have some gaps.

THE POST-FLOOD GENEALOGY

The post-Flood genealogy in Genesis 11 appears to be missing one name. The Gospel of Luke provides the ancestry of Mary, the mother of Jesus, going back to Adam. Luke includes the name of Cainan, son of Arphaxad, Noah's grandson. Cainan is not included in the Genesis 11 genealogy. The reason for this discrepancy is not necessarily that Luke made a mistake, but being a Greek, he had access to the Greek Septuagint version of the Hebrew text. Some versions of the Septuagint include Cainan in the Genesis genealogy. The Septuagint translation was created two to three hundred years before Christ in order to meet the need of the growing number of Greek speaking Jews. Alexander the Great had Hellenized his empire to the point that Greek was the preferred language throughout most of the known world. The Septuagint, rather than the Hebrew text, was generally referred to by New Testament authors and early Christian fathers. It is thought today to have had fewer errors than the Hebrew texts (none considered major), a result, perhaps, of the tumultuous times of the Jewish nation in Judea.

Regardless of whether Cainan belonged in the genealogy, Moses may have known this and other names, but he kept to the pattern of ten names because ten was symbolic of divine completion. Matthew followed the same idea, except his number was fourteen, in which the factor seven was the number for spiritual perfection. In the first chapter of Matthew, there are three groups of fourteen names in the genealogy from Abraham to Jesus. In order to maintain fourteen names in the middle group, Matthew omitted three descendants of Jehoram, although Matthew must have known that these names were included in 1 Chronicles 3. It is reasonable to assume that other names were omitted in the post-flood genealogy to keep the list to ten names.

Another issue in the Genesis genealogy is that different versions, such as the Hebrew, Septuagint and Samaritan Pentateuch, have different ages for persons in the genealogies. These differences appear to be copying errors, and they are not really significant unless one is trying to determine the exact age of the earth, clearly an exercise in futility. Just as Cainan may have been omitted from Genesis 11, upsetting Bishop Ussher's calculations, we can see that other names may have been omitted; the big question is, how many?[2]

A strong candidate for missing generations is Eber, who lived 464 years. His offspring, Peleg and then Reu, lived only 239 years each, and their descendants even less. This steep drop in life spans may indicate a gap of many generations in which lifetimes actually fell more slowly. Because the life spans given in Genesis do not follow a uniform decrease, it is difficult to interpolate an average decrease in life span. It is much easier, however, to estimate the average time between generations. Almost all the sons listed in the genealogy were born when their fathers were about thirty-three years old. This is equivalent to thirty generations for each thousand years of history, a number which will be considered in chapter 10 for estimating the timing of the Flood.

Because of the flexibility in meaning of certain Hebrew words, it was possible to create genealogies of ten or fourteen names without appearing to omit generations. In addition to the Hebrew word for *begot* meaning to sire a lineage or a son, the Hebrew words for father and son can also mean ancestor and descendant.

REFERENCES

1. Rana, Fazale, and Hugh Ross. *Who was Adam?* Colorado Springs: NavPress, 2005: 47
2. Aalders, Gerhard. *Genesis Volume I.* Grand Rapids, Zondervan, 1981: 256–259.

9

THE GREAT FLOOD

The busy tribes of flesh and blood
With all their lives and cares
Are carried downwards by thy flood,
And lost in following years.
—Isaac Watts

In this chapter, we will consider the biblical narrative of the Noachian Flood, described in Genesis 6–9. Then in the next chapter, we will consider evidence for the Flood and what evidence might be most appropriate to the Biblical narrative. The story of this catastrophe engenders considerable debate among Christians, almost as much as creation itself. Major issues about the Flood are how it was caused, when it happened, and whether it was global in extent. Also, logistical problems may be hard to understand, such as how all the creatures arrived at the ark, how they survived in the ark, and for a global flood, how all the different species found their appropriate locations across the surface of the globe. Some of these problems appear to have no possible solution unless God intervened. But that is exactly what God did when He brought the animals to Noah and called Noah and his family into the ark. Before considering the Flood in detail, we will look at the circumstances that existed prior to the Flood, which can only be described as epic and legendary.

GIANTS AND ANGELS

The first few verses of Genesis 6 would make excellent material for a Hollywood movie, with giants, beautiful women, bedroom scenes, extreme wickedness, and violence:

> Now it came to pass, when men began to multiply on the face of the earth, and daughters were born to them, that the sons of God saw the daughters of men, that they were beautiful; and they took wives for themselves of all whom they chose. (Gen 6:1–2)

The interpretation of this passage hangs on the meaning of *the sons of God*, for which there are two main points of view.[1] Some Christians understand this phrase to mean just the righteous line from Seth to Noah, excluding the rebellious line of men from Cain. But this hardly fits in with the context of choosing as many daughters of men as they wanted, nor with the outcome of giants mentioned in the fourth verse. Also, daughters of men would then refer only to the daughters from Cain's line, which is strange because daughters were being born to all men descended from Adam. We could also take issue with the assumption that all of the messianic lineage were truly God fearing, making the designation *sons of God* somewhat arbitrary.

The alternative belief is that *sons of God* refers to angels, presumably the fallen angels that Jude described in verse 6 of his epistle: "And the angels who did not keep their proper domain, but left their own abode"[2] Except for these verses in Genesis and Jude, angels mentioned in the Bible are God's servants for blessing mankind. One-third of the angels, however, rebelled under the leadership of Satan. (Rev 12:4) These are the fallen angels who took wives from the daughters of men. More importantly, the only other Biblical instances of *sons of God* refer to angels. (Job 1:6, 2:1)

The argument that angels are purely spiritual and are therefore unable to father children in our material world carries some logical weight, but it is not scriptural. The Bible tells of angels visiting mankind at different times; when they visited Abraham's nephew Lot, they were eating and drinking. (Gen 19:1–3) Angels also had extraordinary supernatural powers, able to cause blindness, disease, and death. Consequently it is reasonable to believe that angels had the ability to have children. And this may be what is meant in Genesis 6:4: "There were giants on the earth in those days, and also afterward, when the sons of God came into the daughters of men and they bore children to them. Those were the mighty men who were of old, men of renown". The Hebrew word for giants is *nephilim*, which does not necessarily mean giants but rather apostates.[3] Nevertheless, in view of their might and renown, the description of giants seems appropriate, in addition to that of apostates.

The existence of giants *afterward* poses a problem if this refers to a time after the Flood, because all the giants had perished. The genes for giant offspring, however, may have been carried by at least one of Noah's three daughters-in-law, or even his wife. It is less likely that Noah and his sons carried such genes because Noah appears to have come from a God fearing family. From time to time, these genes were expressed in certain tribes as The Old Testament indicates, with descriptions of giants existing at various times and localities, including the tribe that inhabited Gath where Goliath lived. The Israelites and other nations repeatedly fought these tribes and their giants, and over time, annihilated the populations that carried the genes responsible for giants.

This intriguing situation about giants and men of renown may well account for legends of giants, gods, and semi-mortal men in Greek, Roman, and many other cultures. They were credited with amazing strength and doing great feats of valor, in addition to their despicable acts that characterized the wickedness of that time. After the Flood, the memories of those times and events were carried down through many generations by word of mouth, with embellishments and omissions, until they were recorded in writing during the Roman and Greek civilizations. These legends, with which many of us are familiar, recall miraculous deeds that are impossible for ordinary humans. Nevertheless, their emotions and their dilemmas reflect life among the rich and powerful throughout the ages.

AS IN THE DAYS BEFORE THE FLOOD

Jesus used the story of the Flood to illustrate His point about the abruptness of His second coming. People were getting on with their lives, eating together, and marrying, and everything looked normal; but the fabric of society was rotten. God saw wickedness at every level. The extent of the wickedness of those days can hardly be imagined from this horrifying description of humanity:

> Then the Lord saw that the wickedness of man was great in the earth, and that every intent of the thoughts of his heart was only evil continually. And the Lord was sorry that He had made man on the earth, and He was grieved in His heart. (Gen 6:5–6)

In addition, violence was continually part of their thoughts. (Gen 6:11) This way of life was recalled by Job's friends, who made reference to it when they accused Job of keeping to the old way of wickedness. Presumably, this was because they themselves did not live that way: "Will you keep to the old way which wicked men have trod, who were cut down before their time, whose foundations were swept away by a flood." (Job 22:15) Noah had many years to warn his family about the universal wickedness that led to the Flood, but he had centuries to tell the Flood story to his descendants. Long after the Flood, those warnings and stories continued to be remembered and handed down through the generations, eventually to Job and his friends. Finally, when Moses wrote about the Flood and the beginnings of mankind, scripture tells us that God inspired him with the truth, so that he did not have to rely on distorted legends. (2 Tim 3:16)

The Flood was a judgment on man's wickedness, which was so great that God was grieved and was sorry that He had created man. Knowing in advance what was going to happen did not lessen God's feelings of sorrow that subsequently arose. He decided that the increasingly wicked human race needed pruning down to one family, in which Noah was in some respects the equivalent of a new Adam. Noah was one of the few who did not succumb to wickedness; but being well behaved was insufficient reason for God to have chosen Noah. The difference was that God gave His grace (unmerited favor) to Noah: "But Noah found grace in the eyes of the Lord." (Gen 6:8) As a result, Noah walked with faith in God. (Gen 6:9; Heb 11:7) This relationship is what allowed him to be just and perfect in his dealings with his family and his neighbors. Perfect does not mean he was without sin but means that he maintained relationships with other people in the fear of the Lord.

The wickedness of mankind had grown through the generations between Adam and Noah, to the point that if it continued, even Noah's family and descendants were at risk. This increase in wickedness implies a genetic influence that, on average, amplified the bad behavior of the previous generation. Recently the new scientific field of epigenetics indicates that nurture, especially lack of nurture, can override nature and influence a person's genome.[4]

At the time of the Flood, God placed a limit of 120 years on man's life. Although men had lived to almost 1,000 years before the Flood, God did not want to continue striving with any man for such a long period. It is as though after a hundred years or so of not living up to God's righteousness, it is better for everyone if God took each person home. The *Guinness Book of Records*, lists only one man in modern times that may have made that ripe old age. This limit on man's lifetime was not implemented immediately, but it slowly took effect over many generations after the Flood.

LOCAL OR GLOBAL

Although, in English versions, Genesis indicates that the Flood appears to have been global in extent, examination of the Hebrew text reveals a vast local Flood may be a better interpretation. There are four considerations that lead to this conclusion.

Perspective: The description of the Flood is written from the perspective of the ark, so that flood conditions beyond the vicinity of the ark can only be inferred from phrases such as the whole earth. The Hebrew word for *earth*, however, can mean simply ground, such as the ground I stand on, or land, such as the land I live in, or the whole earth that circles the sun.[5]

Consequently, the word *earth* in the Flood narrative can mean the land beneath the ark and the floodwater, most likely the whole Tigris-Euphrates river basin, known as Mesopotamia.

Hills or mountains: A clue about the Flood's depth is provided in Genesis 7:19–20: "And the waters prevailed exceedingly on the earth, and all the high hills under the whole heaven were covered. The waters prevailed fifteen cubits upward, and the mountains were covered." *Hills* and *mountains* are translated from the same Hebrew word. By using the same English word for both instances, the meaning now becomes that the high hills were covered, and then another fifteen cubits of water rose above those hills (about twenty-five feet). Mountains are too far away to be visible from most of Mesopotamia, so that it is reasonable to assume that the Hebrew text is referring to hills, perhaps the lower foothills leading to the Zagros Mountains in the east. The extra fifteen cubits covered trees and shrubs, so that nothing could be seen but water. Noah could not have known if the water continued to rise because landmarks were no longer visible.

As the Flood receded, hills became visible: "the tops of the mountains were seen". (Gen 8:5) It might be appropriate to consider that these mountains were the same hills or range of hills that disappeared as the Flood rose. When these hills had been covered, nothing but water could be seen from the ark. The water continued to rise during the 150 days that it prevailed on the earth. During this time, mountains that had not been covered would have been visible only if the ark was close enough to them. This understanding of the Hebrew text is consistent with a local Flood.

Hyperbole: In chapter 3 we considered the use of hyperbole in the Bible; absolute terms such as *all* and *every* are not always absolute in their meaning. For example, when Genesis states that, "all the high hills under the whole heaven were covered", context restricts *hills* and *heavens* to what could be seen from the ark. Although written in the time of Moses, the narrative must be consistent with Noah's awareness of the world. It is unlikely that he knew much if anything about the earth beyond Mesopotamia, so that reading into these verses any meaning beyond his understanding of the world is inappropriate. Similarly, verses that refer to destruction of every animal can be limited to those animals that were destroyed by the Flood.

God's Intent: God's intent was to destroy mankind as stated in Genesis 6:7: "So the Lord said, 'I will destroy man whom I have created from the face of the earth, both man and beast, creeping thing and birds of the air'" Animals were included in this destruction because the wickedness and violence of men had corrupted all creatures associated with them. This corruption was limited to the vicinity of man's activity: "for the earth is filled with violence through them; and behold, I will destroy them with the earth." (Gen 6:13) Consequently, God did not have to flood the whole earth when His intent was to destroy only man, creatures affected by man, and the land where mankind dwelt. This area was probably limited to Mesopotamia, which with the Levant, is known as the cradle of civilization.

With the explanation given above, a local Flood in Mesopotamia is a valid interpretation of the Genesis narrative.[6] This interpretation does not diminish scripture in any way because it is supported by the Hebrew text. Numerous theologians have come to the same conclusion that the Flood was local.[7] Discussion of evidence for local floods is given in the next chapter.

Nevertheless, the alternative of global flooding should not be ignored. Without the four considerations listed above, the Flood narrative would have a global interpretation. Ignoring hyperbole, all creatures would have been destroyed, which implies the highest mountains were covered. In addition the Young Earth model for a global Flood includes deposition of several thousand feet of sediment on the continents, covering the highest mountains. We will examine evidence for this kind of Flood in the next chapter.

FLOOD MECHANISMS

Genesis describes two causes of destruction, rain and fountains of the deep. There is no mention of volcanoes, earthquakes, asteroids, and meteorites. Such catastrophes may have occurred but only to a limited extent in the region where the ark floated; otherwise it is likely they would have been mentioned. These other mechanisms were not the means by which mankind was destroyed, nor were they comparable to the destructive power of the Flood. God said in Genesis 6:17: "And behold, I Myself am bringing floodwaters on the earth, to destroy from under heaven all flesh in which there is the breath of life; everything that is on the earth shall die." This indicates that floodwater was responsible for the destruction, of mankind, not asteroids, not earthquakes, nor volcanoes. Nevertheless, these other catastrophes may have been significant elsewhere, as well as being instrumental in causing the Flood.

Whatever flood mechanisms prevailed at any given location, people tried to save their lives by running to higher ground, or taking to boats. Some succeeded for a while, but mudslides, flash floods, shipwreck, and privation eventually overtook all, except those in the ark.

Rain: Rain does not raise sea levels overall because rain water comes from clouds that are generated by the oceans and seas. Nevertheless, rain causes significant local flooding in which people and animals die, especially when associated with storm surges. Such local flooding, caused by rain and high winds, was not the major factor for Noah's Flood.

A total of forty days of rain is reminiscent of heavy monsoons, which are not normally serious in Mesopotamia. Monsoon activity in Arabia, however, was much more intense at the end of the Ice Age, and a monsoon could have been instrumental in causing torrential rain in Mesopotamia.[8] Genesis tells us that the Flood started in the spring, when such stalled cyclones tend to occur, although under the hand of God they could have been much more devastating than mankind has experienced since.

Related to rainfall is the snowmelt that occurs each spring. This source of water often causes flooding, sometimes severe after a heavy snowpack. The Tigris is fed from rainfall and snowmelt from the Zagros Mountains, and from the Taurus Mountains as far away as Armenia. Other rainfall that causes some delayed flooding emerges out of springs. This again depends on the amount of prior precipitation and also on the storage capacity of aquifers in hills above the springs. These mechanisms could have contributed little to Noah's Flood.

Fountains of the deep: The phrase, "all the fountains of the great deep were broken up" implies that whatever held the water back was destroyed. (Gen 7:11) The Hebrew word for broken can mean bursting or breaking through.[9] This interpretation will be considered for the location of the *deep* in chapter 10. The *fountains of the deep* were much more likely than rain to have been the major cause of mankind's destruction, whether in a global or a local flood.

Flood abatement: God mentioned only one mechanism that caused the waters to subside: "And God made a wind to pass over the earth, and the waters subsided." (Gen 8:1) The Flood depth did not decrease after the rain was stopped and the fountains of the deep were closed; only the wind caused the Flood to subside. This means the fountains of the deep did not take back the water they had expelled.

If the Flood were local, then in the seventy-three days during which the wind blew and the waters subsided before the ark touched down, the water level dropped to some extent because of evaporation. Winds would have blown around the earth and rain would have fallen elsewhere. Winds by themselves, however, could not have caused the Flood level to decrease by more than a few feet during those seventy-three days because loss of water by evaporation is relatively limited; typical evaporation rates are about one third of an inch per day. There had to be another mechanism that caused the waters to subside, for which an explanation is given in the section on Local Floods in chapter 10. If the Flood were global in extent, then there is even less likelihood that the wind in itself caused the waters to subside; the winds would have caused rain to fall elsewhere on the oceans.

THEY WENT IN TWO BY TWO

A likely location for Noah to have built the ark is close to the Tigris River, which would have enabled him to transport many large trees that were to be used. We do not know what technology Noah had at his disposal to build the ark, but Genesis notes that before the Flood, some craftsmen were skilled with bronze and iron. In addition, the Gilgamesh epic includes the use of copper, gold, and silver by the antediluvian residents. Whatever wealth Noah may have had, all could have been used on the ark project because money and precious materials had little value for a long time to come.

Pictures of animals entering the ark two by two is well known by all those who have attended Sunday school. The first of two descriptions of animals entering the ark is in Genesis 6:19–20, which essentially states that the animals were to enter in pairs. The second description in Genesis 7:2–3 gives more detailed instructions; seven pairs of each clean animal entered the ark but only one pair of each unclean animal.

Some of the biggest mysteries are exactly what species were brought to the ark, where they came from, how they got to the ark, how they survived in the ark, and how they ended up in their final home after the Flood. Concerning the different species in the ark, the global Flood interpretation is that the ark was filled with every species of land dwelling creature from all over the globe.

The alternative view, for a widespread but local flood, would mean the ark contained only those creatures that inhabited the flooded area. The words *every living thing* would simply mean every living thing in the land that was flooded. Another possible restriction is that God may not have brought carnivores into the ark. Such an arrangement would make sense because Noah had to provide food for the animals, and food for carnivores does not keep very long without going rotten. Also, when the animals left the ark, the herbivores would not have become extinct as a result of releasing hungry carnivores from the ark. This approach is appropriate in a local flood scenario because carnivores would eventually repopulate the flooded area from distant lands, after herbivores had established a sustainable population. The presence of carnivores in the ark would not have been a problem under the conditions that may have prevailed in the ark, which are described in the next section.

Animals that entered the ark included all domestic kinds because they were essential for the survival of Noah and his family after the Flood. God led wild species to the ark from their native habitats, and perhaps He supplied appropriate foods when none was otherwise available on the journey. Even though the world may have had a relatively uniform and temperate climate, some animals are able to survive only in unique conditions, such as polar or alpine regions. Noah did not have to determine what species to load on the ark because God brought each one to the ark.

Noah was instructed to load food on board before the Flood arrived. Although the next section will make the point that food may not have been necessary during the Flood, a need for provisions existed while loading the ark and also after the Flood, before crops could be planted and had time to grow. Such food storage was vital for Noah and his family and also for their livestock. After the Flood, food for wild animals became available as the land dried out and recovered. This may have required a phased release of the different species from the ark. Certain foods for humans and livestock can be stored for long periods of time, but many species require fresh food, a problem discussed in the next chapter.

Genesis 6:19 provides a criterion for the species brought into the ark, with the words *living thing*. This expression means a creature with a soul, or Mammals and Birds, as discussed in chapter 3. It is fitting that the very creatures that God wanted Noah to save were those he could relate to, the same kinds that had God created on the fifth and sixth Days of creation, and from which Adam sought a helpmate. Sufficient numbers of other land based creatures, such as reptiles and amphibians, could have survived the Flood by floating or hanging on to floating trees and debris. Aquatic creatures needed no such provision, although many must have died by any one of several mechanisms in the turbulent waters.

A YEAR AT SEA

Ocean going ships are designed with systems for managing food, water, waste disposal, adequate ventilation, and illumination below decks. Except for food, there is no mention of any of these prerequisites in the description of the ark. Without supernatural help, Noah and his family could not have kept up with feeding and watering the animals, and mucking out the stalls. And all of this was in more or less total darkness because torches could not be used without ventilation. Ventilation was limited because only one small window existed, which appears to have been kept closed. (Gen 8:6) Various authors have suggested that Noah's task was made manageable by the phenomenon of hibernation. The problem with this suggestion is that most species do not have special metabolic processes for hibernation, and mammals that do hibernate only do so for a few months. Otherwise, this might be a viable solution.

A better answer to this problem is provided by God's presence. He resided in the ark: "Then the Lord said to Noah, 'Come into the ark, you and all your household'" (Gen 7:1) God invited Noah and his household into His presence when all the animals had already settled in. This situation is similar to the time when God commanded Moses into His presence on Mount Sinai, where Moses stayed for forty days and nights. (Ex 24:18) Moses did not know how long he would spend with God, and probably he had limited supplies with him. In fact, Moses neither ate nor drank during that time. (Ex 34:28) He could not have survived forty days without water unless he was the recipient of divine help: God placed Moses in a state of supernatural suspended animation. This state was not only for Moses' physical survival but also to satisfy God's holiness. God was very particular about human cleanliness, having given strict instructions to the High Priests for when they entered the Holy of Holies each year. In the ark, God could have kept all the animals in a similar state of suspended animation.

Similar to, but more effective than hibernation, suspended animation avoids the great variety of problems associated with housing so many animals in such confined quarters for so long. Prodigious amounts of fresh food and water (the latter not mentioned in Genesis) were not required. Cleaning the stalls would only have been necessary when embarking. After the ark landed, an extension of this state for carnivores would have been useful, allowing herbivores to leave the ark first, followed by the carnivores a year or two later, in order to protect the herbivores.

HOW HIGH THE MOUNTAINS, HOW DEEP THE OCEANS?

We have already examined the possibility that a local Flood merely covered hills and foothills, rather than all the high mountain peaks. A flood that did not at least cover foothills would not have accomplished God's intention of destroying mankind. The depth that may have been reached in global flooding is discussed in the next chapter. One of suggestions for the Young Earth model is that the highest mountains were relatively low before the Flood, a few thousand feet perhaps, and then reached tens of thousands of feet after the Flood as a result of a temporary increase in tectonic movement. If this were true, the amount of floodwater necessary to cover the mountains was considerably less than would have been required with today's topography. Nonetheless, the source for even this lesser amount of water for a global Flood has not been identified, and there is no evidence that the world's mountain ranges rose by as much as 20,000 feet over a period of a few hundred years. Geological evidence points to slow tectonic processes that are observed today. For example, the Himalayas are still rising at about 0.5 inch each year.

WHAT DIED IN THE FLOOD?

All of mankind died in the Flood, except for Noah and his immediate family. This was God's intent, and the outcome is stated explicitly:

> All in whose nostrils was the breath of the spirit of life, all that was on the dry land, died. So He destroyed all living things which were on the face of the ground: both man and cattle, creeping thing and bird of the air. They were destroyed from the earth. Only Noah and those who were with him in the ark remained alive. (Gen 7:22–23)

Two conditions are given for creatures that were to be destroyed; they had to dwell on land and breathe through nostrils. Although drowning was a likely cause for their demise, starvation and exposure was also instrumental for those not immediately swept away by flood waters. Many reptiles and amphibians that usually reside in water, and others that normally live on land, could have survived unaided. Insects were not included in the destruction because they do not have nostrils; instead they breathe through multiple body orifices. Some may have found sanctuary on the ark, for as we all know, it is not easy to keep out flies, spiders, and other bugs from our dwellings. Many could have survived on floating debris.

The animals present in the ark were Mammals and Birds:

> Then God spoke to Noah and to his sons with him, saying: "And as for Me, behold, I establish My covenant with you and with your descendants after you, and with every living creature [*nephesh chay*] that is with you: the birds, the cattle, and every beast of the earth with you, of all that go out of the ark, every beast of the earth. (Gen 9:8–10)

After the Flood, God stated that the rainbow was to be the sign of His covenant not to flood the earth again. He made this covenant with Noah, all his descendants, and *every living creature* (Mammals and Birds). God emphasized this covenant with Noah and *every living creature* by mentioning it three more times in Genesis 9. The kinds of creatures specified are birds, cattle, and beasts of the earth. The ark rescued only Mammals and Birds, the same kinds of creatures that God described in Genesis 1 for the creation week.

LANDFALL AND THE OLIVE LEAF

After 150 days afloat, the ark settled on the mountains of Ararat. The Hebrew text does not state that the ark settled at the very top of the highest peak in that mountain range.[10] The Hebrew word for *mountains* means both hills and mountains, so that the location of the ark could have been anywhere on the Ararat mountain range, including its foothills. From the ark's landing site, Noah could have looked up towards the peak of Mount Ararat itself, although it was probably too far away to be visible. After the ark went aground, the waters continued to recede, and then seventy-three days later, tops of hills (*mountains* in Genesis) became visible. The hills that appeared were much lower than the place where the ark landed, because they appeared seventy-three days later, during which time the flood had been subsiding.

After another forty days, Noah opened the window and released birds to find out if the land was habitable. Perhaps Noah could not see the landscape sufficiently well from his vantage point on the ark. The dove he sent out returned at the first attempt, but after the second flight a week later, it returned with an olive leaf. Olive trees are subtropical and grow up to about 5,000 feet altitude. Finally, when released a third time, the dove was content with the environment and did not return. This was 103 days after landfall, sufficient time for plants to have grown and produced the grain that doves feed upon.

Genesis 8:5 states: "the tops of the mountains were seen." Bearing in mind that the Biblical description of the Flood was written from the perspective and viewpoint of the ark, the meaning is that the hills below the ark were not just visible, they were actually seen. The hills above the ark had been visible all along. The only people alive who could see these hilltops were Noah and his family. The view from the ark was limited by the curvature of the earth, which limited the distance from which the hills could be seen to about eighty miles, depending on visibility.

THEY WENT OUT TWO BY TWO

One can imagine how Noah's family rushed out of the ark when they first opened the ark's door. Dry land and fresh air may have seemed almost like a new garden of Eden. Perhaps the animals inside wanted to rush out as well, but Noah had a year at sea to think about that. He had a zoo full of herbivores and perhaps carnivores as well. Which of these should he let out first? Common sense would indicate that the herbivores should leave first, and then some years later, the carnivores could leave. By then, the herbivores would have reproduced sufficiently to provide adequate prey for the carnivores. The Bible discreetly does not mention this logistical problem or its solution. Assuming they were in a state of suspended animation during the Flood, carnivores could have remained in that condition until the time came for them to leave the ark.

Another logistical problem is how smaller creatures made their way to far off places, and how creatures with unique diets found sustenance on their journeys. But just as God led different species to the ark, we can assume that God could have taken them to their new habitats after the Flood, especially if the Flood were global. We have to appeal to God's intervention because it was impossible for Noah's family to have managed such problems. Exactly how God did this is an unexplained detail, made much simpler in the situation of a local flood. God's instructions on leaving the ark were to multiply:

> Bring out with you every living thing of all flesh that is with you: birds and cattle and every creeping thing that creeps on the earth, so that they may abound on the earth, and be fruitful and multiply on the earth. (Gen 8:17)

At this time, Noah and his family were given a new diet that included all living creatures: "Every moving thing that lives shall be food for you. I have given you all things, even as the green herbs." (Gen 9:3). In the short term, Noah had access to the meat from the sacrifices that he made; it was common religious practice, including that of Israel, for those performing the sacrifice to eat portions of meat that had not been burnt in the sacrifice.

SACRIFICE AND COVENANT

> Then Noah built an altar to the Lord, and took of every clean animal and of every clean bird, and offered burnt offerings on the altar. And the Lord smelled a soothing aroma (Gen 8:20–21)

Noah was kept quite busy at first by sacrificing one or maybe two of every clean animal and every clean bird. He was able to do this and leave enough to breed and multiply because there were seven pairs of each clean animal. Noah was familiar with the distinction between clean and unclean animals and birds. Later, when the Jewish nation was formed under Moses, God gave detailed instructions about ceremonially clean and unclean animals. Clean animals were not carnivores, carrion eaters, nor animals that rummage for food in the ground. Clean animals ate only vegetation. From this we see that God chose creatures for sacrifice that avoided contact with death and decay; ceremoniously unclean features of our natural world. Although Genesis does not state what animals were clean, God had made such information known to mankind from the very first. A full list of clean and unclean animals was later given to the people of Israel through Moses; it is recorded in Leviticus 11. The concepts of clean and unclean had relevance to sacrifice and also to defilement.

Animal sacrifices were not new, and the need for them was appreciated by both Abel and Noah. They served to remind people that God took sin seriously, and that a permanent solution was needed to restore fellowship with Him. One might object to animals being used this way, but all creatures belong to God, and they are His to dispose of as He desires. Anyway, in the continuous cycle of life and death, most animals die without living full natural life spans.

Animal sacrifice served God's purpose. In contrast, God does not treat humans in this utilitarian way, because they are made in His image and likeness. God is opposed to murder, and requires judgment on murderers, even from animals that killed humans. (Gen 9:5–6) Animals that were sacrificed were supposed to be free of any physical blemish; equivalent to being free from sin in human terms. This pointed to the ultimate sacrifice of Jesus, a man who obeyed God in all He did. Animal sacrifices reminded God's people that they were all sinners, and eventually the real price was to be paid for their sinfulness. Each sacrifice was temporary soothing of God's anger at man's wickedness. For the reader who wants a full Biblical treatment on Jewish sacrifices, the Epistle to the Hebrews gives a clear comparison between the ceremonial sacrifices of animals and the atoning sacrifice of Jesus.

Defilement was caused by contact with death or disease; this was codified later by Moses for the nation of Israel. There were many rules for dealing with defilement, including a restriction on eating the meat of unclean animals. This ban was lifted after the crucifixion of Jesus, when Peter had a vision that all creatures were henceforth considered clean for the new Jewish Christians. With the work of Christ completed, they were not obligated to observe the old ceremonial religious activities.

Before God provided the Jewish people with laws and ceremonies through Moses, people had been carrying out religious activities from the time of Adam; two of these, sacrifices and tithing, are mentioned in Genesis. Nations that did not have a relationship with God worshiped idols instead. Many of them sacrificed animals, and even people, for the sake of transitory favor with their gods. Tithing is first mentioned in the life of Abraham, and continued through to the end of the Jewish nation in Jerusalem. Tithing, however, still is

God's method to provide for ministers who serve Him. Sacrifice and tithing were more than mere rituals. They were intended to build and maintain a relationship between God and his people, in recognition of God's providence.

FAIR GAME

After the Flood, God gave mankind the right to take animals for food, "every moving thing that lives shall be food for you" (Gen 9:3) Again, the use of the word *every* should be understood in its context, which in this instance would include what is safe to hunt and nourishing to eat. Not all species meet these criteria, which must have been true in Noah's time as well. As mankind migrated over almost the world's entire land surface, lifting the restriction from eating meat was essential. In desert places, where insufficient food grows for humans, herds and flocks eat grasses and coarse vegetation, providing meat, dairy, and other animal products that can be vital for human survival. Similarly in polar and mountainous regions, hunting animals allows mankind to live in otherwise inhospitable climates. In temperate and tropical zones where fruit and vegetables are abundant, man could probably survive quite well without any meat or animal products, as many vegans do.

In addition to being used for food, animals serve several other purposes for humanity, including transport, clothing, tools, and pets. After the Flood, God stated that all animals were to be afraid of men; perhaps because they were not created that way, and perhaps animals on the ark had become too accustomed to Noah and his family as they took care of them in the ark.

God made a covenant with mankind and Mammals and Birds, promising to never again destroy all flesh, using the rainbow as a sign of His promise. (Gen 9:15) We still have to endure local flooding, but regardless of ongoing wickedness, mankind does not have to fear extinction by water. When God spoke to Noah about the rainbow, one may have appeared at that time. It was not, however, the first rainbow ever seen because rainbows are caused by the simple physical phenomenon of refraction, requiring just sunshine and rain.

CAPITAL PUNISHMENT

Having evicted mankind from the garden of Eden, God did not make any laws for man to keep, until after the Flood. He then gave Noah two laws, one of which said: "Whoever sheds man's blood, by man his blood shall be shed; for in the image of God He made man." (Gen 9:6). Making man in His own image was the high point of God's creation, and anything that might damage His image was of vital concern to God, and still is. This concern includes marriage because God's image is expressed as male and female.

The other law prohibited eating meat with blood because blood contained the life of the animal. In essence, mankind was commanded to have respect for life, at least for creatures in which blood circulated. This commandment also goes back to the creation narrative, where God first gave life to Mammals and Birds. Many generations later, when God took charge of the nation of Israel through the leadership of Moses, He gave a more comprehensive set of laws for His people to follow. The two commandments given to Noah were included.

AFTER THE FLOOD

The first recorded event after the world had recovered from the Flood occurs in Genesis 11, which is about the Tower of Babel. This tower, built of bricks and pitch, was one of many ancient ziggurats built in the vicinity of Babylon. Currently, there is no archaeological evidence that any of the existing ziggurat ruins is the Biblical tower. The purpose of these towers is captured in their name, which conveys the concept of a stairway to heaven. Many ancient narratives have been discovered from all across the world that describe such towers, built to reach the gods. Some accounts include its destruction, followed by diversification of languages. Others refer to towers of bricks and pitch, even though pitch was not available locally at those locations.[11]

After the Flood, the first few generations spoke the same original language as their ancestor Noah. The growing population migrated east from the landing site of the ark on the foothills of Mount Ararat. Later they went back to the land of Shinar where Babylon was located. Noah's descendants did not want to be separated from each other, thinking naturally that they had strength in numbers. Eventually they built a city and then the tower with its religious significance. It is worth reading God's commentary about their intentions:

> But the Lord came down to see the city and the tower which the sons of men had built. And the Lord said, "Indeed the people are one and they all have one language and this is what they begin to do; now nothing that they propose to do will be withheld from them. Come, let Us go down and there confuse their language, that they may not understand one another's speech. (Gen 11:5–7)

We may wonder why God was concerned that mankind, seemingly primitive in technology, could achieve very much, let alone anything that they might propose. One answer is to note that their abilities were dependent on a higher power, one that could release what they needed. Also, their ability to acquire this power depended on their unity, which in turn depended on a common language. Consequently, I think that they, or at least their leaders and priests, were attempting to tap into supernatural power, which would have been satanic in nature. People have tried this approach to gain power through the ages, and some still try today.

Pyramids and ziggurats have been built in many places around the world; all dedicated to local gods, and most, if not all, were sites of human sacrifice. Even lesser edifices, such as Stonehenge, are thought to have been used for human sacrifice. Some of these structures were built with massive stone blocks, weighing up to 1,000 tons, procured from quarries that might be many miles or even hundreds of miles away. Seams between the blocks in some structures were often so precise that modern masons would be unable to equal their workmanship. Such technology indicates the possibility of supernatural help, which may have been obtained from Satan. He had, and still has, a vested interest in keeping people's attention away from the true God. Babel's tower was the forerunner of pyramids, ziggurats, and henges that were eventually built across the globe. The similarities between them and their alignment with the stars was the result of a mankind's common experience back at Babel.

The city of Babel was the origin from which mankind migrated to the three contiguous continents, Africa, Asia, and Europe. From these continents, migrations continued until men and their families had filled every habitable corner of the globe. These migratory patterns are being confirmed by modern genetic studies, described briefly in chapter 11.

REFERENCES

1. Ross, Hugh. *The Genesis Question*. Colorado Springs: NavPress, 1998: 127.
2. Phillips, John. *Exploring Genesis*. Grand Rapids, Kregel Publications, 1980: 78–80.
3. Wilson, William. *Old Testament Word Studies*. Grand Rapids: Kregel Publications, 1978: 185.
4. Uddin, Monica, et al. *Epigenetic and immune function profiles associated with posttraumatic stress disorder*. Proceedings of the National Academy of Sciences, 107.20 (2010): 9470–9475.
5. Snoke, David. *A Biblical Case for an Old Earth*. Grand Rapids, Baker Books, 2006: 158–175.
6. Ibid., 165–168.
7. Thompson, Bert. *In Defense of … the Genesis Flood, Part 1*. Apologetics Press: Reason & Revelation, August 1998: 18.8:57–63. <www.apologeticspress.org>.
8. Hill, Carol. *Qualitative Hydrology of Noah's Flood*. Perspectives on Science and Christian Faith. 58.2 (2006): 120–129.
9. Wilson, William. *Old Testament Word Studies*. Grand Rapids: Kregel Publications, 1978: 49–51.
10. See Reference 1, 147.
11. Frazer, Sir James. Folk-lore in the Old Testament: Studies in Comparative Religion, Legend and Law. London: Macmillan, 1919: 360–375.

10

LEGENDS AND EVIDENCE FOR THE FLOOD

At thy rebuke the floods retire.
Thine are the fountains of the deep;
By thee their waters swell or fail;
Up to the mountain's summit creep,
Or shrink beneath the lowly vale.
—John Quincy Adams

GREAT FLOOD LEGENDS

In his book *Moons, Myths, and Men,* H. S. Bellamy identified flood legends from over 250 peoples scattered across the globe. An almost universal theme in these legends is destruction of mankind, except for the rescue of one man and his family through the building of a large vessel. Other common themes include divine cause and warning, a rainbow, sending out birds, the saving of animal and bird species, and sacrifices made after landfall. Most of the other forty or so elements of the Biblical story are embodied in more than one of the legends. Nations in the Americas even include the division of languages and separation of tribes, which occurred after the Flood at Babel. Perhaps the most famous alternative to the Bible, and one of the closest to the Biblical narrative, is contained in the Babylonian Epic of Gilgamesh, written on stelae (large stone blocks). Fragments of the earliest versions have been dated to about 2,000 BC, whereas Moses wrote the Book of Genesis about 1,400 BC. The earliest record of the Flood is a fragment of the Sumerian Eridu Genesis, dated about 2,800 BC.

Neighboring civilizations might be expected to have similar Flood stories. Although the Babylonian version was earlier, it does not necessarily mean that it was more accurate. Moses had the advantage of divine revelation, which is the hallmark of the Old Testament.[1] After the Flood, consensus about the deluge would have existed among the tribes for many generations. Divergence accelerated after the Tower of Babel, when different languages were visited on the original tribes. (Gen 11:7) As tribes and nations migrated from the Middle East, variations increased, especially as they gave up monotheism and believed in the fantasies of polytheism, with the associated bizarre behavior of its gods.

PHYSICAL EVIDENCE

Currently, no incontrovertible scientific evidence exists for the Biblical Flood; instead, considerable evidence exists for numerous localized floods, all over the world. Geologists have not found evidence for a worldwide flood that covered all mountains within the timeframe of humanity. Nor is there conclusive evidence for a local flood that closely meets the Biblical Flood story. In recent years, the Creation Research Society established an initiative to understand the geologic column within the perspective of a catastrophic and recent global Flood. As yet, they have no conclusive evidence to report on a global flood that deposited almost all fossil bearing sedimentary layers.[2] In contrast to this model, a less catastrophic worldwide flood need not leave much sediment behind, as detailed later in the chapter in the section on Global Flood Mechanisms. Having said that, there is a good case for the existence of a Biblical Flood, based on the evidence presented later in this chapter. Such a Flood, however, does not fit the Young Earth catastrophic model or that of relatively small local floods that we experience today.

Archaeological evidence for the ark and its location is extremely controversial. Potential sites include the top of Mount Ararat at about 17,000 feet, Mount Nemrut and Uzenzili, both at about 6,000 feet,

Durupinar at about 4,000 feet, Mount Judi at about 2,000 feet, and sites at lower elevations in Mesopotamia.[3]

CONDITIONS FOR THE FLOOD

Although many suggestions have been made as to how the Flood may have occurred, none so far have satisfied all the conditions that the Bible imposes, the known findings of archaeology, and at the same time the physical constraints of nature. A solution is presented in the rest of this chapter that meets these Flood conditions, which are summarized below:

- The location should include Mesopotamia, where Adam's descendants are most likely to have dwelt.
- The Flood must have occurred prior to established civilizations that indicate knowledge of God and the afterlife. Evidence of pre-Flood civilization, if it exists, would be limited to Mesopotamia.
- The Flood must have occurred after the ice age; otherwise most of the available water for flooding would have been frozen.
- Plausible locations for both the source and the sink of the floodwaters must be identified.
- The Flood must have been at least high enough to strand the ark at the southern boundary of the Urartu kingdom, close to modern day Mosul.
- Sources of water must be identified that had had sufficient volume to cover Mesopotamia, at least as high as Mosul.
- A barrier must be identified that dammed the Flood for many months.
- A mechanism must be identified that allowed winds to release the floodwaters.

LOCAL FLOODS

Many theologians and scientists believe that the Flood was local. And indeed, there is considerable evidence for several vast but localized floods. Major floods have occurred across the world, including the Middle East, the Mediterranean Sea, the Black Sea, the Caspian Sea, and the lower Tigris-Euphrates basin down to the Persian Gulf. The Mediterranean flood occurred at a time much earlier than any human occupation. The Black Sea and connected Caspian Sea floods are possible candidates for the Noachian Flood, as many have suggested. Mesopotamia, stretching the length of the Tigris, is a better alternative considering its location as the likely habitation of mankind at the time. This whole Arabian basin is surrounded by mountains and hills, except for the Strait of Hormuz in the southeast. This is a narrow stretch of water that long ago had been closed off by sand dunes, so that any significant flooding in Mesopotamia would have had nowhere to drain away.[4]

The catastrophic collapse of glacial dams and the overflow of glacial lakes have been major causes of flooding in many places across the world. A well known example is the Missoula Flood, which inundated what are now large parts of Oregon and Washington. Over 500 cubic miles of water, which had previously backed up in Lake Missoula, poured into the Pacific.[5] As the last ice age came to an end, this lake is thought to have breached glacial dams more than once. Several mechanisms can contribute to the rupture of glacial dams, including a warming climate that increases the amount of water and pressure at the bottom of the glaciers. In addition, heat from the earth and seismic activity may be involved. A glacial dam begins to collapse as small water channels cut through cracks at the top, side, or bottom edges of the glacier. The process rapidly escalates until the glacial dam is breached, and hydraulic processes destroy the whole dam. As melt water rushes out of the bottom of a glacier, under very high pressure, it could well be described as a *fountain of the deep*, where the *deep* signifies the lake held back by the glacier.

Other instances of the collapse of glacial dams are known to have occurred across the Northern Hemisphere, one of which is suspected of flooding central North America all the way south into the Gulf Mexico. Another may have traveled west from Europe, washing out the English Channel, and leaving Great Britain separated from France. Lake Agassiz, which lay over five states and provinces of the USA and Canada, is believed to have had more water than all lakes of today combined. It appears to have broken out in different directions at different times. Glacial lakes in Siberia are thought to have flooded southwards through the Aral and Caspian lakes into the Mediterranean. These and others may have released massive amounts of water into the oceans at about the same time, but they could not have flooded the whole earth to thousands of feet.

Glacial dams are not confined to the ice age; they have been observed within the last few decades. Hubbard Glacier in Alaska has repeatedly dammed up large volumes of water, which then flooded the terrain beneath it as the glacial dam was breached.[6] This occurred at sea level, but glaciers in Swiss mountains have also collapsed and caused flooding in the valleys beneath them.[7] Even after decades of disappearing glaciers, glacial dams are still a threat to populations in mountainous parts of the world such as the Caucasus, Andes, and Himalayan mountains.

WATER GAPS AND WIND GAPS

When torrents of water spill out of lakes they erode whatever rock formations are in their path, creating canyons and rivers. One example of such canyons is a gorge, hundreds of yards wide and up to fifty feet deep, that was created over a few weeks as flood water in Canyon Lake, Texas, poured over its spillway in 2002. Another is the canyon, up to 140 feet deep, caused by the Spirit Lake flood of mud and water that occurred after the Mount St. Helens volcanic explosion in 1980. Canyons, created by torrents of water, are known as *water gaps* when rivers continue to flow through them. Otherwise, if the sources of water cease to exist, they are known as *wind gaps*. More than a thousand of these gaps have been found all over the world in mountainous areas.

Frequently, wind gaps appear to have been blasted through rocks that were higher than the surrounding terrain, where rivers would not normally flow. This has been an enigma to geologists, which some Young Earth scientists resolve with a two phase global Flood hypothesis.[10] The collapse of glacial dams, however, offers a more likely explanation; especially because these water and wind gaps are known to have formed repeatedly in the locations of glacial dams. Rivers flow downhill over existing landscapes under the pull of gravity, reaching relatively low velocities. Even so, they are able to carve canyons through rock over long periods of time. In contrast, the water pressure at great depths behind a glacier can generate much higher velocities, so that water ejected from the bottom of glacial dams has considerably more power to erode rock formations.

Water escaping from the bottom of glacial dams has high velocity because it is forced out at very high pressure. As a result, it continues in the direction it started because of its momentum. Unlike a river, it is not constrained initially by gravity to follow the contour of the earth's surface. Consequently, canyons can be cut through rock at elevations well above normal river beds, depending on the direction and height of the ejected water. Where rock surfaces face a glacial dam failure, the torrent of high speed water will cut through those rocks, instead of merely falling downhill under gravity.

In addition to being a cause of local flooding, the collapse of glacial dams offers an explanation for the water gaps and wind gaps found in mountainous areas, where glaciers have come and gone for tens of thousands of years. They provide an explanation for wind gaps, where rivers appear to have cut their way through ridges and escarpments for which there is no apparent source of water.

MESOPOTAMIA

Mesopotamia is a special candidate for a catastrophic local flood caused by the collapse of glacial dams. To the east and northeast lie the Zagros Mountains, which are known to have had huge glaciers. Almost one-third of the world's 1,000 water and wind gaps are located in these mountains, indicating considerable flood activity in the past.[9] The Taurus Mountains lie to the north of Mesopotamia, stretching from Iran all across southern Turkey. Many glacier covered mountains exist along this chain, including Mt. Ararat. A few hundred miles further north are the Caucasus Mountains, which still have destructive floods generated by the collapse of glacial dams.[11] Smaller mountains, which lie along the western side of Mesopotamia next to the Mediterranean, also had glaciers, but these were small by comparison and could not have contributed significantly to the Flood.

Further to the east, massive flooding took place in the vicinity of the Altai Mountains, some 12,000 years ago. It was possibly the largest single flood that has ever occurred on the earth. It started about 2,000 miles east of Mesopotamia and appears to have progressed westwards, engulfing the Aral Sea, the Caspian Sea, the Black Sea, finally pouring into the Mediterranean Sea.[10]

In the south of Mesopotamia, the Tigris and Euphrates Rivers join together, becoming the Shatt al Arab, which empties into the Persian Gulf. The Persian Gulf in turn flows into the Gulf of Oman through the narrow Strait of Hormuz. Towards the end of the ice age, the Persian Gulf was dry because of an arid climate, and also because the sea level had fallen as a result of so much water being locked up in glaciers and the ice caps. The Gulf of Oman had receded far from the Strait of Hormuz. In addition, the Strait of Hormuz was filled with sand because of prevailing winds that created great sand dunes from the immense amount of sand lying on the dried up bed of the Persian Gulf. These sand dunes also ran across the southern hills of what are now Oman, the United Arab Emirates, and Saudi Arabia.[12] Under suitable conditions, such sand dunes can reach heights that exceed 1,500 feet.[13]

Mesopotamia was essentially landlocked at the time of the Flood. When God released the fountains of the deep, massive torrents of water gushed out almost horizontally from the bottom of some of the glaciers, sending many cubic miles of water cascading down the valleys, which overwhelmed the Tigris and Euphrates rivers. A flood level of only 1,300 feet of water above sea level would have flooded the Tigris River all the way into Turkey. The town of Cizre in Turkey is located just where the Tigris elevation is at 1,200 feet.

As the ark floated on the floodwaters, winds from the south blew it northwards towards Turkey. If it remained somewhere in the middle of the flooded area, Noah could not have seen any mountains because of the curvature of the earth. Mountains less than 15,000 feet higher than the ark, and more than 150 miles away from the ark, could not be seen.

SPEAKING VOLUMES

Having said all that, we need to get an estimate of the volume of water necessary to flood Mesopotamia to a depth of 1,300 feet, in order to determine if such a flood is feasible with natural sources of water. We will consider two flood depths, 1,300 feet that would reach beyond Cizre, and 750 feet that would reach just beyond Mosul. This city is the lowest in elevation that fits the Biblical description of where the ark landed. Mosul is on the southern boundary of Urartu, the region that encompasses Mount Ararat. The original Hebrew word for Ararat, which had no vowels, could equally well refer to Urartu, a kingdom that surrounded Mount Ararat, and which existed at the time of Moses. The Hebrew word translated Ararat is the same word translated Armenia in 2 Kings 19:37 and Isaiah 37:38. This is because the land of Urartu eventually became known as Armenia,

Mesopotamia can be modeled with simple geometric shapes in order to estimate the volume of water required to flood it. Considering the lower end of the Tigris, the Shatt-al-Arab rises merely 50 feet over a distance of 240 miles upstream from the Persian Gulf. The river basin along that stretch is about 90 miles wide. To the east and west, the hills rise approximately 750 feet for every 55 miles away from the river. Further upstream, the river rises 700 feet in 320 miles, and then another 550 feet in just 80 miles. In these two sections, the land on either side of the river can be modeled as a simple valley. In the lower section of the model, it is 200 miles wide at the southern end, tapering to zero width at 750 feet altitude. The upper section, which applies only to the 1,300 foot flood depth, has a width of 325 feet, decreasing linearly to zero at 1,300 feet altitude.

The Persian Gulf, which has a surface area of 92,000 square miles, would have had the same flood height as that reached by the floodwater in Mesopotamia, adding substantially more water to the total flood volume. In addition, the land of Saudi Arabia, which surrounds the Persian Gulf, would have been flooded. Using the distances mentioned above, the volumes of water necessary to flood Mesopotamia and the Persian Gulf are given in Table 1, where volumes are measured in thousands of cubic miles.

The total Flood volumes for the selected depths of 1,300 feet and 750 feet are 54,000 cubic miles and 26,000 cubic miles.

Flood depth above sea level, feet	750	1,300
Volume of water in Tigris river basin, cubic miles	9,000	25,000
Volume of water over Persian Gulf, cubic miles	13,000	22,000
Volume of water around Persian Gulf, cubic miles	4,000	7,000
Total volume of water for Flood, cubic miles	26,000	54,000

Table 1: Water volumes required to flood Mesopotamia and Persian Gulf

We can now determine if rain and melting glaciers might provide flood water to equal at least 26,000 cubic miles. The combined watershed from all regions that feed Mesopotamia is about 1,500,000 square miles. If all of the Tigris-Euphrates and Persian Gulf watersheds received an average of twelve inches per day for forty days, the total volume of rainwater would amount to about 11,000 cubic miles. Such rainfall rates occur naturally for two or three days over much smaller areas but not for forty days over the larger area being considered. If rainfall produced flooding anywhere near this upper limit of 11,000 cubic miles, God must have intervened to maintain a suitable weather pattern over Mesopotamia for forty days.

The glacial dam flood from Missoula Lake has been estimated to have discharged 843 cubic miles; the Altai flood released about 530 cubic miles. Although the Lake Agassiz flood has been estimated to have discharged about 5,040 cubic miles, this was from a lake with the enormous area of 365,000 square miles, although at a relatively low altitude. In contrast, the Taurus and Zagros mountain ranges provided even larger areas that could have harbored many lakes held back by glacial dams. Mountain chains surrounding Mesopotamia are about 1,000 miles in length, and vary in width from about 200 miles to 400 miles. The total mountainous area around Mesopotamia is about 400,000 square miles. In comparison, Lake Missoula has an area of about 3,000 square miles, and lay among peaks that rose to about 10,000 feet. The mountains occupy an area that is about 200 miles long by about 100 miles wide, equivalent to an area of 20,000 square miles.

These measurements indicate that the mountains surrounding Mesopotamia could have produced at least twenty concurrent floods similar in size to the Missoula flood. Because the mountains surrounding

Mesopotamia are significantly higher than those surrounding Lake Missoula, they held more water, possibly as much as 1,000 cubic miles for each Missoula size lake. The combined flood volume from glacial dam collapses could have been as much as 100,000 cubic miles. Therefore, it is reasonable to conclude that sufficient water, from the collapse of glacial dams, was available to cause a flood with a depth of 750 feet, and even enough for 1,300 feet. Rain increased the flood depth by about 200 feet at the most.

WINDS OF CHANGE

After the Flood had peaked, the waters subsided because God had made a wind. (Gen 8:1) This wind could have been the Shamal, which blows from the northwest along the Zagros Mountains.[14] It would have created large waves that caused the partially consolidated sand dunes in the Strait of Hormuz to crumble. After the dunes had been breached, further erosion quickly followed, and they were completely swept away, leaving little trace of their existence. This explanation is attractive because it matches the only mechanism given by the Bible that caused the waters to subside.

The description given above provides not only a qualitative explanation but also a quantitative solution that fits the geography of Mesopotamia. Calculations of water volumes are necessary because the Bible gives only a brief description of what happened. Other phenomena may have been involved, and such possibilities should be explored.

Because Mesopotamia was landlocked, a modest rise in the worldwide sea level could not have been a contributory cause for the Flood depth. After the last glacial maximum, sea levels rose by about 600 feet; but the level relative to any given coast line would also have been affected by isostatic depression and rebound as the glaciers melted.

GLOBAL FLOOD MECHANISMS

The Young Earth Flood model proposes that water covered the whole earth, including the highest mountains, although they may not have been as high as they are today. In addition, all sedimentary layers that contain fossils were deposited in catastrophic flood conditions that prevailed during and after the Biblical Flood. One of the difficulties with this concept of a global Flood is that an adequate source of water has not been identified. Rain simply recycles water from the oceans, without raising sea levels. The water canopy theory, which proposed that the outer layer of water that God created in the second Day was several miles thick, has been discarded by almost all scientists for a variety of reasons. Consequently, the only other source for water had to be deep beneath the earth's crust.[15] Immense pressures and high temperatures exist far below the earth's surface that could have forced huge plumes of water and steam into the oceans, if aquifers existed at those depths. Certain types of rock under the earth's crust may store water with aqueous densities up to about three percent by weight. Such rocks lie deep in the earth's mantle and have sufficient volume to store much more water than our existing oceans contain. This and other evidence suggests that there are great quantities of water trapped in the earth's mantle.[16] Models of our solar system indicate that the earth originally should have had much more water than is thought to exist on and in the earth's crust. One problem with this source of water in the mantle is that no mechanism exists for the mantle rock to release its water sufficiently rapidly for the Biblical Flood.

Springs on land do not produce significant volumes of water; they are fed by gravity from hills above, flowing through complex aquifers. Gravity keeps water in relatively shallow aquifers below the land surface so that in general they are not available to flood the earth. Deeper aquifers are at very hot temperatures. Geysers such as Old Faithful eject steam and very hot water at over 200 °F, as a result of ground water percolating down into regions where there is hot magma. That is the reason for geysers being found only in volcanically active sites. The magma may be above sea level, or below the bottom of the deepest ocean. In the latter situation of hydrothermal vents, water is emitted at temperatures as high as 750 °F, constrained as water instead of steam because of the very high pressure at the bottom of the oceans.

The oceanic crust is about 23,000 feet thick on average. It reaches temperatures at the boundary with the upper mantle of between 350 °F and 650 °F, although much higher temperatures are found close to rifts and cracks in the crust.[17] If vast sources of water existed in the middle of the earth's crust, they would have an average temperature of about 500 °F. The average depth of our oceans is about 12,000 feet and covers 71 per cent of the earth's surface. Currently, the average height of earth's land surface is a little more than 2,500 feet. Therefore, if the oceans were to have risen by only 6,000 feet and covered the land to the same level, an additional amount of water equivalent to about two-thirds of existing oceans must have come from inside the earth. Moreover, almost all the of the oceanic crust must have been aquifers, except for about 1,000 feet of rock to cap the aquifer and about 50 percent of the aquifer volume to be rock pillars. These would have been necessary to support the weight of water above. If the oceans had an average temperature of 40 °F, and if the fountains of the deep were emitted at an average 500 °F, the final average temperature of the oceans would have been a little over the boiling point of water, 212 °F. If flood levels were higher than 6,000 feet, more hot water and steam would have been ejected, so that the oceans would have been even hotter. The whole earth's surface would have been cooked before any significant cooling took place. Unless scientists can discover a cool source of water that exceeded about half the volume of our oceans, and then determine how it retreated, there is not much hope for the global Flood model.

As stated above, in order to raise the sea level by 6,000 feet would have required all of the oceanic crust to be an aquifer. Much of the ocean floor, however, has been drilled for geological research, without any evidence being found for vast aquifers. If *fountains of the deep* were indeed aquifers under the oceans, water escaping from them would behave like water escaping from hydrothermal vents at the bottom of the ocean. They could not have spurted high into the sky as depicted by Young Earth flood models. This is because water is more or less incompressible, so that it could not expand violently upward through thousands of feet of ocean into the atmosphere.

A more likely cause of global flooding is melting of glaciers and polar ice caps as the earth warmed at the end of the Ice Age. This mechanism, however, produced a rise in sea level of only a few hundred feet, over a period of many decades. Its effect was more pronounced than if it occurred today because the weight of glaciers and ice caps had depressed much of the earth's crust. This allowed deeper flooding over some continental surfaces. As the ice and glaciers retreated, the crust did not rebound immediately because of the very viscous nature of the crust and underlying mantle. In fact, the earth is still rebounding, quite slowly now, from the depressions caused by the last Ice Age. Where the ice was thick, land was 3,300 feet or more lower than today.[18] By about 13,000 years ago, the earth had warmed considerably from the coldest phase of the Ice Age, and considerable amounts of water were available to raise sea levels.

Young Earth. There is some consensus among Young Earth scientists about the catastrophic flood model and the initial geological layer laid down by the Flood. Although some of these scientists suspect the starting point to be as low as about 375 miles into the earth's mantle, most Young Earth scientists believe that the lowest sediments deposited by the Flood were the Paleozoic and Mesozoic layers.[19] Paleozoic strata are visible in the Grand Canyon, where the total of the Paleozoic and Mesozoic layers averages about 5,000 feet in thickness. About 1,000 feet of Mesozoic strata are visible at the top of the Canyon, but the remainder, about 2,000 feet, has been eroded away. All vegetation that was not floating during the Flood would have been buried under thousands of feet of sediment. This is not consistent, however, with the Biblical narrative, which states that the dove Noah released was able to find a fresh olive twig; presumably from a living tree that was not buried under thousands of feet of sediment.

The Young Earth Flood model describes overwhelming hydraulic activity that eroded huge quantities of sediment from the oceanic crust. These sediments were subsequently deposited on the continents, but strangely, not in the ocean depths. The model also requires the movement of tectonic plates to have accelerated by a factor of about 30 million from today's speed. The individual continents would have separated from the original single landmass over a period of just a few months.[20] The Flood and separation of the continents would have occurred less than 5,000 years ago, over a period of a few hundred years. This model is called Catastrophic Plate Tectonics (CPT), which has some interesting features. But if anyone should think that it is even close to realistic, the words of Paul Garner in his book, *The New*

Creationism, should be a caution: "While many of the details remain to be worked out, catastrophic plate tectonics is a very promising theory." The problem is that the devil may be in the details, such as the inability of CPT to explain the presence of animal tracks in Paleozoic and Mesozoic sediments.[21]

Another detail that has not been worked out concerns the differences in the geology of oceanic and continental crusts. The oceanic crust is made of basaltic rock, heavier and thinner than continental crusts. Except for sediments washed from the land, deep oceanic floors have no significant limestone, sandstone, or shale type sedimentation.[22] These sediments make up the majority of the geological column on land, formed by erosion of existing continental rocks and by precipitation of water born minerals. If the *fountains of the deep* had broken through the ocean floor, creating sands and particles from the oceanic crust by hydraulic processes, continental sediments could not have been included. Whatever sediments were created by the *fountains of the deep*, they must have fallen back down to the bottom of the ocean because of their weight. Moreover, no mechanism has been proposed by which many thousands of feet of sediments were pushed up onto land. If a satisfactory mechanism were to be found, such as the action of very violent waves and currents, then it could not explain the uniformity over thousands of miles of many of these discrete sedimentary layers, quite a few of which can be formed only in calm and shallow waters.

The recent global Flood model does not provide explanations for several geological features that have been listed by two Christian geologists, Davis Young and Ralph Stearley in their book, *The Bible, Rocks and Time*. This book reveals significant problems with the Young Earth Flood model.[23] The following list outlines some of the issues that were examined:

- Regularity of strata over large continental distances, indexed by thin synchronous layers caused by asteroid impacts; a violent global flood would have caused considerable chaos to these layers.
- Many sedimentary strata and sequences of lava flows could

not be deposited physically in just a single year, or even hundreds of years.

- Countless volcanoes worldwide have been covered up by sediments and lava flows: there should be much more visual evidence for these volcanoes after a recent global flood.

- Scientists have identified about 150 major asteroid impacts across the face of the globe. If the earth were very young, they must have all struck the earth in a very short period of time after the Flood, along with the eruption of dozens of major volcanoes. Except for microbes, life could not have survived anywhere in the world. In addition, almost all impact craters and volcanoes should appear to have the same age, showing the same degree of erosion over the last few thousand years. That is not the case.

- Overwhelming and complete evidence for faunal succession, in which various fossil types are found only in a restricted range of strata, never below these strata. (Some species have survived to modern times and have no upper boundary.) The lowest fossils that have been identified with any certainty are small soft-bodied creatures in pre-Cambrian layers. Multitudes of larger fossils have been found in the Cambrian explosion. Above the Cambrian layers, fossils of very large sea creatures exist, such as bony-sided fish. Most if not all of these are extinct. Above all of these we find fossils of cetaceans (mammalian sea creatures) and modern scaly fish. In the Young Earth global Flood, all these creatures would have coexisted in the oceans. Nevertheless, not one of the modern species is found in the lower fossil layers. If the Flood caused their demise, there is no reason why all these fossils should not be mixed up.

Similarly on land, there are no elephants found with dinosaur fossils. Why are the fossil layers so clearly separated between later existing species and earlier or extinct reptilian species? One suggestion is the separation of different sized animals by classification, which is caused by rapidly moving water. But this does not work for similar sized animals or objects. Another is ecological zoning, in which elephants would be found in one locality and dinosaurs at another. This is a very artificial explanation without any evidence, especially in light of recent analysis of fossils found in the Western United States. At least one type of dinosaur was distributed over a wide geographical area with many different ecological zones.[24] The only reasonable explanation for the fossil record is that creatures which had died and formed most of the older fossils were extinct at the time of the Flood. Some species survived catastrophes that have afflicted the earth, such as the so-called fossil fish, the Coelacanth. In this vein, it is intriguing to speculate about dragons and Loch Ness monsters; but other books pursue these legends.

Other problems for which the Young Earth model does not provide explanations:

- Although a catastrophic flood could explain the existence of fossilized bones in some circumstances, many fossilized dinosaur footprints exist that do not appear to be compatible with a violent global flood. In several places across the world, dinosaur tracks have been found in multiple strata, one layer on top of the other. I have seen good examples at Dinosaur Flats in Texas. These tracks are well detailed, which means they had to have dried out over several days, before becoming inundated and covered with more sediment. Evidence of wind blown dust can be seen in the footprints, contrary to the effect of waves that would have erased them as floodwaters continued to rise in a catastrophic global flood.

- Recognizing that continents have drifted thousands of miles, Young Earth creationists propose that they did so over a period of a few months. This is equivalent to their moving at a rate of about one foot per second instead of the current rate of about one foot per year. The problem is that the viscosity of the asthenosphere, the part of the crust immediately below tectonic plates, would need to have been reduced by a factor of some 30 million. The viscosity of lava can be reduced substantially by very high temperatures and when water is embedded in the lava. No known mechanism exists, however, for such changes to have occurred over so much of the asthenosphere in such a short time, and then changed back again so quickly. Because of its immense size, thermal changes occur too slowly in the asthenosphere to allow the changes suggested by the Young Earth model.

- Vast amounts of erosion have occurred over many thousands of years, reducing the original sedimentary layers on the earth's surface to a fraction of their original volume. A Young Earth explanation is that as the Flood waters receded, they washed the recently formed, soft sediments downhill into the oceans. The weakness of this argument is that it does not work for igneous rocks that become relatively hard once they have solidified. For example the magnificent scenery of the Hawaiian chain of islands is due in part to erosion that could not have taken place over a mere few thousand years.

- Upright fossilized trees exist in dozens of sedimentary layers at Specimen Ridge in Yellowstone Park. These have been used as an argument for catastrophic global flooding on the basis that such trees have no root balls, and they must have been transported and then deposited in an upright position. This phenomenon of upright trees was observed at Spirit Lake, after the volcano of Mount St. Helens exploded in 1980. The trees in Yellowstone, however, actually prove they were not the result of a catastrophic flood because the deposition of upright trees requires calm water, as occurred at Spirit Lake. Also, most of the upright trees at Specimen Ridge do have root balls, some with soil horizons.

- Permafrost, where soil and rock are always below freezing point, exists at depths below 5,400 feet in Siberia.[25] This is quite remarkable, considering the warmth rising from the earth's core. It would be more amazing if permafrost reached those depths after a global catastrophic Flood that occurred a few thousand years ago. The Young Earth position is that there were no ice caps prior to the Flood, and that they were formed as result of the Flood. This leads to an impossible situation for the Young Earth model because scientists have calculated the length of time for permafrost to sink deep into the earth's crust. Using thermal conductivity, a basic property of matter, the time it would take for permafrost to reach the measured permafrost depth of 1,778 feet at Prudhoe Bay is over 500,000 years.[26] On the other hand, if it were argued that God created the world 6,000 years ago with such deep permafrost already in place, then there could be no explanation for the multitude of fossils found in these frozen arctic regions. The conclusion must be that polar ice caps could not have been caused by a recent global flood because there would have been insufficient time for permafrost to have penetrated over 1,000 feet.

Old Earth. If sources of water were to be found that had sufficient volume to cover the whole earth to 6,000 feet or more, flooding could not have been catastrophic as required by the Young Earth CPT model. Instead, it would have had a low impact, in which the fountains of the deep welled up into the oceans without spurting high into the atmosphere. The sea level would have risen about fifty feet per day. Water would have slowly covered the existing sediments and geological formations on the continents. There would not have been any significant sedimentation, or any lasting destruction of the landscape. This approach to a global flood allows vegetation to have remained alive and to have quickly recovered so as provide food for the thousands of animals that disembarked from the ark. In many parts of the world, significant floods have occurred in historical times because of slowly rising water, then after a few years, no significant and lasting trace of flooding can be found. For example, where sea level has risen and then fallen considerably in the past, scientists look for old beach erosion patterns because there is no other evidence in situ. Such global flooding, however, is not consistent with the Biblical Flood.

A PERFECT STORM

The Bible narrative indicates the Flood was at least hundreds of feet deep where the ark floated, almost certainly in the river basin of

Mesopotamia. Shallower flooding would have allowed some of mankind to escape by climbing nearby hills. In addition, the ark landed in the vicinity of Mount Ararat, which means the ark rested no lower than its foothills. They could be as far from Mount Ararat as modern day Mosul. The rest of the world may have endured other calamities that are not mentioned in the Bible, which we may be able to discover from geological studies. Worldwide flooding may have occurred but not measured in thousands of feet. Currently, geological research is finding evidence that is applicable to a likely timeframe for the Flood. I will attempt to summarize a combination of conditions that may have occurred prior to Noah's Flood. It is based on several related events that took place when the Younger Dryas cooling period was about to start. Before that time, the polar ice caps had made their furthest advance during the Last Glacial Maximum (LGM) some 4,000 years previously. The earth had been warming considerably, but the ice cap had only partially melted into the oceans, causing a modest rise in sea level.

The Flood may well have started approximately 12,900 years ago, when the fragmented remains of a large comet struck North and South America and Western Europe.[27] The immediate and local effect of the multiple impacts was the collapse of glacial dams in the vicinity of the impact zone. In addition, impact blasts caused fires across the North American landscape, where debris from the impact in Canada were scattered across the Eastern states of North America.[28] The swarm of comet fragments extended into Siberia and the Middle East.

In contrast, a single enormous comet would have left a very large impact crater, which has not been found. A swarm of smaller comets or comet fragments is considered more likely; these would have struck the earth over a much wider area, including the Middle East. Smaller comet fragments that crashed into the ice cap produced less impact debris, which contain chemical signatures that characterize impacts to the earth's surface. The 1908 comet explosion over Tunguska is a small example of this kind of impact.

At the time of the comet impact, Lake Agassiz was breached, releasing massive amounts of cold water into the North Atlantic. This halted the normal oceanic currents and precipitated the Younger Dryas cold spell. Similar flooding from glaciers close to Siberia might explain the extinction of the Siberian mammoths, many of which show evidence of having drowned.[29]

A second outcome of comet impacts were fires that were started across North America. The remains of these fires were eventually buried, forming black mats that have been discovered at many sites across much of the United States.[30] Recently, they were associated with the comet impact and the extinction of most of the mega-fauna of that time. One or more of such catastrophes is believed to be the cause for the extinction of thirty-five of the larger mammal species at the beginning of the Younger Dryas cold spell.[31]

In addition to the disappearance of mega fauna in North America, the combination of catastrophes initiated by comets is thought to be responsible for the decline of the Clovis culture, possibly to the point of extinction.[32] Many scientists assume that Clovis people were humans. Unless they were descended from Adam, however, they must have been hominids, even though they appear to have made stone tools and painted simple pictures on rocks. The Clovis culture gives no firm indication of any awareness of God, of idol worship, or the concept of an afterlife. These defining characteristics for the descendants of Adam can be applied to archaeological sites across the world.

Meanwhile in the mountains surrounding Mesopotamia, glacial dams had collapsed due to comet strikes, emptying glacial lakes into the land locked basin of Mesopotamia. The cradle of civilization was flooded as high as about 1,300 feet above sea level. At the end of the Flood, God caused a wind to blow, producing waves that broke down the partially consolidated sand dunes to the south; and then the floodwater drained into the Arabian Sea, as described earlier in this chapter.

Prior to the younger Dryas, rising sea levels around the world were causing enormous ice bergs to break away from the continental shelves that had been exposed as the sea level dropped during the ice age. As these icebergs entered the oceans, up to 90%percent of their volume sank so that sea levels rose even more. An increase of even 100 feet would devastate our modern civilization, but at that time it merely caused animals to move further inland. Even though some ice had melted after the Latest Glacial Maximum, isostatic adjustment was minimal for many years, and land surfaces close to the glaciers were as much as 2,500 feet lower than they are today. The global pattern was that of temporary high sea levels coinciding with greatly depressed land surfaces that were under or close to the ice caps.

As the Younger Dryas rapidly progressed, probably with the help of an impact winter caused by comet impacts, water became locked up in the polar ice caps again. Sea levels dropped, leaving little evidence of its brief excursion inland.

GENETIC AND CULTURAL EVIDENCE

Recent discoveries from genetic science about our ancestors indicate a recent bottleneck, in which only a few humans existed over several generations. In addition, the Out of Africa theory indicates that we all came from one locality. The evidence, however, is also consistent with the human race spreading out from the Middle East rather than from Africa, and from one man instead of many. Details are given in the next chapter.

NOAH AND THE FLOOD

It was early summer, and there had been a few rain showers. Noah had noticed that these had been increasing over the last few hundred years, as had the spring run off from the glaciers in the mountains. Some of the wise men had been saying that the glaciers would cease to exist within a hundred years as a result of earth warming. But none of this was of much concern to Noah because God had already told him that a great flood was coming. It was going to destroy all mankind except for Noah and his family; they would survive aboard the huge ark he had finished building several weeks ago.

He knew that he would not have to wait much longer for the coming deluge. All the animals that God had brought to him were now loaded on board and settled down in their stalls. As he made final preparations, he looked frequently with concern at his village, where two of his relatives had been married that week. Life had been good for the inhabitants of the cradle of civilization, but some ominous signs had occurred. Travelers had reported two massive floods further down the Tigris River. They described how huge fountains had broken out from the bottom of the mountain glaciers and then cascaded across the river valley. Everything was swept away by the floods, which eventually drained downstream into the desert in the far south.

Villagers had marveled at the sight of so many animals migrating from all directions towards the huge boat in Noah's yard. But they did not appreciate Noah telling them why all this was happening. Finally every animal was onboard, and it was time for Noah and his family to enter the ark. As they stepped onto the deck, they found themselves in the presence of God. He had called them into the ark, and after they were all on board, closed the great door behind them. For seven days they dwelled in communion with God, ignoring the taunts outside from local villagers and tourists who had come to see the unusual attraction.

And then the rain started, unusually heavy and persistent. That morning Noah peeked out of the window and glancing up north, he saw with fear and excitement a wall of water rushing towards them. As high as the trees and rushing forward faster than a galloping horse, the villagers had no hope, especially because an even higher wave followed behind the first onslaught. The roaring of the flood and cries of the villagers were muffled by the stout walls of the ark. Soon the ark shifted slightly as the torrent crashed against it, and then it rose with the flood to begin its long journey on top of the floodwaters. Noah suspected that glaciers further up the Tigris valley had collapsed and poured their contents into the cradle of civilization.

Looking out of the window on occasion, Noah could see that not only was the ark afloat on turbulent waters, but rain continued to pour down. That year, he and all of mankind were unaware that the Indian monsoon had come early, much further to the west, and with extra ferocity. He saw at one point that the hills he used to walk on were being covered by the flood, and then soon after, the trees on top of them were covered. After that, Noah had no way of knowing how much higher the flood rose.

Waiting for the rain to stop and then for the water to abate, day after day and month after month, would have been stressful; except Noah and his family, along with their cargo, were in the presence of God. Peace and joy were continual, even when strong winds blew across the ark.

These winds eventually brought about a steady drop in the height of the floodwater, which became evident when Noah felt the ark bump. Noah did not know why the floodwater subsided, causing the ark to run aground. The ark had ridden the wind driven waves with little movement; those waves however, had pummeled and broken through the sand dunes at the southern end of Mesopotamia.

They had landed north of where their voyage started and at a higher elevation. Even so, there was water almost everywhere they looked. Seventy three days later, Noah saw the tops of hills appearing above the water's surface. The ground close by was still sodden, and nothing appeared to be growing. Noah sent out a raven and a dove to explore the land that was out of sight from the ark. The raven was a scavenger and could find its own food. Nevertheless, it returned to the ark until the ground was dry enough for its liking. The dove, however, could not find any suitable food, and it also returned. A week later the dove flew north to where the ground was dryer and found an olive tree sprouting, from which it plucked a twig for Noah. The leaves on the twig indicated that trees were beginning to grow again, as had plants that had already flowered, producing seeds that had begun to ripen. After another week, the dove found that the seeds that it liked to eat had fully ripened, so it did not return to get food in the ark. Eventually, Noah released all the animals, waiting until each species was able to find the food on which it lived. The Flood was over.

DATING THE FLOOD

The Flood probably occurred about 12,900 years ago after comet fragments struck the northern hemisphere. In principle, however, it could have occurred about 8,000 years ago, soon after the Mesolithic ice age, also known as the 8.2 kiloyear mini ice age. Prior to this cold spell the earth had begun to warm up after the previous cold spell of the Younger Dryas. If the Flood had not occurred about 12,900 years ago as suggested previously, the Straits of Hormuz would still have been blocked by sand dunes. Mesopotamia would have remained comparatively dry, and when the Mesolithic ice age ended, glacial dams could have collapsed, releasing floodwaters and filling the Mesopotamian valley, as described above. The later date, however, is not consistent with the 11,600 year old temple at Göbekli Tepe in southern Turkey and the evidence of civilizations with advanced agriculture that existed before 8,200 years ago.

If the Flood occurred about 12,900 years ago, at the time of comet impacts and the extinction of many larger mammalian species, about 250 generations are missing from the genealogy in Genesis 11. If the Flood took place about 8,200 years ago, there are only about 100 names missing, most likely between Eber and Peleg, as explained at the end of chapter 8.

The first humans were farmers; Cain grew crops, while Abel raised livestock. They dwelt in homes and some lived in cities (more like a community than a present day metropolis). Noah's father tilled the ground, and Noah was a farmer. From time to time, these early humans also hunted and gathered, just as we do today. They were not, however, part of the hunter gatherer culture that had existed before them. Archaeology indicates a hiatus about 8,000 years ago between the hunter gatherer culture and complex farming civilizations that dwelt in villages. Hunter gatherers had existed for tens of thousand of years with very little change in their culture. They were competent in making simple stone tools but show none of the intelligence and religious awareness that existed with the subsequent Neolithic farming communities. Hunter gatherers disappeared at about the time farming civilizations began to proliferate, replaced by early farmers that were anatomically modern humans who had descended from Adam.

The earliest known domestication of crops is thought to have taken place about 11,000 years ago, in the Karacadag Mountains of southern Turkey.[33] This fits in well with my proposed time for the Flood of 12,900 years ago, and with the location: these mountains are about 100 miles northwest of Cizre in southern Turkey.

REFERENCES

1. McDowell, Josh. *Evidence that Demands a Verdict*. San Bernadino: Here's Life Publishers, 1979: 141–176, 267–320.
2. Reed, John, and Michael Oard. *The Geologic Column*. Chino Valley, Creation Research Society Quarterly, 2006: 124;

Hunter, Max, Michael Oard, and Carl Froede. *The Pre-Flood/Flood Boundary and the Precambrian.* Creation Research Society Quarterly, 46.1 (2009): 56–71.

3. Basaran, Cevat, Vedat Keles, and Rex Geissler. *Mount Ararat archaeological Survey.* Associates for Biblical Research, Bible and Spade 21.3, 2008: 70-96. <www.biblearchaeology.org/publications/bibleandspade.aspx>.

4. Sanford, Ward. *Thoughts on Eden, the Flood, and the Persian Gulf.* Geological Society of America, Newsletter of the Affiliation of Christian Geologists 7.1, 1999.

5. Baker, Victor, R. Craig Kochel, and Peter Patton. *Flood Geomorphology.* New York: Wiley, 1988: 450–451.

6. Lawson, Daniel, et al. *Hubbard Glacier update: another closure of Russell Fiord in the making?* Journal of Glaciology 54.186 (2008): 562–564.

7. Haeberli, Wilfried. *Frequency and Characteristics of Glacier Floods in the Swiss Alps.* Annals of Glaciology 4 (1983): 85–90.

8. Oard, Michael. The Origin of Grand Canyon Part III: A Geomorphological Problem. Creation Research Society Quarterly 47.1 (2010): 45–57.

9. Ibid.

10. Lee, Keenan. *The Altai Flood.* Colorado School of Mines, Department of Geology and Geological Engineering. 4 Oct. 2004 <geology.mines.edu/faculty/Klee/AltaiFlood.pdf>.

11. Petrakov, Dimitry, et al., *Debris Flow Hazard of Glacial Lakes in the Central Caucasus.* Debris-Flow Hazards Mitigation: Mechanics, Prediction, and Assessment. Netherlands: Millpress, 2007: 703–714.

12. See Reference 4.

13. Dong, Zhibao, Tao Wang, and Xunming Wang. *Geomorphology of the megadunes in the Badain Jaran Desert.* Geomorphology 60.1–2 (2004): 191–203.

14. Hill, Carol. *Qualitative Hydrology of Noah's Flood.* Perspectives on Science and Christian Faith 58.2 (2006): 120–129.

15. Anderson, Wm. Scott. *Solving the Mystery of the Biblical Flood*. Bloomington: Xlibris, 2001: 38–45.
16. Bergeron, Lou. *Deep Waters*. New Scientist, 155.2097 (1997): 22–26.
17. Hekinian, Roger. *Petrology of the Ocean Floor*. Amsterdam: Elsevier, 1982: 289–290.
18. Anderson, John. *Antarctic Marine Geology*. Cambridge: Cambridge University Press, 1999: 59.
19. Garner, Paul. *The New Creationism*. Darlington, England: Evangelical Press, 2009: 199.
20. Ibid., 187–189.
21. Froede, Carl. Animal *Tracks and Catastrophic Plate Tectonics*. Creation Research Society, Creation Matters 17.1 (2012): 1-4.
22. Vardiman, Larry. *Sea Floor Sediment and the Age of the Earth*. El Cajon: Institute for Creation Research, 1996: 25–36.
23. Young, Davis, and Ralph Stearley. *The Bible, Rocks and Time*. Downers Grove: Intervarsity Press, 2008: 78–111.
24. Vavrek, Matthew, and Hans Larsson. *Low Beta Diversity of Maastrichtian Dinosaurs of North America*. Proceedings of the National Academy of Sciences 107.18 (2010): 8265–8268.
25. Kotlyakov, Vladimir, and Tatyana Khromova. *Description of Russian Permafrost*. National Snow and Ice Data Center. 2002. <http://nsidc.org/index.html>.
26. Lunardine, Virgil. *Permafrost Formation Time*. Defense Technical Information Center. 1995. <www.dtic.dla.mil>.
27. Isabel Israde-Alcántara et al. *Evidence from central Mexico supporting the Younger Dryas extraterrestrial impact hypothesis*. Proceedings of the National Academy of Sciences. 109.13 (2012): 4723-4724.
28. Napier, Bill. *Was a Giant Comet Responsible for a North American catastrophe in 11,000 BC?* Royal Astronomical Society. 1 April 2010. <http://www.ras.org.uk>.
29. See Reference 15, 74–76.
30. Firestone, R. B., et al. *Evidence for an extraterrestrial impact 12,900 years ago that contributed to the megafaunal extinctions*

and the Younger Dryas cooling. Proceedings of the National Academy of Sciences 104.41 (2007): 16016–16021.

31. Faith, J. Tyler and Todd Surovell. *Synchronous Extinctions of North American's Pleistocene mammals.* Proceedings of the National Academy of Sciences 106.49 (2009): 20641–20645.

32. See Reference 30.

33. Heun, Manfred, et al. *Site of Einkorn Wheat Domestication Identified by DNA Fingerprinting.* Science 278.5341 (1997): 1312–1314.

11

REVELATION IN CREATION

For since the creation of the world His invisible attributes
are clearly seen, being understood by the things that are made,
even His eternal power and Godhead,
so that they are without excuse (Rom 1:20)

The most adamant atheists find they must make excuses for the appearance of design, which scientists find throughout nature. For example Richard Dawkins wrote, "Biology is the study of complicated things that give the appearance of having been designed for a purpose".[1] Similarly, Francis Crick, the Nobel laureate for DNA's structure wrote, "Biologists must constantly keep in mind that what they see was not designed, but rather evolved".[2] This appearance of design is found from the physics of minute subatomic structure, throughout cellular biology, throughout our solar system (anthropic principle), to the grandeur of cosmic physics.

Although it is said that God works in mysterious ways, we can determine from the Bible some of what God did in the past. In addition, we can discover from scientific studies the laws that God imposed on the properties of matter. All of these laws show no significant variation with time, so that scientists believe that they can be applied since our world existed. Although Young Earth scientists have speculated that basic physical constants changed dramatically soon after creation, a few thousand years ago, they have not found any significant evidence. This is not surprising because the world and its creatures could never have existed with some of the changes suggested by Young Earth scientists.

MULTIPLICATION

God could have created the world full of people and animals. Instead, He chose to establish mankind with just a single mating pair, and in the case of animals, either a single pair or perhaps just a few pairs, commanding them to multiply and fill the earth. In the beginning, God created only Adam and Eve for the human race. They began to fill the earth until God started over with Noah and his seven family members. God chose to fill the world through reproduction again, repeating his command to be fruitful and multiply. In a similar way, Jesus started His church with only twelve apostles, using them to preach the gospel so that His church could multiply throughout the remainder of history.

DIVERSITY FROM SIMPLICITY

God created great diversity from the simplicity of just a few building blocks. The examples listed below do not include the 25 known fundamental particles such as quarks, or the variants of DNA base molecules. At the subatomic level, three major particles, proton, neutron, and electron, combine in different quantities and give rise to ninety-four naturally occurring elements. These elements combine in countless ways to form millions of different organic and inorganic molecules and compounds. At the molecular level, DNA is configured from just four types of base molecules (A, C, G, and T), which are arranged in billions of different sequences that program all the different species and all the different individuals within those species. In addition, the amazing diversity of organic chemistry is based on the ability of the single element carbon to form three-dimensional molecules, from a few atoms up to many thousands of atoms. The different three-dimensional arrangements of proteins are almost limitless, perhaps as many as 10 million being found in nature. All these are made from only twenty amino acids. At the plant level, diversity is staggering; classification is continually being revised to make sense of all the variations within the different species.

Can we apply these concepts to the story of creation? In places where there is ambiguity, we can appeal to the methods that we know God has used elsewhere. In particular, after God created birds and sea creatures, He commanded them to multiply, implying that God created only one pair or perhaps a few families. Similarly, God made only one male and one female for mankind, commanding them to multiply. Although Genesis 1 does not provide the same instructions for animals, we can assume God commanded them to multiply in the same way; just as He did after the Flood. We can extend the argument to flowering plants and seed bearing trees; they would have spread over the earth by reproduction, taking many years in the process.

This approach for creation eliminates the 24-hour Day model, which requires very large numbers of plants and trees to have been in place on the sixth Day, to provide food for land creatures and birds. If only a few plants of each species had been created initially, a few large animals would have demolished many species of plants, and then starvation would have followed for all.

God designed many genes to be common in different species but with different expressions of those genes, to create the diversity of form and function that we find in nature For example, the genome for sea anemones is nearly as complex as that of humans; we share more than 80%percent of non-coding genes and more than 40%percent of protein coding genes.[3] This commonality is separated by about 700 million years, implying a designer who used common DNA designs for new species that were introduced over such a long period of time.

THE DATING CONUNDRUM

A myriad of difficulties complicate direct radiometric dating of ancient fossils. Measurable trace amounts of elements, such as nitrogen or fluorine, are so ubiquitous that definitive results are impossible. Such fossils are usually dated from the age of the sediment in which they are found, which in turn depends on other dating methods.

Slowly accumulating sediments gave rise to many of earth's geological layers, while catastrophic events such as flooding and volcanism deposited other layers and structures. When lava flows over existing surfaces, almost all evidence of the original surface organic material is incinerated and lost. On the other hand, sediments and volcanic ash often cover dead animals, preserving them as fossils in certain circumstances. Particles of rock that eventually formed sediments had been eroded from previous sedimentary deposits, volcanic lava, or perhaps one of the oldest rock formations that existed on the earth's surface. Limestone, however, is the result of organic processes such as accumulation of dead diatoms, or chemical reactions that lead to precipitation.

When radiometric means are used to date a sedimentary layer, the result is the age or ages of the original sedimentary materials. Consequently, fossils in sediments cannot be dated by the age of those sediments. For example, fossils may be found in sediment caused by a flood that took place within the past 10,000 years. If those sediments were previously eroded from rocks that were millions of years old, it would not be possible to date the flood and its fossils from the radiometric ages of the individual sedimentary particles. In contrast, lava contains minerals that can provide an accurate radiometric date in some circumstances. As a result, a sedimentary layer can be given an approximate age if it is next to lava that has been dated.

Animal remains, buried and fossilized within the last few thousand years, can often be dated quite reliably using carbon–14 dating. Although there are numerous special circumstances that give spurious results, the art of this science is in perceiving when conditions may have corrupted the minute quantity of the original carbon–14 with which the creature died. Carbon–14 has a half-life of 5,730 years, so that after ten half lives (57,300 years), only about one thousandth of the original quantity of carbon–14 remains. In the atmosphere and in terrestrial organisms, this is typically somewhat less than one trillionth the quantity of normal carbon–12. The quantities of carbon–14 are minute, and they are susceptible to leeching and contamination. Nonetheless, scientists have obtained consistent dates for many fossils and other organic materials that died over the past 20,000 years or so. Carbon–14 dating can be used occasionally for materials going back 50,000 years, but beyond that, there is not enough carbon–14 for consistent measurement.

Carbon–14 is generated by the effect of cosmic radiation on nitrogen in the upper atmosphere, and is therefore independent of the amount of carbon-12 in the atmosphere. Carbon-14 quickly combines with oxygen to form carbon dioxide ($_{14}CO_2$), which is then taken up by plants and distributed through the food chain, along with normal carbon dioxide ($_{12}CO_2$). The rate at which carbon-14 is generated depends mostly on cosmic radiation, which has short term fluctuations as well as variations over the long term; the percentage of nitrogen in the atmosphere does not vary significantly. As a result, the ratio of carbon-14 to carbon-12 in the atmosphere varies to a small extent over time, causing the same variation in the ratio assimilated by plants and animals. This means carbon-14 dates have a small but varying difference with true chronological dates; carbon-14 dates, however, can be calibrated with artifacts of known age, allowing quite accurate dates going back a few thousand years.

CARBON-14 IN A YOUNG EARTH

Young Earth scientists agree with the dating of fossils going back to about the time of the Flood, about 4,500 years ago. Prior to that, carbon-14 dating in the Young Earth model does not seem possible because of unknown conditions before and during the catastrophic global Flood. Plenty of fossils, however, have been found with apparent ages from 4,500 years ago back for tens of thousands of years. Consequently, Young Earth scientists have proposed at least five mechanisms to account for fossils with carbon-14 dates that are apparently much older.

The basic premise is that carbon-14 levels before the Flood were much lower than today. A simple calculation using convenient numbers provides an idea of what is involved in the Young Earth model. Consider a fossil that was buried when the earth was only 5,730 years old and carbon-14 was 100 times today's value. It would appear to have an age of about 38,000 years.

The first mechanism depends on the reasonable assumption that God created the world without carbon-14, and then the background level slowly increased because of cosmic radiation. A rough estimate of carbon-14 generation is 2 atoms/cm/cm/sec, based on neutron flux measurements.[4] Converting this rate to metric tonnes yields 0.0075 tonnes worldwide per year. The reservoir of carbon in atmospheric carbon dioxide is thought to be about 800 GtC (800 billion tonnes of carbon), of which one trillionth, or 0.80 tonnes, is carbon-14.[5] In other words, the atmosphere gains carbon-14 at an annual rate of about 1 per cent. The reservoir, however, remains fairly constant because the 1 per cent gain is offset by losses, most of which is assimilation by vegetation and absorption by the oceans. Radioactive decay accounts for only about 1 per cent of carbon-14 loss in the atmosphere; carbon-14 turns back into nitrogen with a half-life of 5730 years. The ocean depths and soil act as reservoirs for carbon dioxide, where some carbon-14 decays before it can return to the long term carbon cycle.

If God had created the world without carbon-14 in the atmosphere, it could have led to carbon-14 levels that would indicate a Young Earth. But this approach for a Young Earth leads to problems. If God had made the world without isotopes that can only exist as a result of prior radiation, Young Earth scientists would have to explain the countless number of dates determined for rocks that are millions of years old. These involve elements with half-lives that are millions or billions of years, which do not allow meaningful ages that are just a few thousand years. They have an ingenious proposal that God temporarily accelerated radioactive decay shortly after creation, which is explained in Appendix D. It has serious side effects for which no solutions have been found.

The second suggestion for low levels of carbon-14 is that the Young Earth proposal of a water canopy above the atmosphere, mentioned in chapter 3, reduced cosmic radiation and therefore the rate at which carbon-14 was created. The idea of a water canopy, however, has been thoroughly discredited and is no longer considered by most Young Earth scientists. A third mechanism would have occurred if the earth's magnetic field were much larger than it is today, reducing cosmic radiation and the formation of carbon-14. This idea was inferred by extrapolating backwards from measurements of the earth's magnetic field that were taken during the last two hundred years, showing a gradual reduction. However, the earth's magnetic field has varied through reversals many times without achieving the very high values that are required to significantly inhibit cosmic rays.

The last mechanism concerns biomass. Young Earth scientists suggest that the pre-Flood biomass was much larger than it is today, by a conservative factor of 100, with an associated 100 fold increase in atmospheric carbon dioxide. This would serve to reduce the carbon-14 to carbon-12 ratio so that any pre-Flood fossils would have ages of less than 6,000 years. In addition, this enormous biomass would have been buried in a Young Earth global Flood, providing material for fossil fuels, discussed later in this chapter. The global climate would have been warm and wet, allowing plenty of vegetation to grow, and supporting vast herds of herbivores with numerous predators and scavengers. The situation with marine life is complicated because some microorganisms acquire carbon from minerals, which have little if any carbon-14.

Even if we accept the assumption that the biomass in pre-Flood times was 100 times as big as it is today, the associated 100 fold increase in atmospheric carbon dioxide is debatable. The overall carbon cycle of flora and fauna is currently almost balanced, and is likely to have been similar before the Flood, although some increase in carbon dioxide is likely with a much larger biomass. As flora and fauna absorb carbon dioxide, almost exactly the same amount is given back to the atmosphere through respiration and from decaying organic matter.

PUTTING THEORIES TO THE TEST

All these ideas about carbon-14 before the Young Earth Flood are hypothetical, but the outcome is testable. Old Earth creationists have been answering criticism by evolutionists about lack of scientific methods by showing that their ideas are not only testable but survive testing. Hugh Ross has spearheaded this movement with his book *More than a Theory: Revealing a Testable Model for Creation*. Testing scientific theories is part of the scientific process that eliminates poor theories and establishes strong theories. Moreover, a valid theory should be able to predict consequences that have not been previously observed, for which measurements would provide proof.

One test for the recent global Flood theory is to examine the temporal distribution of fossil remains in the period before, during, and after the Flood. By considering the number of fossils buried per year, or buried over 500-year periods for convenience, we should find a marked reduction in fossil remains during the period after a recent global Flood.

On the other hand, there should be a fairly flat distribution of fossil remains for an Old Earth that had only a local Flood.

Variations in the quantity of fossil remains are to be expected with changes in climate, in particular during the peaks of the Ice Age and during the Younger Dryas cold spell. In the Young Earth situation, the number of fossils buried per year is the same as with an Old Earth, back to about 4,000 years ago. Immediately after a recent global Flood, the quantity of fossils buried would be considerably reduced for decades, perhaps hundreds of years. The surface of the earth would initially be like that of Mars, with only the animals on the ark available to repopulate the earth. All previous flora and fauna would have been buried under thousands of feet of sediment. Only seeds that had floated and survived a year of soaking could have germinated, allowing vegetation to start flourishing. Prior to, during, and for a while after the Flood, carbon-14 levels would have to be interpreted differently from conventional methods.

In 1975, an early analysis in this regard was carried out by Robert Whitelaw in his book, *Speak to the Earth*. He did indeed show that there was an apparent reduction in fossil remains between 4,500 and 5,000 years ago.[4] He made various corrections, however, to the raw carbon-14 data to account for an earth that was just 7,000 years old. Apart from the assumptions he used to make the data fit his theory, the data he used were not accurate. All measurements had been acquired prior to 1970, when carbon-14 dating was still in its infancy. Since then, scientists have determined many avenues through which samples may become contaminated or lose carbon-14, and the processes by which measurement equipment can insert contamination. As a result, complex protocols now exist for reliably determining carbon-14 dates. In addition, carbon-14 dates have been calibrated to reflect the actual changes of carbon-14 in the atmosphere, using artifacts with ages determined by other means.

Recent studies of fossil organic matter, going back 12,000 years, show that there has not been a marked reduction in fossilized remains during the proposed time of a recent Flood, approximately 4,500 years ago. Obtaining statistically valid samples of animal and human remains over any given period of time is not easy because both human and animal populations move and migrate over time spans of hundreds of years, and they are found in small discrete locations such as caves. A better resource is pollen, which is ubiquitous in the areas that trees and plants grow.

Glendalough Lakes, located in a glacial valley of Ireland, have provided pollen samples for dates back to 12,000 years ago. Some species of pollen show continuity back to 6,000 years ago and others back to 10,000 years ago. At that time, the climate had changed dramatically as the Younger Dryas came to an end. During that cold period, of some 1,300 years, completely different species predominated. Similar temporal distribution studies have been made with wood samples from large oaks. These indicate that there has not been any hiatus in the burial of oak trees in fluvial sites, where they are often well preserved. Trees that grow in such environments do so over long periods of time; their fossil abundance gives some idea of climate variation.

The data from this type of research are consistent with other climate data such as temperature and dryness, and with the changes of flora that match each change of climate. During the last 12,000 years in the far northern hemisphere, the climate changed from cold and dry, then to warm and wet, and finally to cool and wet. This sequence is clearly evident in the fossil record, where the flora associated with these conditions change from grasses and sedges, to birch, willow, and heath plants, and then to alder, spruce, and heath plants. The recent global Flood model, with an ice age that followed, has not demonstrated that these three climates, with the spread of associated flora, all occurred since the Flood, some 4,500 years ago.

The study of pollen fossils (palynology) reveals different species of pollen are found in discrete bands throughout sedimentary and other accumulated layers, in clear sequences throughout time. These bands correspond to climatic conditions for those layers and to fossilized wood when present. Banding of pollen fossils would not have been possible in a global Flood that deposited many thousands of feet of sediment. All the pollen species would have been mixed together.

FOSSIL FUELS

Many scientists believe that both oil and coal were created through biogenic processes from organic sources that were originally on the earth's surface. An alternative view is that oil is slowly derived from abiogenetic processes deep below the earth's surface, and then it rises until it is trapped by suitable geological formations.[5] On the other hand, there is little debate about the origin of coal, which is derived from vegetation. We will examine the Young Earth model first, in which coal was formed from vegetation, whereas oil was formed mostly from animal residues.

The Young Earth model states that substantially all oil and coal reserves were formed by the action of heat and pressure on organic sources that were buried by sediments caused by Noah's Flood. We can make some simple and approximate calculations to determine if there could have been sufficient flora and fauna on the earth at the time of the Flood to account for all the oil and coal that has been discovered. Because dead plants and animals usually decompose and get recycled in a matter of years, we are considering only one generation of dinosaurs and other animals. The bodies of animals that had been recycled through decay, or had become fossilized, could not have contributed to oil reserves.

Total oil reserves before the industrial revolution have been estimated at about $3,600 \times 10^9$ barrels of conventional oil, and $6,800 \times 10^9$ barrels of oil in shale and tar sands, yielding a combined total of about $10,400 \times 10^9$ barrels of oil.[6] This is equivalent to $1,650 \times 10^9$ cubic meters. This is a conservative estimate because additional reserves are frequently being discovered. If we assume the dimensions of an average dinosaur were 10 meters by 2 meters by 1.5 meters, and its carbon content was one-third of its 30 cubic meter volume, it would have required the death and decomposition of 165×10^9 dinosaurs to form the total of all known oil reserves. If these dinosaurs required about 5 acres each of vegetation on which to feed, they would have needed a total land area of 825×10^9 acres, or about 1.3×10^9 square miles.

Only 60×10^6 square miles of land exist on the earth's surface, much of it not able to support large animals. If we make the reasonable assumption that half the earth's land surface was not suitable for grazing and browsing, then there would have been ten times more dinosaurs than the earth was capable of supporting. To make matters worse, numerous fossil graveyards contain millions and possibly billions of jumbled skeletons of dinosaurs and other animals; these are supposed to have died in the Flood and are not associated with oil deposits. The case for drowned dinosaurs turning into our oil deposits as a result of a recent Flood fails to account for more than a fraction of known oil resources.

Studies about the origin of coal show that tropical forests can support trees with a carbon content of up to 52,000 metric tons per square mile, representing the highest biomass the earth can produce.[7] Biomass below the surface of the ground accounts for no more than 25 percent of the above ground biomass, so that the total possible carbon in vegetation could have been 65,000 metric tons per square mile. If half the earth's land surface were grassland or desert, forests could have accounted for no more than $3,900 \times 10^9$ metric tons of carbon on the earth's surface. Even with the very unlikely assumption that all this vegetation were to be buried in the Flood, it could not account for the total carbon content in the world's coal fields, estimated to be about $8,100 \times 10^9$ metric tons.[6] In addition, the extreme assumptions made by the Young Earth model about the amount of forestation before the Flood are not realistic. Today's carbon inventory on the earth's surface is only about 5.6×10^9 metric tons, a factor some 700 times less. If we include the carbon content of natural gas reserves, a significant fraction of fossil fuels, the situation becomes worse. The case for the Flood burying forests, which formed all the known coal fields, fails to account for a fraction of known coal reserves.

One calculation by Young Earth scientists is that it would take only about 233 years for the earth to grow sufficient biomass to account for all fossil fuels.[8] This neglects, however, to account for the earth supporting a limited amount of vegetation at one time, with no more than $3,900 \times 10^9$ tons of carbon, as stated above. The existing annual growth of terrestrial carbon in vegetation has been estimated to be no more than 180×10^9 metric tons of carbon, of which 53×10^9 tons is the net increase, the rest being recycled.[8] This growth is currently due largely to cleared land becoming reforested and to an observed increase in CO_2. With this growth rate, it would take only seventy-four years to accomplish the maximum sustainable biomass, which could go no further because the biomass would have been continually recycled. In other words, the high growth rate of carbon content in the Young Earth model would have been applicable only until the biomass reached steady state; after that, any increase in carbon was offset by recycled carbon dioxide. These calculations show that the Young Earth model fails to account for fossil fuels from terrestrial sources.

Other significant sources of biogenic material for fossil fuels are diatoms, algae, and plankton, which died and sank to the ocean floors. These tiny creatures need sunlight to survive and propagate, and so they live only in shallower depths, no further than 100 to 400 feet, depending on water clarity. In principle, sufficient carbon content to account for all known oil reserves could have accumulated on the ocean floors in about 1,500 years after creation, just before the Young Earth global Flood. Because they would have been buried among sediment in the oceans, they could not account for oil fields on land. Recognizing the difficulties of finding sufficient material for pre-Flood sources of fossil fuels, the Young Earth model assumes that fossil fuels were the result of Flood or post-Flood activity. One proposal is that dense masses of plankton bloomed during the Flood, when nutrients might have been abundant.[8] The problem here is sufficient sunlight was unlikely to have been available in view of the countless volcanoes and asteroid impacts that Young Earth scientists believe occurred at that time.

Having said all that, there is another possible obstacle to the Young Earth position; oil may not be derived from organic sources. Most of the earth's oil reserves may have accumulated over billions of years from abiogenetic reactions deep underground. This idea has been proposed by geologists who provide chemical and geological evidence to support their view.

GRANDFATHER AND GRANDMOTHER CLOCKS

In the last few years, scientists have been determining DNA mutation rates that can be used as separate genetic clocks for males and females.[10] Mitochondrial DNA is passed on only by the mother, so that variations in mitochondrial DNA over a selected population allow geneticists to determine the number of generations back to the earliest common ancestor. In the case of mitochondrial DNA, this ancestor is the most recent common grandmother, at a time when a bottleneck existed in the population.

Similarly, a grandfather clock is established by the Y-chromosome, which is passed on only by the father, giving a clock that determines the number of generations since the most recent common grandfather. Many assumptions and unknowns affect the accuracy of determining our genetic history. The general conclusion by evolutionary scientists at present is that mankind originated in Africa fewer than 200,000 years ago and then spread out in a series of migrations into Asia and Europe. Because of the uncertainties in current genetic research, it is entirely feasible that the starting point was Mesopotamia, and the initial event was fewer than 50,000 years ago.[11] In addition, new research is consistent with a bottleneck that occurred more recently, in which the human race was restricted to one man and three women.[12] This would, of course, be Noah for the male lineage, and his three daughters-in-law for the female side.

The fairly recent time frame shown for Noah's family, and by implication Adam and Eve, is reinforced by the difference between the numbers of mutations found in human DNA compared to the DNA of other primates. Far more mutations exist in non-human primates, implying that a considerable time lag occurred between the creation of primates and the creation of humans; the conclusion must be that creation Days were much longer than 24 hours.[13]

ASTEROID

Young Earth scientists estimate that the earth has had over 36,000 major asteroid and meteorite strikes, based on the number of craters on the moon's surface.[14] About 160 of these asteroid craters are still visible today, the others have disappeared through erosion or subduction at tectonic boundaries. If they had all happened a few thousand years ago, as Young Earth believers claim, then there should be about 36,000 craters visible today. Large numbers of asteroid and meteor collisions are indeed part of the conventional history of the earth, but they occurred some 4 billion years ago in the Late Heavy Bombardment.

The 1977 movie *Asteroid* depicts the threat of human extinction from a single asteroid impact. The question for Young Earth believers is would anything be able to live through 36,000 major impacts from asteroids and meteorites, as well as some 40,000 volcanic eruptions and associated seismic activity, all occurring within a few decades? Historical records and geological evidence show that only a tiny proportion of these catastrophes occurred since the Young Earth date for the Flood, some 4,500 years ago. Consequently, if the earth were only a few thousand years old, the vast majority of impacts, volcanic eruptions, and earthquakes must have occurred at the time of the Flood, or soon afterwards.

In addition, there is evidence for about 40,000 volcanoes on the earth's land surface, of which about 1,500 are still active today.[15] Most of these volcanoes would have erupted during the same period as the asteroid impacts in the Young Earth model, adding to the total destruction of the earth's surface. Significant seismic activity would have added to the havoc. The ark would surely have overturned under huge waves and tsunamis, and then the occupants would be cooked by hot water, then frozen by a volcanic/impact winter, and finally starved to death for lack of anything to eat. Well, you get my point. There is no physical evidence for the doomsday aftermath of 36,000 impacts and 40,000 volcanoes that occurred a few thousand years ago.

THE BIG PICTURE

The major events recorded in the Bible are part of a symmetrical pattern of God's intervention in the history of mankind. Similar to the menorah type of literary structures (Semitic Inclusions) found in some Bible narratives, God appears to have arranged His story of mankind with mirror symmetry. The center of history from a Christian perspective is understood to be the cross. Christians look back to it, and God's people in Old Testament times looked forward to it. Prior to the cross, the major events were the deliverance of Israel from Egypt and Israel's conquest of the Promised Land. This occupation is mirrored today by the creation of the State of Israel in 1948, and divine protection against overwhelming odds during the recent wars waged against Israel.

Before the nation of Israel came into existence, God had confused the speech of the different tribes at Babel as they attempted to be like gods and do whatever they pleased. The symmetry here is that nations are converging on a common language, English, and at the same time achieving whatever they please through modern day technology. And as at Babel, where people looked for satanic power, so will the antichrist, who is associated with ancient Babylon in the Book of Revelation. Before the world's population was dispersed from Babel, now called Babylon, God had judged the world through the Flood. The next great event will be the final judgment of the world in the last days, after the modern version of spiritual Babylon finally materializes. The original event for mankind was the creation of Adam with his bride, both sinless. The final event will be the appearance of the bride of Christ in heaven, spotless and without wrinkle. One could draw too much from this pattern, but it is interesting.

GOD IN GENETICS

The difference between the male and female versions of our twenty-third chromosome bears witness to both the creation of Adam and Eve and also to the incarnation of Jesus. As a male, Adam was created with both X- and Y-chromosomes, so that when God took a piece of Adam from his side to create Eve, God simply had to delete the Y-chromosome and duplicate the X-chromosome in order to create a woman.

Jesus did not have an earthly father, as was spoken by the angel Gabriel to Mary, "And the angel answered and said to her, 'The Holy Spirit will come upon you, and the power of the Highest will overshadow you; therefore, also, that Holy One who is born will be called the Son of God.'" Returning to genetics, Jesus was born to a virgin, who as a woman had two X-chromosomes. It was God who provided the Y-chromosome necessary for the conception of a male, replacing the second X-chromosome provided by Mary. This was opposite to the situation in the garden of Eden, where God replaced Adam's Y-chromosome, which only men possess, with an X-chromosome in order to create Eve.

GENESIS AND SCIENTIFIC CHRONOLOGIES

I have left this section toward the end, although it is perhaps one of the more important topics. If my interpretation of Genesis is correct, then the sequence of creation events is exactly synchronized with established scientific chronology. Creation events in the Bible are listed below in Table 2, alongside the corresponding events and times determined by science, most of which are available from the *Wikipedia* internet site. (Times given below are approximate and change a little from time to time with new discoveries.)

The key for this agreement between Bible and science is that all the creatures described in the creation verses of Genesis 1 are extant Mammals and Birds, as explained in chapter 4.

Extant sea mammals appeared mostly during the Oligocene epoch, birds during the Miocene, and mammals from the end of the Miocene, through the Pliocene and into the Pleistocene.

Scientists have proposed that the earth was covered in thick ice from about 800 million to about 600 million years ago. If this were true, it is appropriate that land appeared on Day 4 as the ice melted, allowing new land to rise as a result of glacial isostatic adjustment.

Event	Genesis 1	Science	Time
Creation of the universe	v1	Big Bang Theory	13.7 bya
Primitive earth in solar system	v2	Nebular hypothesis	4.6 bya
Anaerobic chemoautotrophic bacteria		Fossil evidence	3.9 bya
Light penetrates early atmosphere	v3	Unknown	
Photosynthetic bacteria		Fossil evidence	3.0 bya
Multi-cellular marine organisms		Fossil evidence	580–542 mya
Cambrian explosion in seas		Fossil evidence	530 mya
Appearance of land	v9	Fossil evidence	580–500 mya
Primitive land plants		Fossil evidence	434 mya
Finned fish		Fossil evidence	420 mya
Amphibians		Fossil evidence	365 mya
Reptiles		Fossil evidence	305 mya
Flowering plants and trees	v11	Fossil evidence	130 mya
Transparent atmosphere	v14	Unknown	
Extant cetaceans (sea mammals)	v20	Fossil evidence	35–25 mya
Extant birds	v20	Fossil evidence	20–25 mya
Extant land mammals	v24	Fossil evidence	10–0.2 mya
Man	v26	Fossil evidence	<50 kya

Table 2: Genesis creation sequence compared with science

REFERENCES

1. Dawkins, Richard. *The Blind Watchmaker.* New York: W.W. Norton, 1996: 1.

2. Crick, Francis. *What Mad Pursuit.* New York: BasicBooks, 1988: 138.

3. Putnam, Nicholas et al. *Sea Anemone Genome Reveals Ancestral Eumetazoan Gene Repertoire and Genomic Organization.* Science Magazine, 317.5834 (2007): 86–94.

4. Key, Robert. Eds. J. Steele, S. Thorpe and K. Turekian. *Ocean Process Tracers: Radiocarbon.* Encyclopedia of Ocean Sciences. London: Academic Press, 2001: 2338-2353.

5. Riebeek, Holli. *The Carbon Cycle.* 2011. <http://earthobservatory.nasa.gov/Features/CarbonCycle/>.

6. Whitelaw, Robert. Ed. George Howe. *Speak to the Earth.* Terra Haute: Creation Research Society Books, 1989: 331–375.

7. Keith, Stanley, and Monte Swan. *Hydrothermal Hydrocarbons.* 2005. <http://www.searchanddiscovery.net/documents/abstracts/2005research_calgary/abstracts/extended/keith.htm>.

8. Holt, Roy. *Evidence for a Late Cainozoic Flood/post-Flood Boundary.* Journal of Creation, 10.1 (1996): 155.

9. Houghton, Richard, et al. *The spatial distribution of forest biomass in the Brazilian Amazon: a comparison of estimates.* Global Change Biology, 7.7 (2001): 731–746.

10. See Reference 8, 159.

11. See Reference 5.

12. Rana, Fazale, and Hugh Ross. *Who was Adam?* Colorado Springs: NavPress, 2005: 55–67.

13. Nelson J. Warren. *Genetics and Biblical Demographic Events.* Journal of Creation, 17.1 (2003): 21–23; Carter, Robert. *The Neutral Model of Evolution and Recent African Origins.* Journal of Creation, 23.1 (2009): 70–77.

14. Carter, Robert. *Adam, Eve and Noah vs Modern Genetics.* Creation Ministries International, 11 May 2010. < http://creation.com/noah-and-genetics>.

15. Schroeder, Gerald. *The Science of God*. New York: Simon and Schuster, 1997: 117.

16. Oard, Michael, and Carl Froede. *The Pre-Flood/Flood Boundary and the Precambrian*. Creation Research Society Quarterly, 46.1 (2009): 57–69.

17. Duncan, Hamilton. *Volcanism, "Fountains of the Great Deep," and Forty Days of Rain*. Creation Research Society Quarterly, 47.1 (2010): 9–19.

12

MINDLESS EVOLUTION OR INTELLIGENT CREATION

Thus god himself
Was too kind to remain idle
And began to plan the Game of Signatures
Signing His likeness unto the world.
—Johannes Kepler

Kepler was inspired by his view of God as creator to search for laws of planetary motion. He believed that God had ordained creation to operate within the boundaries of laws, which he was determined to discover. He expressed his concept of finding these laws as the *game of signatures*. Many other scientists since Kepler had the same motivation and discovered many more signatures in the laws of nature.

A few thousand years ago, someone learned first hand how the world came to exist: "Who is this who darkens counsel by words without knowledge"? God said to Job (perhaps thundered at him). Job had been implying that he was the equal of God in some respects. God then proceeded to question Job, asking him if he knew much about creation and how animals got their instincts. My point here is that in addition to giving Job a lesson in humility, God was asserting that creation was not an accident. God told Job that He used His immense wisdom and power to create the constellations, our wonderful planet, and the creatures that inhabit it. God has always revealed His attributes in creation, and no matter how much we find out about nature, there are always more wonders to behold. God has signed His handiwork everywhere in nature, proclaiming the awesome expression of His creativity.

ALL WE WANT ARE THE FACTS, MA'AM

During the 1950's, detective Joe Friday in Dragnet was not interested in opinion or hearsay; he wanted to know exactly what happened. The District Attorney would examine statements and evidence for prosecution, and then a jury would examine the evidence for possible conviction. Sometimes, detectives and the legal system conclude a person's guilt when facts do not come to light, resulting in a miscarriage of justice. Facts that might determine the origins of life can also be hard to find and are likely to be circumstantial.

Observations made from repeatable experiments in natural sciences show that laws exist controlling the behavior of matter on every scale. In contrast, no one observed prehistoric events on earth. We must rely on observations made from scientific tests performed on the residual materials left after such events, and then we must use some imagination to interpret any preserved evidence. Preconceived points of view and worldviews are likely to drive the process.

Atheists, who do not accept the existence of God, necessarily must believe that evolution of life is a fact and interpret relevant evidence accordingly; however belief is not the cause of truth. People, who believe in the existence of God, are much more likely to interpret evidence of origins in terms of creation. Agnostics, however, should be able to evaluate scientific evidence on life's origins without excluding the possibility of divine creation.

EVOLVING EVOLUTION

The idea of evolution may conjure up pictures of dinosaurs and the gradual transition from sponges to humans. Most people have seen suggested sequences of fossils that illustrate supposed transitions. They can be very appealing, and some have the appearance that evolution did occur. The fossil record does indeed demonstrate that most species were eventually replaced by others. The evidence, however, may have different interpretations; either God created new species with suitable genetic changes at appropriate times, or we and other amazing organisms are purely the result of trillions of random genetic variations.

As mentioned earlier, it is important to separate the concept of the origin of life from the concept of evolution of species. Evolution of life and evolution of species are opposite in their boundary conditions. For life to evolve, random chemical reactions must overcome the natural tendency for other reactions and energy to destroy any complex molecular structure. The governing laws of nature work against the assembly of specifically complex molecules that are necessary for life. On the other hand, living cells have many built in mechanisms to preserve them from deteriorating or even evolving, albeit specific mechanisms permit limited variation within each species.[1]

When Darwin started his work on evolution he was probably a Deist, assuming that primitive life already existed by divine creation.[2] Despite the title of his work, *On the Origin of Species*, he did not deal with the origin as such; instead he considered causes that might explain changes in the morphology of fossils. In other works, he suggested that fictitious entities called *gemmules* transferred novel characteristics between species.[3] He proposed that a very slow accumulation of mutations together with natural selection were the causes of common descent from primitive life forms to all higher species. However, he was unaware of the fatal results of almost all significant mutations. If a variety of chemicals had arranged themselves into a primitive life form that was able to reproduce, we would then have the starting point for Darwin's *Theory of Evolution*, or *common descent* as he called it.

The fossil record does not support his thesis because vast quantities of fossils showing continuous variations from one species to another over long periods of time do not exist. Instead, all kinds of species exhibit a long period of stasis, typically over several hundred thousand years, and then quite different species appear over much shorter but undefined time periods.[4] As a result, Niles Eldredge and Stephen Jay Gould attempted to explain these sudden jumps that are found in the fossil record in their book, *Punctuated equilibria: an alternative to phyletic gradualism,* published in 1972. This theory is crumbling because it is really a much more improbable version of Darwin's original idea. Other evolutionists have rejected punctuated equilibrium and related forms of neo-Darwinism that rely on mutations as the cause for evolution with this observation: "Development of superpowers through chemical- or radiation-mediated mutation – theoretically giving rise to new species – is a phenomenon found mostly in comic books".[5] The reason for this assertion by Lynn Margulis and Dorion Sagan is what every scientist studying evolution must already know: "New mutations generate variations in members of the same species but the accumulation of mutations has never been shown – in laboratory organisms or in the field – to lead to crossing of the species barrier.[6]

As a result of this rather bleak outlook for a valid mechanism of evolution, Lynn Margulis and Dorion Sagan suggested a new approach in their book *Acquiring Genomes.* They present considerable evidence for species change among microbes through direct acquisition of genomes, from one microbial organism to another. Such changes among bacteria and other microbes may have occurred as they suggest; it is not a theory to which creationists might object because the Bible does not address this issue. Their primary thesis in favor of evolution, however, is the acquisition of genetic material within the cell nucleus, which is merely circumstantial. They refer to a discovery that 250 of the approximately 30,000 protein coding genes in humans are closely related to those same genes in bacteria, admitting that no one knows how the genes were acquired and guessing that viruses were involved.[7] These authors provide some awe inspiring descriptions of symbiotic relationships among microbes and higher organisms.

The response from a creationist perspective is that a good designer does not have to keep reinventing the wheel; God simply re-used genes that He had previously designed and implemented. Nevertheless, this leaves evolution without any known mechanisms for both the origin of life and the progression of species. Current thinking among evolutionists is that evolution may be a combination of all previously suggested mechanisms. Such an approach may work when attempts at hitting a target can be combined quantitatively but not when there is overall qualitative failure of each mechanism, which is the situation for evolution.

LIFE FROM SCRATCH

The emergence of life from naturally occurring chemicals continues to present problems that defy natural solutions. The mechanisms by which inorganic chemicals might have assembled themselves into highly complex self-replicating molecules remain undefined after decades of research. Several possible steps have been identified, but none have been shown to be viable, even inside select laboratory environments. The difficulties are enormous, and there is no compelling reason, or even encouragement, for thinking that scientists will succeed in creating living organisms from scratch. Recognizing the improbability of abiogenesis on earth, scientists are left with two extra-terrestrial options, divine creation or panspermia (life from outer space). But the latter is really jumping from the frying pan into the fire, as most people realize.

The Achilles' heel of natural evolution is that there is no evidence for abiogenesis, life from chemicals. This is well known to scientists, as Richard Dawkins, the eminent British evolutionist, admitted in his interview with Ben Stein in the 2008 movie *Expelled: No Intelligence Allowed*. Although this movie was somewhat humorous and even had a touch of the bizarre, its subject matter was serious. Part of the interview went as follows:

Stein: Well, then, who did create the heavens and the earth?

Dawkins: Why do you use the word "who"? See, you immediately beg the question by using the word "who".

Stein: Well, then, how did it get created?

Dawkins: Umm, well, by a very slow process.

Stein: Well, how did it start?

Dawkins: Nobody knows how it got started. We know the kind of event that it must have been. We know the sort of event that must have happened for the origin of life.

Stein:	And what was that?
Dawkins:	It was the origin of the first self-replicating molecule.
Stein:	Right, and how did that happen?
Dawkins:	I told you, we don't know.
Stein:	So, you have no idea how it started?
Dawkins:	No, no, nor has anybody.

Of course, it is not that simple. But one valid conclusion is that the emperor of evolution has no clothes. Scientists have proposed about a dozen necessary steps for chemicals to assemble themselves into a rudimentary cell, which would be able to both consume energy and reproduce. Laboratory experiments, however, have failed to demonstrate the feasibility of even one of the steps in their proposed pathway. There is great diversity of opinions on how life might have started, which is not encouraging to anyone who hopes that abiogenesis will prove to be viable.

Atheists such as Richard Dawkins have an untenable philosophical position; they do not know and cannot show how life started, and their fundamental assumption, that there is no God, has no scientific foundation. Perhaps that is why the idea of life originating from outer space is so popular with atheists; they do not have to prove anything. Panspermia is such a leap of imagination that it begs the question as to how life actually started. The Biblical account of creation presents no scientific proof, but it does have a wealth of supporting evidence throughout nature.

All ideas for the appearance of living molecules from mere chemicals rely on time, lots and lots of time, hundreds of millions of years. Nevertheless, as long as that may be, it will probably take longer for scientists to figure out how it could have happened without a creator. There are lots of ideas but no consensus; which is not surprising because there are so many opposing requirements to assemble such complex molecular machinery and such specific DNA information in chemically hostile environments. Abiogenesis must climb some insurmountable walls if life had to rely on lady luck.

A few scientists have calculated the odds of abiogenesis from several different perspectives, and all of them find that it is just too unlikely to have occurred.[8] As a result, it was suggested that the origin of life must have occurred elsewhere in the universe, the panspermia hypothesis. Mars was a favorite for a while, but recent probes to Mars have diminished hope of finding any kind of life there, especially because the seas of long ago were found to be too saline for life. The difficulties of transporting any kind of life through millions of light years of space make panspermia a very unlikely candidate for life on earth.[9] No one disputes the difficulties, but the fact is, abiogenesis is a long way from being proven. No compelling reason exists to doubt that there is a God who created life.

Belief in abiogenesis is modern-day alchemy. Starting hundreds of years ago, scientists investigated matter in order to transmute one metal into another, particularly to transmute a base metal into gold. All they needed to do was to find the right chemical mixtures for the process to occur. But because they did not know much, if anything, about atomic structure, they were continually doomed to failure and disappointment. In a similar way, evolutionary scientists try to create life from basic chemicals, without regard for the overwhelming complexity and interlocking molecular dependencies of living cells and the mutually exclusive nature of many of the hypothetical steps.

MICRO OR MACRO

For a given species, changes in morphology from one generation to another can be described as steps in either microevolution or macroevolution, depending on whether speciation takes place. The former can be conveniently defined as changes below the species level as a result of mutation, or the more likely process of variation caused by normal genetic processes that occur typically over a few generations. Such changes can lead to what might be called sub-species that may revert back again, which has been observed many times.[10] For example, the well known finches in the Galapagos Islands that supposedly proved evolution, have now been shown to have not evolved. In recent years scientists have spent extended periods of time evaluating these finches.

They found that beak sizes changed from generation to generation, according to environmental pressures, and then changed back as the climate reversed.[11]

An example of directed microevolution is the great variety of dogs that have been bred from wolves, producing enormous differences in behavior, skills, size, shape, color, and hair structure. If scientists had found fossils of present day dogs, they might have given them names for many different species because of their great diversity. This kind of error in identification has occurred sometimes with ancient fossils, and then with further research, the actual underlying species discovered. Whenever microevolution has been observed, new species have never appeared, whether through natural selection or directed selection by humans, including the breeding of dogs, horses, cattle, sheep, goats, and many other species over thousands of years.

Another well known example of microevolution is seen with the two colors of peppered moths that are found in England. It appeared that moths became darker during the industrial revolution and so had the advantage of better camouflage in the dirtier environment. This was claimed to be a proof of evolution. It was found later, however, that this moth always has had light and dark phases within its gene pool, and still does. Some of the so-called science of where these moths could be found in daytime was fraudulent anyway; dead moths had been glued to trees. Macroevolution or speciation of this moth has not been observed.

Macroevolution is defined as genetic changes that result in a new species. Has macroevolution been observed? It depends on the definition of the word species, which has become very elastic, as witnessed by ever changing classifications of similar species, especially in the vegetable kingdom. If macroevolution has occurred, it cannot be shown to have occurred through long periods of microevolution in the fossil record, as discussed above. Where the fossil record indicates that one species has replaced another, it could be called macroevolution or it could be called creation. It depends on one's worldview as to how the evidence is interpreted. For macroevolution to have occurred, huge genetic barriers must have been surmounted for every new species. In contrast, creation of species is the result of whatever mechanism God used, perhaps as described later in this chapter.

Regardless of what methods God used, all of creation reveals His amazing wisdom.[12] The natural laws that God orchestrated leave evidence for His creation of life, with many phenomena that display divine signatures. Fortunately, macroevolution does not take place, with its possible outcome of nature running amok and away from God's intended design and purpose.

The existence of microevolution, which is minor adaptation of morphology and behavior within species, is important for survival because it allows species to adapt and survive in changing environments. The media frequently report on microevolution but with the overt or implied conclusion that evolution in the macro sense has been observed. Most people are unaware that speciation is not occurring. The proper distinction between observed adaptation and unobserved macroevolution is consistent with creation, in which God created nature with the most wonderful designs, variations of which are limited by the constraints of His genetic design principles.

Another aspect of macroevolution is that in addition to there being no proof that it actually happened, scientists observe that it has clearly not happened for many species that continue to exist today. Journals frequently report on fossils that are tens or even hundreds of millions of years old, which appear to be almost identical to their modern counterparts. These reports include dozens of species of every kind, some of which survived catastrophic times such as the K/T boundary (a thin layer between the Cretaceous and Tertiary periods), when speciation is thought most likely to have occurred. Although such evidence does not prove that evolution failed to occur, it does establish that there is no mechanism that forces evolution to take place, even over hundreds of millions of years.

An example of well documented evidence that demonstrates macroevolution has not occurred is in the fossil record of fish. Scientists have found that over a period of about 360 million years, no gradual macroevolution occurred, as revealed by a very complete fossil record.[13] Not only are known fossil fish virtually identical to modern fish, but the earliest fossils appear suddenly without any sign of ancestral species.

Many other species appear suddenly in the fossil record without any trace of evolutionary ancestors that might otherwise explain their existence. As a result, scientists have invented *ghost lineages* to unknown imaginary ancestors in order to maintain the evolutionary paradigm.[14] These transitional ghosts have not been found, and in view of the well established fossil record, it is unlikely that they will be.

STUCK ON SQUARE ONE

Abiogenesis might be a more viable solution for the origin of life if each of the countless small leaps, required for molecules to assemble into a living cell, did not fall back before the next leap could take place. If there were numerous islands of molecular safety, where increasingly complex molecules could be protected before the next leap, then there might be some hope for abiogenesis. Scientists have conducted many thousands of experiments in which basic building blocks of life have been assembled from just simple chemicals. Molecules which are necessary for life, and which have already been produced in the laboratory, include ribose type sugars, phospholipids, nucleic bases, and several but not all amino acids. They were created, however, in highly selective environments, different for each type of building block. Their formation, long-term survival, coexistence, and combination in a real world environment are, practically speaking, impossible.

The properties of matter do not support life emerging unaided from earth's lifeless resources. This view, which has not been successfully challenged, was expressed back in 1984 by Charles Thaxton, Walter Bradley, and Roger Olsen in their book *The Mystery of Life's Origin: Reassessing Current Theories*. Since then, appreciation of the difficulties for generating all the basic building blocks has only increased. Scientists keep trying to do what seems impossible; sometimes succeeding in small ways but without solving the overall objective of creating life. Many miracles would be required for self-assembly of a prototype cell, starting with all the necessary organic molecules in place, then assembly of appropriate proteins and a simple form of self-replicating RNA, followed by an outer casing to enclose all the components. So far, laboratory experiments that start with raw chemicals have been unsuccessful in anything beyond basic building blocks. Even these are not useful, being found in racemic mixtures (see the section on Mirror

Images later in this chapter) and amongst other compounds that inhibit further progress.

THE COW JUMPED OVER THE MOON

Some scientists believe that the most likely self-replicating component of the first living cell is RNA, in particular rRNA that carries the templates for proteins and helps support self-replication. The appearance of RNA in a chemical soup has yet to be demonstrated. Moreover, if nature did have the ability to assemble all necessary complex molecules for a living cell in one location, despite their diverse requirements for stability, it would need to make a miraculous leap forward. This leap for life would have started by gathering all the necessary molecules into one very small place, 10 to 100 times smaller than the thickness of a human hair. Then a complex membrane structure of lipids would have had to grow by chance in the same place, encapsulating these precious molecules, somehow omitting any chemicals that would have adversely reacted with the necessary components. Would there have been life at this point? Not by a long way! Such a happenstance accumulation of unstable molecules would be poised only half way in the leap to life. To complete the leap it must first have acquired the functions and molecular components for procreation and metabolism; the latter being the ability to assimilate food and energy and to excrete waste. Unfortunately, a molecule of self-replicating RNA could not have the complex information that is necessary to metabolize other vital molecules for the rest of the cell; it could only replicate itself.

Metabolism requires suitable entrances in the membrane, proteins to handle the food, and an energy conversion system. In addition, procreation requires the orchestration of thousands of proteins and the ability of the membrane to split and surround two full complements of cellular components. The first RNA molecules could not have had such complex instructions embedded within them by accident. Like the cow jumping over the moon, abiogenesis remains a leap of faith, beyond any hope or imagination; God has signed one of His masterpieces, the creation of life. Further details on the woefully inadequate state of the art for proving abiogenesis can be found in *Origins of Life* by Fazale Rana and Hugh Ross and in *The Cells Design* by Fazale Rana.

If the origin of life could be found in mere chance collisions of molecules, then it is likely that man could find a way to create life. Heaven forbid! Our track record with death has been so tragically grotesque that we could not begin to imagine the horrors that would be unleashed from Pandora's Box of life. We can rejoice; it appears that God arranged His creation so that He does not have to share the glory of creating life with mortal men.

MIRROR IMAGES

Two forms are possible for many of life's basic molecules, each being an optical isomer of the other: that is, they have the same chemical formula. The difference between them is their three-dimensional shapes that look the same when one of them is viewed in a mirror. It is similar to two sailors with semaphore flags, one with his right arm held out, the other with his left arm out. Nineteen of the twenty amino acids found in living cells are left handed in shape; right handed versions of these amino acids do not participate in living cells. Similarly, the sugars in DNA and RNA molecules are right handed. Living cells must always acquire these organic molecules with the appropriate optical isomer (left or right handed). If amino acids and sugars in racemic mixtures (50 percent of each isomer) were to be added to a living cell, it could not survive because cells are unable to properly form proteins or DNA and RNA molecules.

Without the assembly instructions contained within DNA, nature always produces racemic mixtures of both left and right handed building blocks. Some bacteria, which do not ingest amino acids, avoid the problem of finding amines and sugars with the correct optical isomers by building their own. They assemble optically correct molecules through assimilation of CO_2 and inorganic nitrogen compounds. Perhaps God introduced these bacteria as the first life forms on earth. God has left another signature in living cells, which all require amino acids and sugars with the correct optical isomers.

EARLIEST EVIDENCE

The three forms of the earliest known single cell life are bacteria, archaea, and eukarya. Each of these has distinct ribosomal RNA (rRNA), which is one reason for these three classifications. Multi-cellular organisms have the more complex eukaryotic cells, which are believed to have appeared later than the other two. These three cell types, which are similar in many respects, are believed by many evolutionists to have a common ancestor, although the eukaryotes are more closely related to archaea than bacteria. Evolutionary scientists agree that such complex life forms could not have arisen directly three times, or even once, from inanimate matter. One proposal is that there must have been an earlier living organism, a proto-cell that evolved into three separate domains of single-cell life. This proto-cell must have existed and multiplied over millions of years and occupied many different environments as it changed into the three extant forms of single cells. Anything that survived long enough to mutate successfully must have been relatively hardy, so there is no reason to suppose that it became extinct; simpler organisms have higher chances of survival in destructive environments. Nevertheless, there is no evidence for the existence of a proto-cell, past or present, which is an enigma for believers in abiogenesis. This lack of a previous life form is consistent with creation, rather than evolution. In God's economy, a simpler life form was not needed, even though it may have been possible for God to have created it. Because no relict proto-cells exist, we can see that God has left another signature in the complexity of the earliest life forms.

IRREDUCIBLE COMPLEXITY

As scientists probe the structures and mechanisms of living cells they continuously uncover more levels of complexity. Moreover, what they find is that the multitudes of processes in cells are designed for optimum functional capability, near optimum or optimum efficiency, and amazing reliability.[15]

Michael Behe first brought serious attention to the concept of irreducible complexity in his book, *Darwin's Black Box*. As noted before, Darwin had no idea of the staggering complexity of cellular components and processes. For his generation and others afterwards, living cells were the equivalent of a simple electronic black box, which contained nothing more than wires; whereas cells are now known to be the equivalent of a modern black box, with thousands of diverse components, including many microprocessors. In recent decades, science has discovered that living cells have multitudes of systems and processes, each of which has dozens of different protein components that function properly only when all components are present. In other words, there could not have been any intermediate stages in any proposed evolutionary path from much simpler cells. Some evolutionists claim that simpler systems may have evolved first, perhaps with unrelated functions, then two or more of these simpler systems combined forces, evolving into the ultimate system. These simpler cells, however, would also be governed by irreducible complexity, so that the problem does not disappear. Conceptually, natural selection would favor the simplest life form that did not waste energy and resources on unnecessary structures and processes. In this way, evolution would lead to irreducible complexity, but only if chemicals were able to assemble living cells without divine aid.

The problem of irreducible complexity is applicable to proposals for abiogenesis. All of the stages that might have led up to the first evolved life form have minimum requirements. A certain number of proteins and cellular functions would have to be self-programmed into RNA for a minimal life form to replicate. Therefore evolutionists really do have to deal with the problem of irreducible complexity in their belief that life arose from mere chemicals.

Many examples of irreducible complexity exist that are not related to cellular functions but exist within behavioral patterns. As with living cells, such irreducible complexity is also encoded within the genome. One of these behaviors is the method that the Japanese honeybee uses to kill giant hornet scouts, made public with a video by the BBC. Scout hornets look for bee hives, and when one is found, the hornet enters the hive in order to leave a pheromone for its colleagues to pick up and attack en masse. Normally a dozen or two of these huge hornets would completely destroy the bee colony, which may have 30,000 bees, taking the larvae to feed their own young. Instead of attacking the scout hornet as it arrives, the bees allow the hornet to enter the nest, using signals to delay their attack. Once inside, the bees simultaneously swarm on to the hornet in hundreds, but they do not sting the hornet; its exoskeleton is too thick anyway. At this point, they vibrate their abdomens creating heat. They cause the temperature inside the swarm to reach almost 115 °F, sufficiently high to kill the hornet, which can only withstand 114 °F at the high levels of carbon dioxide created by the bees. The bees can survive 123 °F under the same conditions.[16]

Although one might argue with difficulty that genetic modifications may result in beneficial morphological changes, such arguments are impossible to make for behavioral adaptations that must be synchronized over a large group. An argument for evolution of this phenomenon must explain, in terms of genetic mutations, the following events with the correct sequence:

1. All the bees waiting until the hornet is inside the hive, with a warning signal both given and understood.
2. Large numbers of bees simultaneously attack by swarming on the hornet.
3. Bees vibrate their abdomens instead of attempting to sting the hornet.
4. Bees remain in the swarm for some minutes until the hornet dies.

If one or more of these activities were missing, the hornet would survive and fly back to alert its colleagues, and then all the bees would be doomed, along with any behavioral advantage gained by that one hive. All four behavioral characteristics must evolve in the correct sequence or be programmed together in their DNA. Any of the four activities are of no value by themselves and could not be inherited. These four behavioral patterns must have been programmed into the bee's DNA together, unless the bees are much smarter than we realize.

THE COMMON SENSE OF COMMON DESCENT

The evidence for abiogenesis is overwhelmingly negative, as indicated above. Scientific evidence from fossils, however, is more favorable for Darwin's evolution of species from existing simple life forms. If there were no God, and initial life forms were freaks of nature, then the evidence for evolution would include many transitional fossil sequences over long periods of time. Nonetheless, whatever evidence has been found, which might be used in arguments for evolution, is all circumstantial and better explained by creation.

The concept of evolution relies on combinations of beneficial mutations, even though the proportion of beneficial mutations is miniscule. However, the premise of multiple beneficial mutations, ignores the possibility that such combinations combine without overall detriment to the organism. Evidence from genetic studies indicates that combinations of neutral and mildly beneficial changes actually work against each other.[17]

More damaging to the concept of evolution are genetic studies determining the limits of viable changes in genomes. Without testing the limits of microevolution and examining mechanisms for punctuated equilibrium, the assertion that microevolution and punctuated equilibrium lead to macroevolution, is not proper science. We see organisms change, but are those changes really leading towards a more complex or competent organism, are they just expressing variations encoded within their genomes, or have they simply become defective in some way? An attempt at defining the limits of genetic changes was made by Michael Behe in his book, *The Edge of Evolution – The Search for the Limits of Darwinism.* Although this book argues strongly that random mutations do not enhance species, even over the long term, he shows that there is a case for another aspect of Darwinism, common descent.

The combination of these two positions, creation and common descent, may seem contradictory, but that's where God comes in. Instead of common descent by natural mechanisms, a creationist explanation for the progression of species is common design, with divine adjustment of genomes for each new species. The fossil record shows that at the end of a period of stasis, during which no significant changes occurred for a given species, a new species appears with considerably different morphology and behavior. The necessary complex genetic changes are beyond the mechanisms explained by Darwin. Nor has neo-Darwinism been able to show how such changes in genetic structure may have occurred. Genomes include very powerful mechanisms to prevent speciation. In contrast, the God of creation simply made all the necessary and complex modifications to the DNA of an existing species, both male and female, creating a new species. The word *simply* here is, of course, somewhat of an understatement. This approach to common descent is a much better explanation of incremental introduction, (sudden jumps in the fossil record), than resorting to impossible combinations of beneficial mutations in genomes that were designed to prevent such processes occurring.

God's genetic design principles allow species to adapt only within certain limits, so that each species can survive a range of environments. Without these limits, creation might run amok. Further evidence that evolution does not occur, even when predicted to do so, has been found with lizards in geographic isolation from each other over the last seven million years.[18]

A PURPOSE DRIVEN UNIVERSE

The universe reveals at least two levels of purpose. The most obvious is that the universe is able to support mankind in relative safety and with lots of resources; this is known as the anthropic principle. The other level concerns the question, why would God want to create man in the first place? This was answered in chapter 4; He has declared His desire to develop an intimate relationship with those who love Him.

For atheists and others, who do not believe in creation, the origin of the universe and the origin of life share the same prime cause: the random movements of matter and energy. The earth, the solar system, and the universe, however, are full of features that indicate they were intelligently designed. The concept of intelligent design started when a group of scientists found that science for evolution was lacking in substance; instead, they found considerable evidence of design. Scientists for evolution do not deny the appearance of design, which is found throughout creation; instead, they exhort each other to ignore such evidence.

Intelligent design science does not normally say much about the nature of God or about the age of the earth. It focuses instead on the attributes of living matter and the universe as a whole, revealing evidence that contradicts the ideas of naturalistic and accidental origins. The intelligent design movement started in biological sciences, and has since found evidence for design in all other natural sciences including astrophysics. An early landmark defining intelligent design was *The Creation Hypothesis*, edited by J. P. Moreland. Shortly afterwards Fred Heeren published *Show Me God*, which has a cosmological perspective. A few years later biological evidence for purposeful creation was powerfully presented by Michael Denton in *Nature's Destiny*. Intelligent design is found wherever we might look in nature: nuclear physics, astronomy, chemical elements and molecules, and cellular structures and organs within living creatures.

The Big Bang Theory, held in esteem by almost all scientists, cries out in agreement with the first verse of the Bible: declaring the beginning of all space, matter, and time. The Bible indicates that creation itself has much more to say about the magnificence of God's workmanship: "The heavens declare the glory of God; and the firmament shows His handiwork. Day unto day utters speech, and night unto night reveals knowledge." (Ps 19:1–2)

It is only in recent decades that science has been able to understand the depth of this knowledge and to translate the detailed language spoken by creation. What we find is that the universe appears to have been designed with amazing precision. Two aspects of design are the dozens of physical constants that must have precise values for the universe and life to exist, and the anthropic principle, in which our solar system and even our galaxy appear to be uniquely designed for humans to flourish. Almost everyone agrees that nature presents us with the appearance of design, from stellar physics to molecular biology.

Arguments for and against evolution and intelligent design have raged in professional publications, in school boards, and in law courts. Most of the time, neither party presents a water tight case. Intelligent design is charged with being religious and with not being scientific, neither of which is accurate. Intelligent design science does not prove the existence of God, but does provide evidence for His existence; many attributes of nature look as if someone did design the universe, and even evolutionists agree with that. It is not, however, an issue on which courts should have jurisdiction. The science that reveals the appearance of design is valid, both for Christians and atheists.

It is the responsibility of individuals to evaluate what is known about the universe, based on the evidence and their philosophical positions about the existence and relevance of God. Many people, who believe in God, affirm intelligent design; but that does not make the concept of intelligent design religious. If someone does not believe in God, that person can affirm only the appearance of design. The point that is often overlooked is that science cannot say anything about the existence of God; there are no instruments to measure Him. Consequently, the acceptance or denial of God is a philosophical position, which then leads to a decision about the appearance of design. If intelligent design were to be treated as a forensic science, rather than a religious issue, then scientists should be following the evidence and looking for the designer.

Physicists and astronomers have discovered many physical constants that must have precise values for our solar system and for the universe to exist. Some examples are given below.

Creation of carbon: Carbon, the essential element for life, is also the fourth largest of the elements in abundance. Its existence is owed to a precursor element, a radioactive isotope of beryllium, which is formed from the combination of two alpha particles. This beryllium isotope is created within very hot stars and has a half-life of only 10^{-16} seconds. During its fleeting lifetime, it must add another alpha particle, but it can only do this if both molecules have the same resonant energy level.[19] This is indeed the case: they were given the same energy levels to within about 2 percent. Before normal carbon can exist, one more hurdle exists on the long road to humanity. Normally, the excited carbon atom breaks up into its constituent beryllium and alpha particles But a mere 0.04%percent decay into the normal ground state of carbon, which is sufficient for the abundance of carbon in the universe. This final step is caused by the Hoyle state, a unique resonance of excited carbon atoms, predicted by the famous astronomer Sir Fred Hoyle when he was searching for a reason to account for carbon's prevalence.[20] As a result of his discovering this resonance, he turned from atheism, finding additional scientific reasons to embrace the existence of God.

Ratio of masses between protons and electrons: The proton is 1836 times heavier than the electron. Molecular structures and living organisms could not exist without this precise ratio. Stephen Hawking, the brilliant champion for a non-created universe, determined that "these numbers seem to have been very finely adjusted to make possible the development of life".[21]

The four fundamental forces of nature: The strengths of gravity, electromagnetism, and the strong and weak nuclear forces are in precise balance. Otherwise there could be no galaxies or solar systems.[22]

GENETIC ENTROPY

Recently, some studies have shown that over the last few centuries, harmful mutations have been accumulating in the human genome, which is deteriorating as a result.[23] Originally an atheist, John Stanford wrote convincingly on this topic in *Genetic Entropy & The Mystery of the Genome – The Genome Is Deteriorating*. His research shows that even when harmful mutations are ignored, cells are less likely to fulfill their normal functions. Consequently, sickness will become more and more prevalent in mankind over many generations.[24] Unless medical technology is significantly improved, we may not survive as a species in the long run, unless God intervenes. We should not expect anything else because there is no reason to think that entropy does not apply to DNA. This observation on the deterioration of the human genome has been tested mathematically, the results confirming the eventual extinction of the human race if no intervention occurs.[25] The Second Law of Thermodynamics reigns over all of nature, so that despite the exquisite mechanisms incorporated within DNA to maintain our genome's integrity, it will degrade over many generations.[26]

The possibility of mutations giving rise to a new higher species of man, as Darwin and many others had hoped, is doomed because even if a super-race arose, it would carry with it most of the corrupted genetic information and predisposition to disease. An example is the previously mentioned inability of humans to manufacture vitamin C, possibly inherited from the DNA that God transformed from a previously created species.

As a species ages and genetic defects reduce its average lifespan, survival of that species depends on how quickly each generation can reproduce before succumbing to fatal sickness. Humans are able to mitigate this to some extent with medical technology. Species in the wild avoid this kind of extinction by natural selection. In addition to the Darwinian notion that natural selection eliminates the weakest, it also eliminates defective genes. This is actually Darwinism in reverse, in that natural selection maintains existing genetic codes.

TRUTH OR CONSEQUENCES

In the first of the TV game shows, Truth or Consequences, competitors were asked a difficult question. If they could not give a true answer within the time limit, they had to perform a zany stunt. Life can be somewhat similar. If you do not know the facts about an important issue, you may hold opinions of little consequence, or on the other hand might face severe consequences. Lack of knowledge about driving regulations is one example. Ignorance about topics of creation and evolution is not dangerous, unless being misled about Biblical interpretations and scientific evidence can affect one's faith in God and the benefits that such faith would bring.

In the Star Trek movies and TV shows, Spock is credited with almost completely logical thought processes. One would imagine that faced with the evidence for intelligent design and the lack of evidence for abiogenesis, he would start looking for the creator. He might then look for a suitable religion and its scriptures. He would need to understand permissible meanings of scripture that might be associated with the original language. Having searched the universe for new and unimaginable life forms, he would have little trouble accepting angels, and of course, the God who created them.

REFERENCES

1. Rana, Fazale. *The Cell's Design*. Grand Rapids: Baker Books, 2008: 183–201.
2. Darwin, Charles. *On the Origin of Species*. London: Clowes & Sons, 1859: 484.

3. Margulis, Lynn and Dorion Sagan. *Acquiring Genomes*. New York: Basic Books, 2003: 25–28.

4. Ibid., 82, 83, 96.

5. Ibid., 71.

6. Ibid., 72.

7. Ibid., 76.

8. Rana, Fazale, with Hugh Ross. *Who was Adam*. Colorado Springs: Navpress, 2005: 153.

9. Rana, Fazale, and Hugh Ross. *Origins of Life*. Colorado Springs: Navpress, 2004: 197–207.

10. See Reference 3, 28–32.

11. Grant, Peter and B. Rosemary Grant. *Hybridization of Bird Species*. Science, 256.5054 (1992):193–197.

12. See Reference 1, 269–283.

13. Bergman, Jerry. *The Search for Evidence Concerning the Origin of Fish*. Creation Research Society Quarterly, 47.4 (2011) 283–295.

14. Doyle, Shaun, and Paul Nethercott. *Ghosts in the Rocks*. Creation Ministries International. 14 July 2011. <http://creation.com/ghost-lineages>

15. See Reference 1, 181–182.

16. Sugahara, Michio and Fumio Sakamoto. *Heat and carbon dioxide generated by honeybees jointly act to kill hornets*. Naturwissenschaften, 96.9 (2009): 1133–1136.

17. Doyle, Shaun. *The Diminishing Returns of Beneficial Mutations*. Creation Ministries International. 7 July 2011. <http://creation.com/antagonistic-epistasis>

18. Thorpe, Roger, Yann Surget-Groba, and Helena Johansson. *Genetic Tests for Ecological and Allopatric Speciation in Anoles on an Island Archipelago*. Public Library of Science, Genetics. 6.4 (2010). <http://www.plosgenetics.org/article/info:doi/journal.pgen.1000929>.

19. Schroeder, Gerald. *The Science of God*. New York: Simon and Schuster, 1997: 27.

20. Heeren, Fred. *Show Me God*. Wheeling: Search Light Publications, 1995: 181–182.

21. Ibid., 179.
22. Ibid., 182.
23. Crow, James. *The High Spontaneous Mutation Rate: Is it a Health Risk?* Proceedings of the National Academy of Sciences, 94.16 (1997): 8380–8386.
24. Bergman, Jerry. *The Pleiotropy Problem for Evolution.* Creation Research Society Quarterly, 46.4 (2010): 284–289.
25. Sanford, John, John Baumgardner, Wesley Brewer, Paul Gibson, Walter Remine. *Using Numerical Simulation to Test the Validity of Neo-Darwinian Theory.* Proceedings of the Sixth International Conference on Creationism, 6.15 (2008): 165–175.
26. Bergman, Jerry. *The Elimination of Mutations by the Cell's Elaborate Protein Quality Control Factory: A Major Problem for Neo-Darwinism.* Creation Research Society Quarterly, 43.2 (2006): 68–74.

APPENDIX A
MAJOR BIBLICAL THEMES

The Sovereignty of God. Everything that has ever happened was a result of God's will, manifested through His absolute power, over both natural and spiritual realms, either directly or indirectly. God's power over all things is related to His knowledge of all that happens and all that will happen, even when sparrows fall to the ground.

Having said that, God has given mankind free will, which includes the freedom to ignore and disobey God. In general, God does not override people's decisions, and He does not force them to go to heaven. God was aware that Adam and Eve would sin, but He had already determined His solution for the fall of man. His sovereign will provided salvation for mankind through the cross, for those who believe, as explained in the section on redemption.

Although God created beings capable of choosing evil, and He knew that they would commit evil, they become merely agents in God's overall purpose, as exemplified by the role of Satan in the story of Job. Natural events and processes are agents in God's plan for the overall benefit of the world and to obtain His immediate and ultimate purposes. Such events may cause suffering and death.

If we are tempted to judge God on such issues, we should examine our own attitudes towards these kinds of evil. For example, our highways and vehicles suit our purposes, but they are responsible for an appalling loss of life and limb. Yet we accept these consequences in order to gain the greater good of fast and efficient transportation. Although we condone this kind of expediency in ourselves, we can not accuse God of expediency; after all, in His humanity He suffered torture and death on a cross because of His love for the world. Anyway, there is no other God; without His creation we would not be alive to accept or reject His wisdom and loving kindness. If we accept His benefits, we must also accept the other side of the coin, which involves suffering. The alternative of rejecting God because He allows evil, would also reject Him for His blessings, both in this life and the one to come. More is said about death and suffering in chapter 7.

Relationship. God's desire is to have fellowship with His people. In the Old Testament, God established a covenant with the nation of Israel to bless them and to be their God; but their disobedience and wickedness led to curses rather than blessings. God established a new covenant in Jesus Christ, applicable to all those who believe the gospel about His new covenant. Many people reject the opportunity to have a close relationship with God. Those who seek God and are finally admitted into heaven will find an intimacy without distraction or detriment. The garden of Eden was the first indication of God's desire for fellowship, providing idyllic surroundings for companionship in the cool of the evening. Adam and Eve were created man and wife to portray the oneness of God; the church now portrays that same oneness, even with our fallen natures.

Redemption. The fall of Adam and the subsequent loss of relationship with God affected all of mankind. Adam's descendants are unable to know God through their own efforts. Without knowing God, it is impossible to gain entrance to heaven; but there is a solution. God intended from the beginning to restore His relationship with men and women; it required the death and resurrection of His son Jesus Christ. This is the basis of the gospel, in which Jesus paid the penalty for all sin, thus purchasing or redeeming those who believe in His salvation.

Suffering and maturity. If there were no God, suffering would be at least as commonplace, much more so probably. This is because God has continually provided instruction to men on how to love their neighbors, and also because He intervenes at times to answer prayers to alleviate suffering. On the other hand, God uses suffering to bring maturity to believers. The benefit is that heaven will not be populated with immature and rebellious people. Often, when suffering is borne with maturity, the result is a powerful witness to others about the gospel. Maturity is one of those characteristics that only grow by being exercised.

First the natural, then the spiritual. This is an overriding principle that sheds light on Genesis. It means that life did not start out in a heavenly world or in a paradise. Heavenly places (if place is the right word) are eternal and inhabited entirely by spiritual beings. These beings have bodies that are not composed of flesh and blood that decay. In contrast, God created life in a material world; people are made of flesh and blood, which are subject to corruption and decay.

Justice. The Old Testament is largely a history of Israel, revealing a number of complaints that God had against them. One of the most significant was they omitted to deal justly with each other. Because God requires people to act justly (Mic 6:8), we should consider how God Himself acts justly. We would find that before exacting justice, God is patient and merciful.

Living by Faith. The heroes of the Bible all have the hallmark of faith. Hebrews 11 is devoted to the faith of men and women from many walks of life; patriarchs, kings, and the persecuted. Essentially, they believed that their choice of actions, which often resulted in disadvantage or death, honored God through obedience or through their belief in Him and His promises.

APPENDIX B
GUIDELINES FOR INTERPRETING SCRIPTURE

Three major criteria help in determining the validity of any given interpretation. The first, and most obvious, is the extent to which the Bible text supports that interpretation. For example, the creation story is contained within six consecutive Days, finite periods of time, which could be interpreted as 24-hour days. The Bible, however, provides evidence that the word Day could be figurative, with an unknown length, possibly thousands or millions of years. Other evidence must be used to determine what kind of Day Genesis is all about. An example of a theory that has weak support is a version of Theistic Evolution. In this theory, after God had created the universe, mankind arrived on the scene by common descent through random genetic mutations. Although the Bible does not say exactly how God created animal species, the account of mankind's creation is quite specific. In Genesis 1, we find that God initially created one man Adam and then one woman Eve from Adam's side, with both together in His image and likeness. This is hard to square with random mutation and any attempt to do so distorts the meaning of the text.

The second criterion is silence, meaning the Bible has nothing to say whatsoever on a given topic. An example is the Gap Theory, critiqued in *Unformed and Unfilled* by Weston W. Fields. In this theory, the universe, including the earth, was created billions of years ago. Then

God created animals such as dinosaurs, eventually destroying them along with the habitable surface of our planet, before starting over. This earlier creation would have occurred after the creation of the universe described in the first verse, but before the dark and formless condition described in the second verse, hence the name *gap*. Genesis does not mention an earlier creation, so we can say that the Bible is silent on the Gap Theory and that it does not support this theory. The Bible, however, does not exclude it. Consequently this theory is logically permissible but not appealing to most believers because of the lack of Biblical support and material evidence.

The third criterion is exclusion. To say that the universe created itself would fly in the face of many Biblical passages, notably the first verse. Therefore, this idea that the universe created itself must be excluded from any Biblical interpretation of creation.

In addition to these three criteria, general principles exist for interpreting the Bible.[1] Each of them has relevance depending on the genre or type of scripture, such as narrative, poetic, or didactic. The first principle is context, context, context, similar to the real estate expression of location, location, location. The second principle is to allow clear passages or concepts in the Bible to interpret less clear passages. This approach is justified because we believe that the Bible was revealed by God, the original text was without error, and truth does not contradict itself.

A third principle is to recognize the use of literary techniques. The controversy that ensnared Galileo was in part the result of misunderstood figurative passages; the details are provided in chapter 2.

A fourth principle is to make use of major themes that run throughout the Old and New Testaments. When these are applied to the creation story we get a much clearer picture of what God was saying and doing, allowing interpretations that are consistent with the whole Bible. Such interpretations exhibit strong Biblical support and are more preferable to interpretations that rely on only the text in question. Major themes in the Bible are given in Appendix A.

A final guide for interpretation is to avoid the tendency to understand history with our built in anachronistic bias. The Bible was written long before there was any scientific understanding of our universe, whether of minuscule atomic particles, microbes, or galaxies. It describes what could be seen from the earth's surface with the unaided eye. I find that a rewarding method for understanding scriptures is to imagine oneself in the location and time of the narrative, seeing and hearing what the text describes.

REFERENCES

1. Ramm, Bernard. *Protestant Biblical Interpretation*. Grand Rapids: Baker Publishing Group, 1970: 93–127.

APPENDIX C
A DAY IN CREATION

The length of the creation Day is not likely to be decided from debate on the scriptures because the Bible is not definitive. On the other hand, the weight of science supports an old earth, which in turn indicates that creation Days must be long periods of time. Although we cannot go back and look at the number of sunsets in each Day, Young Earth scientists have not presented sufficient evidence to persuade most people that the earth is only a few thousand years old. Belief in either a 24-hour Day or a figurative Day of thousands of years is likely to depend on one's belief for the age of the earth. This in turn might depend on scientific persuasion or a philosophical view that God did not permit millions of years of death before the fall of man. If the universe were only about 6,000 years old, creation Days of 24-hours would be appropriate, although there is no absolute Biblical substantiation for 24-hour Days during the creation week.[1]

Before considering the issues, it is helpful to understand whether the Genesis text can actually define the length of a creation Day. It is not appropriate to say that each creation Day must be interpreted to mean long periods of time. There is no implication in the text of eons of time. The Hebrew word for Day could be interpreted as a 24-hour day, or it could be interpreted in a figurative sense, without any implication for its duration. There would, however, be little point in adding details of billions of years of history to the creation narrative because it could not have been understood at the time it was written.

It might be argued that the figurative meaning for Day is deceptive, and that God would not leave us in the dark. This same argument, however, fails when it is applied to the geocentric debate of Galileo's time. In this debate, scientists measured the orbits of God's solar system and were able to help interpret ambiguous scriptures. In particular, science threw light on the meaning of scriptures that mentioned the rising of the sun. Everyone understands now that the Biblical language is figurative and records visual appearances rather than scientific explanations of the solar system. These would not have made sense when the scriptures were first written. A similar situation exists today concerning the creation Day; it remains to be seen how this impasse will be resolved within the church at large.

LET THERE BE LIGHT

The size of the universe can be determined from the velocity of light. Scientists have shown that this velocity is constant with very high precision. In order to account for light emitted from distant stars, Young Earth proponents have devised various hypotheses to allow light from distant stars to reach the earth in fewer than 6,000 years. They are forced to do this because there is little debate about the vast magnitude of our universe, with distant galaxies located many billions of light years away.[2]

One of these ideas is that God created starlight from all the distant stars to mimic the billions of years during which they did not exist. Perhaps God created only the rays that arrive on earth, and He did not bother to create light rays for all the other directions in the universe. This idea of appearance of age sounds absurd, and would discredit God with deception. Fortunately, leaders in the Young Earth movement are not promoting it.

A second suggestion is that God caused light to have vastly greater velocity during the creation week. As a result, starlight from billions of light years away arrived within days of the earth's beginning. Since then, the velocity of light was quickly reduced to its present value. This theory has unintended consequences that no amount of additional reasoning can overcome. The velocity of light, c is related to its wavelength, λ and frequency, f by the expression $c = f\lambda$. This basic equation and other laws of physics have been ignored in this attempt to force a Young Earth into reality. For example, sight depends on the wavelength of visible light, which matches the size of optic cells within the eye. If the wavelength of light varied slightly, all creatures would have been blind until the velocity of light became very close to today's value. Also, Einstein's famous equation $E=mc^2$ implies that the nuclear core of the sun would release so much energy it would have instantly exploded. These and other problems make this explanation impossible.

A third suggestion is that the universe started with a Big Bang according to Carmelian Cosmology.[3] This is somewhat different to the Big Bang model which most scientists believe today. The Carmelian theory is consistent with the General Theory of Relativity, and it resolves some of the problems associated with the conventional Big Bang theory. It may turn out to be generally accepted by the scientific community. Although it is similar to the Big Bang model, it cannot be used to support a Young Earth model, as explained in Appendix D.

EVENING AND MORNING

Young Earth believers propose that the phrase *evening and morning* defines the creation Day as a 24-hour period. That might seem strange to us; we think of a 24-hour day as daytime and nighttime. We might add morning and evening if we were being precise about shades of light and dark. The world continually experiences evening and morning all the time. Both of these events occur as bands of twilight that sweep across the earth's surface at about 1,000 mph. At the poles, morning and evening do not exist for three months at time, just continual daytime or nighttime. The first five creation Days have a worldwide perspective, which means they are not specific to any one location. Consequently the words evening and morning do not make much sense as unique times of day in the context of creation, except to define a beginning and ending.[4]

Apart from the six instances in Genesis 1, there are six other verses in the Old Testament of *evening* with *morning* in that order. In all instances, they refer only to events that took place specifically in the evening and also in the morning, or else they refer to nighttime only. There is no sense in which a 24-hour period was being considered in these passages. Thirteen verses in the Old Testament have *morning* before *evening,* and these refer to events that took place only at those times, such as sacrifices, or in two instances that refer to daytime only. The Bible provides no precedent to show that *evening* with *morning* defines or even implies a 24-hour day. The Old Testament meaning of these two words is that of normal nighttime or a sequence of events between evening and the subsequent morning.

Each creation Day started when God spoke that something was to happen. After God completed His work for that Day, evening occurred, and then after an unknown period of night, morning appeared. This is the sequence of events depicted by Genesis. It contains the important information that God communicated for each Day. In the Bible, the words *day and night* indicate a 24-hour period, so that *evening and morning* should not be considered to mean a 24-hour Day.[5]

The phrase that ends each creation Day, "so the evening and the morning were the second day" for example, has not been translated accurately in most versions. A more accurate translation is: *And there was an evening and there was a morning, a second day.* This gives a slightly different sense, and reduces support for attempting to use the phrase as the definition of a 24-hour Day. The Hebrew conjunction that is usually translated *and,* strongly implies sequential chronology. After God completed His work for each Day, there was an evening, which indicates that God had stopped work, then an implied night during which no one works, (as Jesus stated), and then morning, which indicated the night was over. All references to creation Days and parts of creation Days can be considered figurative and extended in time, which is consistent with other Biblical texts, Hebrew language, and with modern English.[6]

THE FIRST DAY

Because the first Day was not actually called the first day in the original Hebrew, but *day one* instead, it could be argued that it was not the first day that ever existed. The logical meaning of *day one* is the first day in a certain sequence of days. This interpretation removes any confusion that the first Day might be considered as the very first day ever. If it were the very first day, God would have used the ordinal number *first* instead of the cardinal number *one*. *Day one* implies others preceded it; the second and subsequent days are then counted with ordinal numbers that refer back to *day one* as the starting point.

The concept of a singular day within a continuum of days is found in one other place in the Bible. In Zechariah 14:7, "the Day of the Lord" is translated from the Hebrew words that also mean *day one*. It is equally a very important day, and thus the words *day one* mark God's involvement in both the beginning of the earth and also the end. In both instances, the length of the day appears to be longer than twenty-four hours.[7]

The first Day does not include the initial creation of the universe and the formless state of the earth, which are described in Genesis 1:1–2. The beginning and ending phrases of each of the six Days are identical, so that including the *ex nihilo* creation event of verse 1 within the first Day does not do justice to the literary structure.[8]

THE SEVENTH DAY

The first six Days all had a beginning and an end. The seventh Day, however, had a beginning, but it does not have a defined ending. On this Day, God rested from His labors and then continued in that state of rest. Consequently, the seventh Day should be considered as on going. This observation was made by the author of Hebrews, who used it along with Psalm 95 to argue that believers can enter the rest of God. This is because His rest still carries on from the beginning of the seventh day. Just as God rested from His works, Hebrews urges us to cease from our own works, which we might otherwise think would gain us salvation by our own efforts.

In addition, there is clear indication that in Genesis 2:2, the word *day*, which embraces all six Days of the creation story, has a figurative meaning of more than twenty-four hours. Therefore, it is not reasonable to deny that any of the six previous Days could have figurative meanings of long periods of time.

THE GENERATIONS OF CREATION

Genesis 2:4 states, "This is the history of the heavens and the earth when they were created, in the day that the Lord God made the earth and the heavens." The words *this is the history* are used for the Hebrew words that actually mean these are the generations. Generations can mean the application to specific persons, grandfather, father, son, et cetera, or generally over a whole population. Sometimes, a period of time can be assigned to a generation, thirty or forty years typically. Some scholars argue that this phrase is a postscript for Genesis 1, so that generations would refer to the Days of creation. Such reasoning implies an Old Earth understanding, although it does not do justice to the real meaning of generations, nor to the way that this phrase is used ten times in Genesis. In each instance, the phrase precedes the names and lives of people, so that it is reasonable for it to do so in Genesis 2:4.[9]

Lending weight to this argument is use of the single Hebrew word for God, *Elohim*, in Genesis 1:1 through Genesis 2:3, whereas the two-word title *Jehovah Elohim* is used from Genesis 2:4 onwards. Almighty is a good translation of *Elohim*, consistent with the creation story of Genesis 1. In Genesis 2 the creation story concentrates on the relationship between God and Adam, for which the more appropriate two-word expression *Jehovah Elohim* is used; *Jehovah* is the covenant name that God gave to Moses in a face to face meeting beside the burning bush. It is the personal part of God's title, appropriately used in Genesis 2 and 3, where God communicated intimately with Adam and Eve in the garden of Eden. After that, the double title of God's personal majesty is no longer used in the Old Testament, except for a few occasions with Abraham, whom God referred to as a friend.

CREATION DAYS IN THE BIBLE

Moses referred to the creation week when he was listing the Ten Commandments. In the fourth commandment, Israel was commanded to work only six days and to rest on the seventh. The reason is given in Exodus 20:11: "For in six days the Lord made the heavens and the earth, the sea and all that is in them, and rested the seventh day. Therefore the Lord blessed the Sabbath day and hallowed it." A similar verse is found in Exodus 31:17 when God spoke to Moses concerning the Sabbath: "It is a sign between Me and the children of Israel forever; for in six days the Lord made the heavens and the earth, and on the seventh day He rested and was refreshed."

Reasons why these two verses should not be taken as a proof texts for 24-hour creation Days are given below.

- For obvious reasons, men normally work less than half of a 24-hour day; God, however, has never been under such a restriction. God's working Day during creation may have been 24 hours or much longer.
- The two verses in Exodus are summaries of the six Days of creation, and as such, do not convey all the information of Genesis 1. Therefore, they should not be used to determine the length of the creation Day.
- God rested on the seventh Day without specifying an ending for the seventh Day, such as the evening and morning format found in the other six Days. The writer of Hebrews determined that the seventh Day is still in existence. Moreover, he pointed out that God's rest continues to this day, implying that the seventh Day is ongoing.
- God was not defining a 24-hour day for men or for Himself but defining the working week for men, namely, six 24-hour days followed by a seventh day of rest.

Another text used as a proof text for a 24-hour Day concerns a question on divorce, to which Jesus answered, "But from the beginning of creation, God made them male and female." (Mark 10:6) At first sight, this appears to mean that Adam and Eve existed from the beginning of the creation week. Adam and Eve, however, were created at the very end of creation, so that the reference by Jesus to the *beginning of creation* must have been about the beginning of mankind's existence, not a literal description of the creation week. Jesus was making a point about the union of Adam and Eve, not the age of the earth. To argue from the Young Earth position that the creation of mankind was in the beginning, with the implication of six 24-hour days for creation, is really not logical. The answer Jesus gave was in recognition that God had planned before creation for man and wife to be one, in the image of God, even as God is one. Regardless of how much time passed between the first Day and the sixth Day, when God created mankind, God's plan for marriages was unity.

A WORKING WEEK

Using the fourth commandment in support for a 24-hour creation Day is not only questionable hermeneutics, it misses the point of the commandment. The two instructions for the Jews were first that they were to work only six days and secondly that they were to rest on the seventh day and keep it holy. Obviously, the only interpretation of the word *day* in the fourth commandment is that it must be one of the seven days of the week. These instructions about man's working week should not be used to define the length of God's working Day.

Although the rest of the world does not appear to have received this commandment, it has great benefit for all mankind. Jewish religious leaders generally took a very legalistic interpretation, whereas not being under Jewish law, the church today is much more liberal for the most part. Jesus spoke strongly against the strict interpretations of the Pharisees that denied human kindness. Nevertheless, it does not seem appropriate to invalidate the underlying principles of the commandment.

From man's perspective, there is no denying the straightforward concept of six consecutive days of 24 hours for a working week. During any given day a man might work only one hour, or all 24 hours until he dropped. The length of the working day is not the issue. However much a man works, dusk arrives, and after some sleep, dawn arrives for another day. On the other hand, God is not bound by time, whether vast or minuscule in duration, nor by tiredness, nor by lack of light. Nonetheless, the sequence is the same. For God, each creation Day started with work, and when the task was completed, evening came followed by morning. The same sequence applies to man; work, evening, an assumed night, and then morning. Jesus had this concept in mind when He said, "I must work the works of Him who sent me while it is day; the night is coming when no one can work." Jesus was not referring to the next few hours but to all the days that were available to Him until He was crucified. Similarly, the previous works He had done in His ministry were done in that same day. Again the length of the task is not the issue.

A full treatment of the length of the creation Day may be found in the fifth chapter of *Science and Faith: Friends or Foes* by C. John Collins.[10]

REFERENCES

1. Aalders, Gerhard. *Genesis Volume I*. Grand Rapids: Zondervan, 1981: 58.
2. Humphreys, D. Russell. *Starlight and Time*. Green Forest: Master Books, 2003: 10.
3. Hartnett, John. *Starlight, Time and the New Physics*. Australia: Creation Book Publishers, 2007: 112–118.
4. Schicatano, Jim. *The Theory of Creation*. New York: Writers Club Press, 2001: 33.
5. Hamilton, Victor. *The Book of Genesis Chapters 1–17*. Grand Rapids: Eerdmans, 1990: 121.
6. See Reference 4, 32–36.
7. Ross, Hugh. *A Matter of Days*. 2004. Colorado Springs: Navpress, 2004: 75.
8. See Reference 5, 118–119; Bavinck, Herman. *In the Beginning*. Grand Rapids: Baker Books, 2000: 101.
9. See Reference 4, 166–167; See Reference 5, 2–11.
10. Collins, C. John. *Science and Faith: Friends or Foes?* Wheaton: Good News Publishers, 2003: 77–96.

APPENDIX D
OLD IS GOOD

The methods that science uses to determine the events of long ago are forensic. Unlike the science of the properties of matter, in which experiments can be duplicated and refined, the study of earth's history can only make use of circumstantial evidence. This evidence is obtained by scientific methods, but it is still circumstantial; there are no witnesses of what occurred long ago.

Many scientific disciplines have been used to obtain data that determines the ages of the earth and the universe, consistently giving time frames of billions of years. Some of the evidence has been challenged by Young Earth proponents with alternative interpretations. Nevertheless, only a small proportion of Young Earth suggestions have anything but limited significance. Considerable scientific background is required to understand some of the issues, but other scientific evidence speaks clearly against Young Earth explanations.

An example is the velocity of light and its use in determining distances to the nearest stars. Distances can be measured optically or with radio signals (both are electromagnetic waves), using the orbit of the earth as a baseline. This distance provides sufficient accuracy only for distances to the nearest stars, such as the Orion nebula, which is 1,270 light years away. Recently the distance to the galaxy NGC 4258 was determined to be about 24 million light years away.[1] This distance was established with the same type of technology used by laser range finders, which rely on basic physical properties of light. In this circumstance, the laser was actually at microwave frequencies, (known as a maser); it is one of the naturally occurring masers that are embedded in many galaxies.

Such measurements provide incontrovertible evidence for stellar distances that far exceed distances of a few thousand light years. Young Earth creationists agree that the edge of the universe is at least 13.7 billion light-years away. Despite this, they disagree with the obvious conclusion that the universe is billions of years old.

The problem for Young Earth scientists is that they need an explanation for how Adam could have seen starlight from stars that were created just days before he was created, and yet that starlight had traversed billions of light-years to reach him. A similar problem would still exist today if the universe were only a few thousand years old. Based on scientific measurements that show the velocity of light is not changing, no credible scientific alternative exists for a young universe. Several hypotheses have been put forward to explain how a young earth might appear to be old. All but one, concerning time dilation, have finally been rejected by Young Earth scientists.[2] The latest work on time dilation, which would have been caused by the intense gravity of the initial phase of the universe, explains how a few thousand years on earth were equivalent to billions of years in the far reaches of the universe.

This new model, expounded by John Hartnett in his book *Starlight, Time and the New Physics,* has the advantage of not requiring dark matter and dark energy, which are somewhat of an embarrassment to the conventional Big Bang model.[3] His hypothesis is similar to the conventional Big Bang model, but he has five dimensions instead of the four used in Einstein's General Relativity. By making a few assumptions, it also allows observers on earth to have seen all visible stars from the first few days of creation onward. Like the Big Bang model, the universe is shown to have expanded, not from a singularity but from an initial radius of 8 million light years. This radius is necessary to allow starlight to reach Adam during the creation week and to avoid a much smaller but uninhabitable universe. The unforeseen outcome of Hartnett's *New Physics* is that the outer galaxies must have traveled almost 13 billion light years in only about 6,000 years, with an impossible average speed in excess of 2 million times the speed of light. The *New Physics* may be fundamentally correct, but it cannot be tweaked to provide a believable explanation for a young earth.

In addition to the well established size of the universe and the strongly implied very long age, reasonable evidence exists for the Big Bang Theory, or something very like it. Although there are weaknesses to this theory, it does indicate that there was a beginning, in agreement with the Bible. New measurements of stellar and galactic events frequently help confirm the Big Bang Theory. Theoretical calculations that simulate the growth of the universe from an initial singularity and the laws that determine how the universe continues to hold together show the most amazing features of God's wisdom. Many physical constants of matter, which can be accurately determined by measurement, are found to be very precise. Consequently, scientists in different fields have deduced that the existence of the universe cannot be an accident, that it must have been designed. This has given rise to a new aspect of science called intelligent design, explained further in chapter 12. The conclusion reached by an increasing number of leading scientists is that there had to be a designer.[4] It is ironic that Young Earth creationists accept intelligent design science but not the ancient universe to which so much of it applies.

The mysteries of Mars. The geological history of Mars is a new topic in discussions about the age of the universe. The robotic explorers, Spirit and Opportunity, have begun to reveal the nature and origin of some of the rocks and strata on Mars. For thousands of years, Mars has been observed with the naked eye to have a red hue. In recent times we have found that this is caused by the red dust on the planet's surface; also there is no liquid water and no significant atmosphere. Preliminary results from exploration of the surface of Mars indicate that in its early history it had large expanses of water and an atmosphere. If this were so within the last few thousand years, then Mars would look more like earth, and it could not have been called a red planet in historical times.

Mars has had many volcanoes, some much larger than those on earth. Its volcanism, however, has largely abated. If Mars had existed in its present state for the last three or four thousand years, there would not have been enough time for oceans, atmosphere, and active volcanoes to disappear in a Young Earth time frame. Consequently, Young Earth creationists are developing new theories that would allow a young Mars to look the way it does today. Early ideas include a catastrophic flood, possibly related to the Noachian Flood.

So many layers, not enough time. Numerous geological features indicate that the earth is much more than a few thousand years old. An example is in the Green River Formation, where over four million varves of sediment exist in a formation that is approximately one mile deep.[5] Varves are discrete thin layers of sediment deposited at the bottom of lakes, with usually two distinct layers each year. Typically, these two layers have different colors and different chemistry as a result of seasonal variations in the particulate matter that settles to the bottom. Multiple layers may be deposited as a result of storms. Even if a varve formed every day, it would take about 11,000 years to complete the Green River Formation. No credible argument exists, however, to show that varves form as frequently as once a day for any long period of time.

Another example of outstanding sedimentary deposits is in the Appalachians; up to 35,000 vertical feet of sedimentary strata exist.[6] These deposits are at least as thick as the height of floodwater proposed in the Young Earth Flood model. Most of these sediments were not deposited in raging waters but slowly over periods of time much longer than can be associated with the Flood. A description of the mechanisms that cause such sediments to be deposited and the length of time involved is available in the on-line book by the geologist Dan Wonderly, *Neglect of Geological Data*. In addition, this book corrects some erroneous assumptions by prominent Young Earth scientists.

Although Young Earth creationists claim there is no geological column, it has been found in over thirty places around the world. The geological column, however, should not be thought of as a fixed sequence of layers that should appear everywhere. Any given location could have varied in altitude with movement of the earth's crust, sometimes under water, sometimes coastal, other times above sea level and susceptible to erosion. Close examination of the many thousands of feet of sediment in certain sections of the column reveals structures and fossils that could not have been deposited by catastrophic flooding but must have occurred over long periods of time.[7] Nevertheless, floods and other catastrophes have occurred at various times and places.

Radioisotope Dating. The decay of certain radioisotopes provides convincing evidence for a very old earth. Measurements of parent and daughter elements of isotopes in several different decay paths provide ages for older rocks on the earth's crust of up to about 4 billion years.[8] Although Young Earth scientists challenge some of these measurements, often for improper reasons, the vast majority are conclusive. Consequently, Young Earth scientists propose that radioisotope decay rates were very much greater during the creation week, but they decreased dramatically since then. Recently, they completed their research program, Radioisotopes and the Age of the Earth (RATE), designed to demonstrate that radioactivity was much higher at the beginning of creation. Nevertheless, the scientific community has not noticed anything of value or of significance in this work.

Science does not support Young Earth ideas about accelerated radioisotope decay rates. Moreover, the hypothesis of accelerated decay rates has major difficulties that have no reasonable explanation. For example, the resulting nuclear reactions in the earth's core would have created a nuclear power plant that would have increased temperatures and radioactivity, prohibiting life. Recognizing this, attempts are being made by Young Earth scientists to develop a scenario that would have allowed reasonable temperatures on earth. However this may turn out, it will almost certainly look like the wheels within wheels of the old geocentric models.

Radiometric dating of uncontaminated rocks from the moon confirms an old solar system. Similarly, isochrons from meteorites provide compelling evidence for an old universe.[9]

The case of the missing isotopes. Eighty-four naturally occurring elements exist on the earth, with another 14 that occur temporarily as a result of nuclear fission. These elements have a total of the 339 isotopes, 70 of which are radioactive. Half-lives of these radioisotopes vary up to about 6 billion years. Radioisotopes that were present at the earth's formation, some 4.5 billion years ago, would immediately have started decaying. After about ten half-lives, traces of radioisotopes are no longer detectable, so that isotopes with half-lives less than about 450 million years would no longer be detectable today. Ignoring five radioisotopes that are continually being regenerated by radiation, it turns out that all radioisotopes with half-lives greater than 450 million years are detectable on earth, but all those under 450 million years are not detectable.

Isotopes that are no longer measurable on earth are being created in stars, where they can be detected by using spectrographic analysis. They are known to exist naturally and have known nuclear reactions for their synthesis.[10] The latter point is important because the solar system is believed to be the result of much older stellar explosions and the accumulation of resulting debris. These missing isotopes are strong evidence for a very old earth. Young Earth scientists counter this evidence with accelerated decay rates, but as explained above, there is no conclusive evidence and problems are insurmountable.

REFERENCES

1. Argon, A. et al. 2007. *Toward a New Distance to the Active Galaxy NGC 4258 I.* The Astrophysical Journal, 659.2 (2007): 1040–1062.
2. Humphreys, D. Russell. *Starlight and Time.* Green Forest: Master Books, 1994: 43–51.
3. Hartnett, John. *Starlight, Time, and the New Physics.* Australia: Creation Ministries International, 2007: 157–180.
4. Ross, Hugh. Ed. J.P. Moreland. *The Creation Hypothesis.* Downers Grove: InterVarsity Press, 1994: 154–155.
5. Snoke, David. *A Biblical Case for an Old Earth.* Grand Rapids: Baker Books, 2006: 33–36.
6. Wonderly, Daniel. *Neglect of Geological Data.* Interdisciplinary Biblical research Institute, 1993: 39–47.
7. Young, Davis, and Ralph Stearley. *The Bible Rocks and Time: Geological Evidence for the Age of the Earth.* Downers Grove: InterVarsity Press, 2008: 213–242.

8. Dalrymple, G. Brent. *Ancient Earth, Ancient Skies.* California: Stanford University Press, 2004: 82–93.
9. See Reference 7, 415–418.
10. Wiens, Roger. *Radiometric Dating: A Christian Perspective.* The American Scientific Association, 2002: 11–12. <http://www.asa3.org/ASA/resources/Wiens.html>

APPENDIX E

THE FOURTH DAY

Genesis 1:1 states that the heavens were created in the beginning, before the Holy Spirit hovered over the face of the deep, and before the first Day when God said "Let there be light." The English wording, however, of Genesis 1:14–19 gives the impression that the heavens were also created on the fourth Day. The key to resolving this apparent contradiction is to understand the peculiarities and limitations of Hebrew grammar. Preachers often study different Bible versions to gain insight about certain passages in the New Testament, which is translated from the well understood, but no longer spoken, ancient Greek language. Greek is similar to English in its grammar. The situation is more difficult in the Old Testament because the Hebrew language has different rules of grammar and some word meanings are not well understood.

HEBREW GRAMMAR

Scholars have identified at least four ways of understanding the crucial sequence of events that unfold in the narrative of creation, from the very beginning to the existence of the completed universe.[1] Two of these, which consider verse 1 to be a temporal clause and subordinate to verse 2, will not be considered because they imply that God did not create the universe *ex nihilo*. In the other two interpretations listed below, verse 1 has an absolute sense, which describes a completed stage of creation:

    A. Absolute meaning, in which verse 1 is an independent clause and subsequent verses are to be read with sequential meaning up to verse 16:

- God created the heavens and the earth (1:1).
- God commented on the intermediate state of the earth (1:2).
- God modified the earth (1:3–13).
- God allowed the heavens to become visible on the fourth Day (1:14–18), requiring the pluperfect tense in English for 1:16.

B. Absolute meaning, in which verse 1 is an independent clause that is a summary of subsequent verses and is not part of the sequential narrative that follows in verses 3–15:

- God summarized creation of heaven and earth (1:1)
- God commented on the intermediate state of the earth but without saying that the heavens were to be created four days later (1:2)
- God modified the earth (1:3–13)
- God created the heavens on the fourth Day (1:14–18)

The reader might ask how the original Hebrew might allow such ambiguity. It probably did not originally. Today most of us do not understand Hebrew grammar, and we must defer to Hebrew scholars who are divided on this issue. Grammatical customs make the problem somewhat complicated. Nevertheless, most conservative scholars, both ancient and modern, accept interpretation A, in which the heavens were created before the first Day.[2] Arguments in favor of the conservative position are summarized below.

- Earlier creation documents, such as the Babylonian Enuma Elish, have been used to suggest that creation was not *ex nihilo* and that verse 1 is a temporal clause. These documents assume the preexistence of the universe and concern the activities of several gods that controlled the earth.[3] If Genesis 1 were just another version of mythical events, then there is little point in treating Genesis seriously.

But Genesis is totally different from these other accounts and contradicts their extravagant myths by naming God alone as creator of the universe. It provides a sequential, technical, and simple narrative of how the earth was formed and then filled with life. Genesis stands alone as the only creation account that is believable and is not in opposition to proven science, when interpreted without unnecessary philosophical assumptions.

- Most conservative scholars, most ancient versions, and the early church affirm that verse 1 is an independent clause with absolute meaning. Attempts in modern times to cast verse 1 otherwise are being increasingly rejected.[4]

- The Hebrew style and poetic structure are elegant and majestic, demanding a straightforward translation that gives God the credit for creation. The unique textual format for the structure of each Day does not lend itself to casting verse 1 as a dependent clause.

In the creation account, God initially created two entities, the heavens and the earth and then described both of them in further detail. Verses 3–13 describe the nature of the earth and its transformation into a habitable world. When the heavens are mentioned later in verses 14–18, it should be understood that the heavens were not being created again.[5] In English, this can be made clear with the pluperfect tense, which incorporates the word *had* to indicate a prior activity.

HEBREW VERBS

Hebrew did not have as many tenses that indicate time as we have in English. Our tenses allow information to be given about the relative time frames of other events. Instead, Hebrew verbs represented the state of completion of the verb, either completed or not completed, corresponding to perfect and imperfect tenses. Information on any relative time frame was supplied by context and grammar.

Languages, such as English and Greek, have more than one type of past tense. Among them is the simple past, also called the perfect tense in English, in which the verb simply indicates that an action has been completed. For example, the boy ran home. No reference is implied about another event or time. The imperfect tense provides a reference time for when the boy was running. For example, the boy was running home when he realized he was hungry. The imperfect verb, *was running*, provides the setting for the second clause about hunger. The tense that concerns us is the pluperfect, which provides a time reference after the boy ran. For example, the boy had run home and raided the cookie jar. In this sentence, we know that he ate the cookies after running home, instead of the other way round.

When the Hebrew text was translated into the Greek Septuagint about 200 BC, the Greek language had a pluperfect tense, but the translators used the simple past tense (Aorist) in Genesis 1. The simple past tense was kept when the Latin Vulgate was written centuries later and also when the King James Version was commissioned.

In Hebrew, the pluperfect sense was usually determined by word order. Normal word order was the verb first, followed by the subject. For the pluperfect sense, the clause for the prior event had the subject placed before the verb, the order used in most English sentences. All sentences in Genesis 1 and 2, however, are in normal Hebrew word order, perhaps to emphasize the unity of the creation narrative. Consequently, the grammar does not allow us to determine if there is a pluperfect sense, and so the reader must resort to context.

Translators have done this for a few verses in Genesis and inserted the pluperfect tense. For example, Genesis 2:5: "For the Lord God had not caused it to rain on the earth"; and Genesis 2:22: "Then the rib which the Lord God had taken from the man He made into a woman". These are translated with the pluperfect tense because the context demands it. In other verses it makes sense to use the pluperfect tense, although it might be debatable whether context demands it.[6] For example, in Genesis 2:8, the New International Version uses the pluperfect tense, where other versions do not: "Now the Lord God had planted a garden in the east", and again in Genesis 2:19: "now the Lord God had formed out of the ground all the beasts of the field". These examples indicate that we should not ignore appropriate use of the pluperfect tense in English translations when determining the correct chronology of the creation account; context must be considered.

THE HEAVENS ON THE FOURTH DAY

Returning to Genesis 1:16, the context is the opening verse: "In the beginning God created the heavens and the earth." Verse 16 is about the sun, moon, and stars that had been created in the beginning.

> Then God made two great lights: the greater light to rule the day, and the lesser light to rule the night. He made the stars also. (Gen 1:16)

Because Genesis 1:1 is an independent clause, the meaning of verse 1 must be that the heavens were created before the six Days of creation, which begin in Genesis 1:3.[7] Therefore, verse 16 must be read with the pluperfect sense; God *had* made the two great lights. It is also necessary and appropriate to translate the opening conjunction with *and* or *now* instead of *then*. Different versions translate the Hebrew conjunction that starts each verse in Genesis 1 with various English conjunctions in order to meet the sense of those verses. They are all translations of the same Hebrew word.

The purposes God intended for the sun, moon, and stars are given in Genesis 1:14–15:

> Then God said, "Let there be lights in the firmament of the heavens to divide the day from the night; and let them be for signs and seasons, and for days and years; and let them be for lights in the firmament of the heavens to give light on the earth"; and it was so. (Gen 1:14–15)

Verse 14 has the jussive command, *let there be*, which should take the alternative translation *let there appear*, found in the Old Testament Hebrew Lexicon (Briggs, Driver, Brown). A more common translation for the Hebrew word is *become*, which is also appropriate in this situation. The heavenly bodies, which already existed, could not be seen until they became visible as lights in the firmament; this was possible after the atmosphere had become transparent.

Many Young Earth creationists insist that the heavens were created on the fourth Day, regardless of the Hebrew meaning and their own understanding that Genesis 1:1 is an independent clause with an absolute sense.[8] The Young Earth position on the age of the earth would not be shaken if it were in agreement with conservative Biblical scholarship and the scientific community about the sequence of creation. Many years ago, the apparent contradiction between verses 1 and 14 first prompted me to investigate the Biblical account of creation, which eventually led me to write this book. I have found it well worthwhile, examining many points of view about Genesis and the evidence that supports them.

REFERENCES

1. Copan, Paul, and William Craig. *Creation out of Nothing.* Grand Rapids: Baker Academic, 2004: 36–49.
2. Hamilton, Victor. *The Book of Genesis Chapters 1–17.* Grand Rapids: Eerdmans, 1990: 107; Young, Edward. *Studies in Genesis One.* Phillipsburg: P&R Publishing, 1994: 1–14; Aalders, Gerhard. *Genesis Volume I.* Grand Rapids: Zondervan, 1981: 50–52.
3. See Reference 1, 30–36.
4. Ibid., 45–49.
5. Bavinck, Herman. *In the Beginning.* Grand Rapids: Baker Books, 2000: 104.
6. Collins, C. John. *The Wayyiqtol as "Pluperfect": When and Why.* Tyndale Bulletin, 46.1 (1995): 117–140.
7. See Reference 1, 42.
8. Morris, Henry. *The Beginning of the World.* Green Forest: Master Books, 2000: 14.

INDEX

A

Abel 115, 116, 117, 118, 120, 122, 141
abiogenesis 204
afterlife 54, 91, 149
alliteration 17
angels 63, 66, 90, 104, 106, 126, 215
appearance of age 24, 83, 226
appearance of design 175, 211, 212
Ararat 138, 143, 148, 152, 154, 165,
    171
asteroid 160, 161, 186, 188
asthenosphere 162
atmosphere 22, 29, 30, 33, 34, 37, 38,
    43, 116, 158, 164, 178, 179,
    180, 182, 236

B

bacteria 22, 30, 38, 39, 41, 46, 50, 198,
    206, 207
beasts of the earth 50
Big Bang Theory 12, 212, 236
birds 46, 47, 48, 49, 50, 86, 87, 138,
    142, 143, 190
Bishop Ussher 122, 124
bodies 41, 62
burial 54, 183

C

Cain 111, 115, 116, 117, 118, 119,
    120, 121, 122, 126
canopy 38, 157, 180

capital punishment 143
carbon-14 178, 179, 181, 182
carnivores 58, 69, 71, 72, 134, 136,
    139, 140
catastrophic flood model 159
Catastrophic Plate Tectonics 159
cattle 45, 46, 47, 49, 50, 52, 85, 86,
    137, 138, 140
cetaceans 50, 161
chiasm 17
chirality 206
circumstantial evidence 2, 3, 148, 196,
    200, 234, 236
circumstantialevidence 9
clothes 91, 200
Clovis 166
coal 184, 185
comet 165, 166, 167, 169, 170
comparable 49, 62, 85, 86, 87, 98, 132
cosmogonies 20
Cosmological General Relativity 36
credibility 24
creeping thing 50
crust 39, 157, 158, 159, 160, 162, 164,
    237, 238
curse 64, 74, 92, 93, 97, 98, 99, 102,
    103, 108, 118, 120

D

Day 18, 21, 33, 58, 225, 228, 229, 241
decay 24, 61, 62, 63, 64, 65, 66, 67,
    73, 74, 75, 95, 97, 99, 101, 102,
    111, 140, 213, 221, 238, 239

diet 56, 57, 71, 122, 140
diversity 176, 177, 200, 202
DNA 28, 70, 74, 88, 89, 175, 176,
    177, 186, 187, 200, 206, 209,
    211, 214
dominion 49, 50, 52, 54, 55, 93
dove 56, 138, 159, 169
dust 22, 28, 33, 46, 64, 81, 88, 98, 162,
    236

E

emotions 46, 49, 53, 87, 127
entropy 73, 214
epicycles 24
Euphrates 84, 150, 153, 155, 168
evening 15, 18, 19, 34, 37, 40, 41, 45,
    82, 83, 220, 227, 228, 231, 232
every living thing 45, 46, 47, 50, 55,
    101, 134, 140
evicted 94, 98, 143
evolution 13, 196
Evolutionary Theory 12
ex nihilo 19, 21, 28, 31, 60, 229, 241,
    242
extant 46, 49, 190, 207
extinction 70, 142, 166, 170, 188, 214,
    215

F

fall 95
firmament 32, 36, 37, 41, 43, 45, 47,
    212, 245
fish 50, 110
fossil fuels 184
fossil record 41, 50, 51, 53, 91, 162,
    183, 196, 197, 202, 210
fountains of the deep 131, 133, 147,
    153, 158, 160, 164
Framework Theory 14
friend 87, 91, 230

G

Galileo 23, 226
Garden of Eden 21, 51, 56, 57, 64, 66,
    67, 74, 79, 80, 81, 82, 84, 92,
    94, 96, 110, 115, 116, 118, 119,
    120, 139, 143, 220, 230
genealogy 24, 121, 122, 123, 124, 170
generations 64, 80, 111, 112, 120, 122,
    124, 128, 129, 143, 148, 170,
    187, 201, 214, 230
genre 17
geysers 157
giants 126, 127
Gilgamesh 133, 147
glacial dams 150, 151, 152, 155, 165,
    166, 169
Glendalough Lakes 183
Göbekli Tepe 54, 170
Gulf of Oman 153

H

Hebrew Language 15
Holy Spirit 23, 30, 104, 189
hominid 89
hominids 53, 54, 87, 89, 91
hyperbole 20, 56, 57, 130, 131

I

image 52, 53, 54, 55, 83, 85, 102, 143,
    222, 232
Imago Dei 53
inclusio 80
Intelligent Design 2, 211, 212, 215,
    236
irreducible complexity 208

J

Job 72, 90, 105, 106, 107, 108, 109,
    111, 128, 195, 219

K

kinds 6, 41, 48, 49, 50, 57, 68, 72, 76, 85, 88, 110, 134, 135, 197, 219, 234
K/T boundary 203

L

land of Nod 116, 119, 120
life spans 63, 65, 124, 141
likeness 52, 53, 54, 55, 100, 195, 222

M

macroevolution 201, 202, 203, 210
mammals 47, 48, 49, 50, 86, 87, 138, 142, 143, 190
Mesozoic 159
Messianic 115, 120, 121
microevolution 201, 202, 203, 210
mirror images 206
mist 80
mitochondrial 186
monsoon 132, 168
morning 15, 18, 19, 34, 37, 40, 41, 45, 168, 227, 228, 231, 232

N

New Earth 63
New Heavens 63

O

oil 51, 184, 186
olive leaf 138, 169

P

pain 61, 62, 63, 64, 65, 66, 74, 75, 92, 95, 96, 97, 102, 103, 106, 110, 115

Paleozoic 159
Pangaea 38, 39
panspermia 199, 201
parallelism 17
Paul 43, 63, 64, 72, 76, 93, 99, 100, 104, 159, 172, 217, 246
permafrost 163, 172
persecuted 110
Persian Gulf 84, 150, 153, 154, 155, 171
perspective 20, 23, 29, 31, 37, 42, 43, 73, 79, 85, 109, 129, 139, 148, 188, 198, 212, 227, 232
pets 49, 50, 142
pluperfect 16, 32, 43, 79, 81, 86, 242, 243, 244, 245
pluperfect tense 16, 32, 43, 79, 81, 86, 242, 243, 244
pollen 183
progressive creation 14
punctuated equilibrium 89, 198, 210, 211
purpose 22, 211

R

radioactive 24, 65, 73, 74, 213, 238
rain 38, 56, 80, 81, 82, 110, 131, 132, 133, 155, 167, 168
rainbow 71, 138, 142, 147
relativistic 24
religion 7, 9, 10, 12, 117, 215
rest 6, 18, 27, 36, 57, 59, 60, 94, 99, 128, 165, 185, 229, 230, 231, 232
rib 88, 244

S

sacrifice 105, 116, 117, 118, 140, 141, 144
sea creatures 28, 45, 46, 47, 50, 68, 70, 161, 177
seasons 32, 41, 42, 70, 245

seed 12, 18, 40, 41, 56, 92, 120, 122, 177
Semitic inclusions 17
Septuagint 16, 123, 124, 244
serpent 85, 89, 92, 97, 110, 120
seven 18, 48, 56, 120, 134, 140, 168,
      176, 211, 232
seventh day 59, 60, 229, 231
Shamal 156
signatures 165, 195, 203
signs 32, 41, 42, 62, 167, 245
sons of God 126, 127
soul 46, 47, 48, 55, 66, 91, 135
sovereignty 219
springs 60, 124, 145, 157, 192, 216,
      233
Strait of Hormuz 150, 153
subside 133, 156
suffering 8, 55, 69, 75, 76, 77, 95, 97,
      102, 103, 104, 106, 107, 108,
      109, 110, 113, 219, 220, 221
symbiotic 58, 97, 198

T

Taurus Mountains 132, 152
temples 54
Theistic Evolution 14, 222
Theory of Evolution 2, 12, 89, 197
thermodynamics 73
Tigris 84, 132, 133, 150, 153, 154,
      155, 168
time dilation 36, 235
Tower of Babel 143, 148
tree of life 66, 67, 81, 93, 94
Tree of Life 93
tree of the knowledge 81, 84

U

unity 22, 52, 54, 85, 144, 232, 244
Urartu 149, 154

V

velocity of light 35, 36, 226, 234, 235
volcanoes 131, 161, 186, 188, 236
Vulgate 16, 244

W

water gaps 151, 152
white hole cosmology 35
wind 133, 151, 152, 156, 162, 166,
      169
wind gaps 152
wisdom 8, 30, 55, 71, 91, 105, 110,
      195, 203, 220, 236
work 21, 232

Y

Y chromosome 88, 187
Younger Dryas 165, 166, 167, 169,
      173, 182, 183

Z

Zagros Mountains 130, 132, 152, 156
ziggurats 143, 144
Zodiac 42, 44

ABOUT THE AUTHOR

Anthony "Tony" Edridge holds a Ph.D. in Physics from the University of Surrey in England and graduated with a Christian Leader's Degree from Hill Country Bible College in Texas. He was employed in various scientific and engineering management positions including Vice President of Engineering and has served as an elder in three evangelical churches over the past 36 years.